# 100 Hikes in™
## CALIFORNIA'S
# CENTRAL SIERRA
# & COAST RANGE

# 100 Hikes in™

## CALIFORNIA'S
# CENTRAL SIERRA & COAST RANGE

### Vicky Spring

### Photographs by Kirkendall/Spring

THE
MOUNTAINEERS

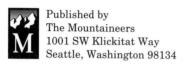
Published by
The Mountaineers
1001 SW Klickitat Way
Seattle, Washington 98134

First edition: first printing 1995, second printing 1997

Published simultaneously in Canada by Douglas & McIntyre, Ltd., 1615 Venables Street, Vancouver, B.C. V5L 2H1

Published simultaneously in Great Britain by Cordee, 3a DeMontfort Street, Leicester, England, LE1 7HD

Manufactured in the United States of America

Edited by Scott Stevens
Maps by Tom Kirkendall
All photographs by Kirkendall/Spring
Book layout by Gray Mouse Graphics
Typesetting by The Mountaineers Books

Cover photograph: Hiker at Ruwau Lake (Hike 36)
Frontispiece: Hiker above Alger Lakes on Koip Peak Pass Traverse (Hike 20)

Library of Congress Cataloging in Publication Data

Spring, Vicky, 1953–
    100 hikes in California's Central Sierra and Coast Range / Vicky
Spring.
        p.   cm.
    Includes index.
    ISBN 0-89886-418-6 (pbk.)
    1. Hiking—Sierra Nevada (Calif. and Nevada)—Guidebooks.
2. Hiking—Coast Ranges—Guidebooks.  3. Sierra Nevada (Calif. and
Nevada)—Guidebooks.  4. Coast Ranges—Guidebooks.  I. Title.
II. Title: One hundred hikes in California's Central Sierra and Coast
Range.
        GV199.42.S55S67   1995                    94-42027
        796.5'1'09794'4—dc20                       CIP

# CONTENTS

# CONTENTS

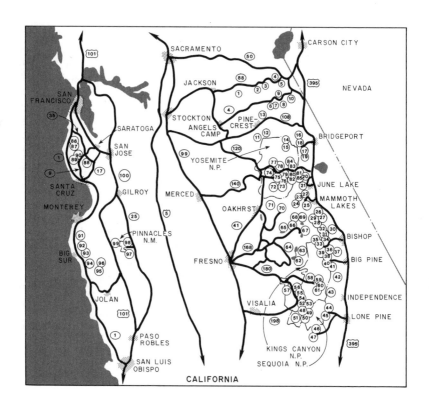

CALIFORNIA

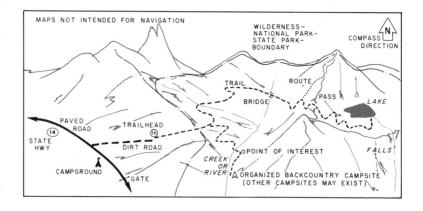

John Muir Wilderness

Golden Trout Wilderness

## Highway 198

Sequoia National Park

Jennie Lakes Wilderness

## Highway 180

Kings Canyon National Park

## Highway 168

John Muir Wilderness

Dinkey Lakes Wilderness

Kaiser Wilderness

John Muir Wilderness

## Highway 41

Ansel Adams Wilderness

Yosemite National Park

7

Yosemite National Park

Portola State Park &
Pescadero Creek County Park

Portola State Park
Castle Rock State Park &
Big Basin Redwoods State Park

Big Basin Redwoods
State Park

Ventana Wilderness

Pinnacles National Monument

Henry W. Coe State Park

# PREFACE

## The Wilderness Act Versus Politics

When the Wilderness Act was adopted, many people settled back and quit worrying about the preservation of the lands now protected by the Act. Since that time, most of the conservation efforts have gone toward adding more lands to the wilderness. Unfortunately, the Wilderness Act, like any written document, is subject to interpretation. With wildernesses now showing signs of extreme overuse and occasional misuse, it is time to take a closer look at the policies and, unfortunately, the politics that have shaped current interpretation of the Wilderness Act.

Beyond a doubt the High Sierra is being loved to death by the hundreds of thousands of visitors. The John Muir Wilderness, in the center of the High Sierra, is the most heavily used wilderness area in the country.

The balance between overuse and over-protection is a fine one. If you cannot get the wilderness permit you want, the rules seem like bureaucratic nonsense. When you arrive at your destination and find all the campsites taken, the rules do not seem strict enough. When you see campers pulling cold food and drinks from coolers that were carried in by horse packers, you wonder how the Wilderness Act could ever have been interpreted to include the luxuries of convenience-store camping.

In an effort to please all users, as well as preserve the resource, the policies governing the wilderness areas have become more political than sensible. For example, tedious miles of nearly level switchbacks have been carved through the wilderness to help horses safely ascend granite cliffs and high passes. Trenches have been blasted into pristine slabs of granite to prevent hooves from sliding on the hard rock. Rocks have been pulled out of trails to prevent horses from stumbling. Shovels throw dirt onto the snow that covers trails in early summer to speed up the melt, so horses can cross.

Another policy that needs examination is the one that determines which creeks will be bridged and which will not. If a horse cannot safely ford a creek, you usually can count on a very good bridge. Many of the lesser creeks have been left unbridged to help preserve the wilderness experience. On paper this policy sounds great, but in reality it leads to far more environmental degradation than it eliminates. Hikers, looking for safe, alternate crossings, create boot-beaten trails along the soft soils at the edge of creeks. Ground is then compacted and vegetation killed in several locations instead of just one. When one foot-log washes away, boots will beat four or five trails to different logs, leaving meadows and the soft soil along stream beds compacted and vegetationless for years. In some areas the problem has been recognized with the creation of separate horse and hiker crossings; however, in most areas the problem is getting worse every year.

In the Mineral King area of Sequoia National Park, the Sawtooth Pass Trail is a mess. The pass lies in the fragile world of the High Sierra and the trail has been overused. On the loose soil of the west side of the pass, the trail has slid away and hikers have created a multitude of paths on the soft hillside. In order to repair the trail, the park regulations require that the trail be upgraded to accommodate horses. The trail cannot be repaired only for the softer footfalls of hikers. One wonders if this policy is in the best interests of the wilderness or if it was written for political reasons to accommodate the economic interests of horse packers.

Horse packers serve a purpose of helping people experience the wilderness who might not be physically capable of going there on their own. However, the wilderness experience of the horse rider must be protected in the same way that the hiker's is protected. If an area or a trail is not suitable for horse use, then horses should not go there. Pristine slabs of granite should not have trenches blasted across them to accommodate hooves (or feet), as has been done on the Pine Creek Trail and the Red Basin Trail, to name just two. The natural snowmelt must not be tampered with to serve the economic interests of the horse packers.

The wilderness is fragile and we must all band together to protect it. We must tread softly, accept the difficulties of an environmentally friendly trail, and be ready to ford creeks in some areas and accept the presence of bridges in other, more sensitive locations. We must learn to limit our impact on the high country. For the individual, that means camping on hard ground, using established campsites, forgoing campfires, staying on the trails, and erasing all traces of your stay when you move on. Forest and Park Service efforts to limit usage must be supported. Equally we must all willingly pitch in and help by carrying out garbage and even our own human waste if need be.

Please let the Forest Service and Park Service know your thoughts about these problems and any other problems you may find as you travel through the wilderness.

# INTRODUCTION

## Before You Leave Home

### HOW TO USE THIS BOOK

If you have never used this type of guide book before, here is a quick orienteering lesson on how to pick a hike suited to your needs.

To start, check the Location Map to find which hikes in this book are in the area you wish to visit. Next, take a look at the list of summary information at the top of each hike. You will want to start off by considering the round trip or loop trip mileage. That is the total number of miles you will need to walk to complete the hike. Because most of the hikes in this book are in the High Sierra, you should also pay attention to the trail's total elevation gain and to the elevation of the highest point reached. Trips that start at, or climb above, an altitude of 7,000 feet require an acclimation period before you set out—please carefully read the Hiking at High Elevation section of the Safety Considerations

*Hiker on Milk Ranch Meadow Trail (Hike 6)*

and Hazards section in this Introduction so that you fully understand the ramifications of hiking at high elevation.

Once you have determined the number of miles to be hiked and the elevation gained, take a look at the hiking time. This is the length of time the average hiker (acclimated to the elevation) will spend walking to and from the destination. If you are driving up from sea level and starting your hike the same day, figure a much slower pace, averaging just a little better than 1 mile per hour. The hiking time does not figure in rest stops, view-gazing stops, or lunch breaks.

Finally, check the section that tells you when the trail is hikable, on an average year. This listing does not mean that the trail will be snow free or that all the rivers will be low enough to hop across with your boots on. Hikable means a hiker can get through to the destination at this time of year. If you are planning just one hike for the summer, check with the Forest Service or Park Service agency that manages the area and find out when the trail is at its best; August and September are usually safe bets.

Maps are very important. The artist's renditions of the trails in this book are not sufficient for navigation and are not designed to be an aid if you get into difficulties along the way. Always carry a map with the contours clearly shown. See the Maps section in the Introduction for more information, and the Appendix for details.

The Reservations and Information section is there to guide you to the Wilderness Permits section of the Appendix, which has detailed information on each hike. Please note that as of 1994 Wilderness Permits were not required for day use on hikes described in this book. Only overnight hikes require a permit.

Finally, the text below the mechanical information section will guide you to your destination and give you an idea of what you can expect to find along the way.

Have a good hike.

## CURRENT INFORMATION

Despite best intentions, maps and guide books cannot keep current with the constant changes effected by man and by nature on forest roads and trails. When looking for the most up-to-date information, you should contact the agency that manages the area, as listed in the Reservations and Information section of each hike and in the Appendix at the back of the book.

## MAPS

The map is one of your most basic and essential pieces of equipment, and you are ill-prepared without it. Experienced hikers usually carry at least two maps covering the same area. One of the maps—such as a Forest Map or a Wilderness Map—will give a large overview of the area, the second will be a detailed topographic map, preferably an up-to-date U.S. Geological Survey (USGS) 7.5-minute quadrangle.

Forest Maps show roads and trailhead access for individual forests. The U.S. Forest Service (USFS) also has a series of maps that cover

*Mount Wallace viewed from shore of Hungry Packer Lake (Hike 33)*

individual wildernesses, showing topography and trails. These maps are sufficient for navigation as long as you travel only on primary trails in well-signed areas. For further information on where and how to obtain the maps you need, see the Appendix.

## WILDERNESS PERMITS

Wilderness permits are required for all overnight trips in national parks and designated national forest wilderness areas (except for the Ventana and parts of the Toiyabe). At the time of this writing day hikers do not need a wilderness permit as long as they are off the trail the same day they started for areas covered in this book. (Watch for possible changes in the future.) Backpackers in the national forest outside of the wilderness areas are not required to have a wilderness permit; however, they must carry a fire permit. See the Appendix for details.

## CLOTHING AND EQUIPMENT

Weather in the central section of the High Sierra is some of the best found in any major mountain range in the world. During the summer, daytime temperatures generally range from a comfortable 60 degrees to 80 degrees Fahrenheit. At night temperatures are in the 30- to 40-degree range, although it can get much colder. However, by September, be prepared for nighttime temperatures in the frigid twenties or the bone-chilling teens.

This ideal weather makes us all a little careless when packing. You tend to forget that the afternoon thunderstorm, which usually passes over in twenty minutes, can last for eight hours. Rain showers can turn to miserable hailstorms or unanticipated snowstorms. Even though you can hike for years and never encounter anything but ideal conditions, you need to be prepared for the worst by carrying winter clothing, a full set of rain gear, and a shelter to crawl into.

Always pack a full set (tops and bottoms) of long underwear. Synthetic long underwear (one of the polypropylene derivatives) is best; however, traditionalists will be well-protected in wool and can occupy their time with itching and scratching. Never use cotton long underwear. Cotton holds water and can cause a body to lose heat rather than retain it. A hat and a pair of gloves are essential for keeping warm and do not take up much room in the pack.

Footwear is a real problem. Since lightweight, relatively inexpensive boots have come onto the market, many people have been seduced by their comfort to the point of jeopardizing their safety. Lightweight boots have their place on day hikes when the trail is in good condition. They do not belong on extended trips in the High Sierra, where the rough trails climb over passes that may be snowbound for most of the summer. Heavy boots are essential when carrying a heavy pack. They strengthen the ankles and help to prevent accidents when carrying a backpack down a steep trail, over a tilting slab of granite, or across a snow slope. The stiffer soles of heavy boots allow you to kick steps into snow and retain your footing once your step is set. When you think about the discomfort of an accident and the expense of a rescue, the cost and extra weight of a heavy boot does not seem so excessive.

Never leave the trailhead without the Ten Essentials tucked into your pack, be it a day pack or a backpack. This list of essentials has been developed by years of hiking experience and by the people who rescue lost and injured hikers. No doubt there are other items which you will find to be essential—throw them in too.

1. Map—it may sound silly, but check before you start off to be sure that the map covers the entire area of the hike. Pack the map in a waterproof bag to protect it.
2. Compass—essential tool for navigation when walking through a cloud in the High Sierra. Be sure and check the declination of the area before you head cross-country. An altimeter is also helpful.
3. First-aid kit—it is not enough to buy one. You need to be familiar with the contents and know how to use them. Excellent first-aid classes are given by the American Red Cross.

4. Extra clothing—carry more than you think you could possibly need even if it does snow.
5. Extra food—you should end your trip with something left over, like a couple of energy bars or granola snacks.
6. Sunglasses—an absolute necessity at high elevations to prevent the eyes from becoming sunburned. Always wear sunglasses when on snow and consider wearing them even on cloudy days.
7. Flashlight—always carry an extra bulb and extra batteries.
8. Knife—has unforeseen number of uses from cutting cheese to first aid.
9. Firestarter—a candle or a chemical paste for emergency fire building with wet wood.
10. Matches—get the waterproof variety.

## On the Trail

### CAMPING

The fragile nature of the High Sierran meadows and lakeshores can not be overstated. At high elevation, plants must deal with the stresses of a short growing season, warm days, cold nights, rain that falls in thundering torrents or not at all, and poor soil. On top of all these stresses, being trampled by feet or crushed by a tent will kill most alpine plants. If several parties camp in the same fragile location, such as a meadow, a bald spot of compacted earth will form and vegetation may not return for many years.

Plan carefully when you set up your camp. If possible, select an already

*To protect the environment, campfires are prohibited in much of the High Sierra. Always use a campstove for cooking.*

established campsite and avoid creating another. Do not dig trenches for tents, remove vegetation, or move rocks. Always camp at least 100 feet away from water or the trail.

Do not camp on and destroy a carpet of soft vegetation. That vegetation is going to send out an army of mosquitos in the evening anyway. If possible, try to camp out of sight of others so that everyone gets the feeling of wilderness. If you get lonely, you can always drop in for a chat about the trail or to inquire if they have a bug repellent that really works.

When possible, find a slab of level granite or a sandy bench to pitch your tent on. Self-standing tents are best for this purpose because they can be pitched anywhere. Carry a foam pad or air mattress to cushion your tired bones from the hard rocks.

Once you have found your campsite, exchange those heavy boots for a pair of softsoled camp shoes. Your feet will thank you and so will the soil and delicate plants around camp. Numerous trips to the creek or lake for water can cause harm to delicate vegetation, so carry a collapsible water bag and make only one trip for water instead of five.

## WATER

Water is one of the best examples of how we have loved our mountains to death. Twenty years ago when we were thirsty in the mountains, we dipped a cup in a clear stream and enjoyed one of the greatest treats nature can offer: cold mountain water. As more people came, we fouled our nest and nowadays no water can be assumed safe to drink unless it has been treated.

The most publicized parasite is *Giardia lamblia,* which can cause diarrhea and other flulike symptoms about two weeks after drinking the contaminated water. There are other less notorious bugs, which will cause similar problems, sometimes within a few hours of ingesting the water. The most effective way of treating water is to bring it to a rolling boil for at least five minutes. Mechanical water purifiers—pumps or drip bags—are also effective but are prone to breakdowns. When added to water, chemicals such as iodine will kill all parasites; however, there is some debate as to their effect on humans.

## GARBAGE AND SANITATION

There is no magic that will make your little campfire hot enough to consume aluminum foil or heavy plastics. That may sound like an obvious statement but there is something about a campfire in the backcountry that makes even the most intelligent people forget what will burn and what will not. Maybe the elevation does something to our fire savvy; someone should study this phenomenon. Think about this the next time you walk by a fire pit and see some aluminum poking out. Better still, stop and fish it out. If you choose to burn your garbage in the campfire, make fishing out the leftovers a morning ritual.

Except for the fire pits, hikers are doing a great job of keeping trails and camp areas clean. We can all pat ourselves on the back because the improvement over the last twenty years has been astounding. There are still a few Neanderthals who are burying their garbage.

Please do not follow suit; that stuff has a way of popping up again in a few years.

If you carried a package of food into the wilderness, you can certainly carry the empty packaging back out. Better still, plan ahead and eliminate all excess packaging before you leave home by taking food out of one or more layers of its bulky wrappings.

Do not wash dishes or your body near a lake or a stream. Carry the water needed back to your camp and do your washing there. Avoid using any type of soap or detergent, including so-called biodegradable soaps, near water. Neither food scraps nor soaps are good for the water. When cleaning fish, do not throw the entrails into the water. You should bury the entrails in a deep hole away from the camp area.

Human waste is one of the messiest problems in the backcountry. As more people become addicted to the beauty of the wilderness, the problem is compounded, fouling the water and continuing the cycle of parasite regeneration. Always carry a small plastic trowel and dig a hole for your excrement 8 to 10 inches deep and at least 200 feet from any water, campsites, or trails. Carry your used toilet paper out in a plastic bag.

### BEARS

Few things spoil a trip faster than watching a bear run off with all your food. And thanks to the availability of human food, the number of bears in the wilderness areas of California is increasing. These bears are intelligent and are following hikers to their favorite campsites, living and traveling at elevations where they are relying on human food for survival.

The best way to eliminate the bear problem and ensure the success of your trip is proper food storage. Counterbalancing food is the recommended method. The equipment required is a 15-foot piece of rope, two food bags equally weighted, a sturdy tree with its first branch at least 18 feet off the ground, and a long stick for balancing the food bags and retrieving them later. (If you do not understand this technique, ask for some explanatory literature with a diagram when you pick up your wilderness permit.)

When there are no trees available, the recommended method of food storage is a bear-resistant canister. These are bulky and expensive and hold about a three-day supply of food for one person. Food canisters are available for rent in Yosemite, Sequoia, and Kings Canyon National Parks. If you find yourself above timberline without a food canister, you should suspend your food over an overhanging cliff, or as a last resort, bury your food under a pile of rocks as far from camp as possible and hope for the best.

Some of the most popular campsites in the national parks have either bear bars, which may require a 25-foot piece of rope for effective use, or food-storage boxes. When bars or boxes are available, you are advised to join the crowds and camp near them. Bears that continually fail to find food will move on, hopefully to search for natural foods.

If a bear comes around your camp, yell, bang cooking pots, and wave jackets in the air. If the bear does not leave, you should. Although the bear is interested only in your food, it is a dangerous animal. Never approach a bear or try and get your food back from it. Leave cubs alone at all times.

## THE SACRED RITE OF THE CAMPFIRE

Fires are an ancient ritual used to ward off evil and give warmth in the night. Unfortunately, this comforting tradition of spending an evening watching shapes and colors dance through the flames is denuding the mountains of wood. The nightly fire requires a lot of fuel, a resource that is slow to replenish in the high country. When you strip the forest floor of dead wood, you are destroying a microhabitat important to the survival of many small plants and animals, which in turn are important to the survival of the entire ecosystem. In the high meadows, a single night's campfire can consume the equivalent of one to two small, sturdy trees. This resource will renew itself—in 70 to 100 years.

Simply stated, there are too many hikers for each of us to have a campfire in the wilderness. Dead wood and other available fuel have been used up in the high country and it will be years before the trees can generate a new crop. The soil in which these trees must grow is now lacking nutrients because wood has been removed and burned, rather than decaying, making regeneration that much more difficult. It is a vicious circle.

To protect the high country, fires are prohibited in most areas above 9,000 feet. In areas that receive heavy use, the restrictions may extend to lower elevations. Where fires are allowed, build them only in an existing fire ring in an established campsite. For your fire, use only dead wood picked up off the forest floor well away from your campsite. Do not break dead-looking branches off trees or snags. And never cut green wood.

Always carry a small camp stove for your cooking, or eat your food cold. For warmth you should rely exclusively on your food and shelter and not on a campfire. Spend your evenings looking at the stars and moon rather than blinding your eyes to the beauty of the night by staring into the fire.

## GROUP SIZE

To reduce the impact of hikers on the wilderness, Forest Service and Park Service rules limit group size to fifteen people. In the national parks and a few high-use areas in the wilderness, group size is limited to eight. This rule was designed for the welfare of the wilderness. Please respect it.

## PETS

Pets are not allowed on trails in the national parks or in the California bighorn sheep zoological areas. Check your map before you start hiking with your pet to be sure your trail does not pass through any restricted areas.

On the trail with your pet, you must keep it under voice control or physical restraint at all times. The pet is not allowed to harass wildlife or hikers. Treat your pet's feces the same way you treat your own: bury it in a hole eight to ten inches deep and at least 200 feet away from all water, campsites, and trails.

The first time you hike with your pet, do not make the mistake of believing voice control is sufficient to restrain your animal. At home your pet may understand where the boundaries are, but the trail will be a new experience for both of you. The dog will be exposed to a whole new world of smells from people and wild animals. Weather and altitude can also affect your pet. Dogs often become possessive of the trail you are walking on or an entire camp area. When dogs meet other dogs and fight for dominance in the middle of a peaceful meadow, you may find yourself in a embarrassing and potentially dangerous situation. Always have the leash handy.

## HORSES AND PACKERS

Horse packers may be found at nearly every popular trailhead in the Sierra. These are knowledgeable, friendly, and almost always helpful ambassadors of equestrian rights in the world. Their services are popular. For a price they will pack you in to a high lake, or you can have your gear packed in while you walk. You can even arrange to be fully taken care of at one of the High Sierra Camps. If you have an accident, need directions, or want information concerning the condition of the trail, talk to the horse packers.

When a hiker sees a horse and rider approaching, it is the hiker's responsibility to move off the trail and let the horse pass. If possible, move off on the downhill side of the trail; however, never endanger yourself to do so. When you see a horse approaching, call out a greeting and let the horse and rider know you are there to avoid spooking the horse. If you are on a narrow section of trail, retreat to a safe place to let the horses pass. When in doubt, discuss the situation with the riders and let them tell you what they can do.

Why do you have to follow these rules? Why do horses get the right-of-way on a trail? The answer is simple: horses may be pretty, but they are much larger than you. No matter how you feel about horses, the trail is not the place to make your point. A little thoughtless action on the part of a hiker could endanger the life of the rider, the horse, and even the hiker. Clients of the horse packers are especially at risk as many are novice riders.

## THEFT

Although not a problem at every trailhead, break-ins do occur in some areas. There is no way to avoid the problem; however, you can reduce your risk by leaving only the old beater at the trailhead. Use a steering-wheel locking device and make sure your car appears empty of personal possessions when you leave. Lock all extra clothes in the trunk and take any valuables with you.

In the Mineral King area of Sequoia National Park, marmots have learned to be proficient trailhead vandals. They chew on hoses, tires, and wires. The only protection against these destructive rodents is to rap a fine wire mesh around the outside of your car. If you do not carry wire, be sure to have plenty of duct tape in your repair kit.

# Safety Considerations and Hazards

## WEATHER AND STORMS

Thunderstorms are the main weather hazard during the summer months in the High Sierra. Storms come up quickly and hikers must be prepared. Think ahead and plan to be in a safe place when a storm arrives. If storms have been building up at a certain time of day, for several days in a row, plan your day's activities accordingly. When a storm hits, the safest place to be is in a forested area away from the tallest tree. Open mountains and ridge tops are the most hazardous places to be in a storm. Other places to avoid are open meadows, caves, edges or bases of cliffs, and anywhere near water.

If a storm catches you in the open, remove your pack and any other metal objects you may be carrying. Put your sleeping pad on a rock that is just big enough to sit on, place only your feet and posterior on the material, and wait the storm out. Do not attempt to quickly put the tent up; the poles may attract lightning.

## SNOW

Early season hikers should arm themselves with ice axes (and know how to use them), wear stiff-soled leather boots for traction, and cover the tops of their boots with gaiters to keep the snow out. They should also be proficient map readers and know how to navigate with a compass when the trail disappears under the snow for miles on end. If you do not have all these skills and the required equipment, wait until midsummer before you head to the high elevations.

By midsummer you will still find lingering snowfields at the higher passes. When at all possible, walk around the snow rather than over it. Old snow can be a tricky thing, with hidden air pockets where you will suddenly and unexpectedly break through. Old snow is often hard and difficult to kick steps into. A slip on old, icy snow will result in a few abrasions at best, at worst you may take a bone-breaking slide to the bottom.

## FALLING ROCKS

Falling rocks are a constant hazard on steep mountain slopes. Most falling rocks are random occurrences. When you hear a rock falling down the hillside above you, look for protection and yell "rock" to warn anyone else in the vicinity of the danger. If you need to cross a rock-fall area, go one at a time, quickly and quietly. Do not rest or camp in old rock fall areas. If you should have the misfortune of kicking loose a rock on a trail, yell "rock" to warn hikers below, even if you don't think anyone is there.

## RIVER CROSSINGS

In order to preserve your wilderness experience, the Forest Service has chosen to leave many creeks unbridged. As a result, trails are usually designed to ford creeks at an area considered suitable for a horse to cross. Hikers are left to enjoy their wilderness anyway they can get across it.

Obviously you are not a horse, so you must set about looking for alternative crossings. In many areas a bit of searching will reveal a sturdy log over the water or a wider point where the water is not flowing as fast.

Before you cross that sturdy log or wade that creek, look around for a long stick that could help you stabilize as you cross. Next, loosen the shoulder straps and unbuckle the hip belt of your pack so you can quickly shed your load if you slip.

Plan all crossings of major unbridged streams for the early morning when the water flow tends to be lower. When crossing deep, fast-moving water, leave your boots on for the best possible traction and wear gaiters to keep from getting too waterlogged. However, these crossings should be rare and are best avoided. Wet boots are an invitation to blisters later. Most crossings can be handled by removing your boots and wearing a pair of water slippers. You should also arm yourself with a heavy stick for balance. Keep the stick on the upstream side to avoid being pulled downstream.

Never tie a rope to someone who is crossing a creek. Ropes have a frustrating tendency to drag people under and a rope may even act as an anchor if it gets caught under a rock. If some members of your party, such as children, have trouble fording a creek, send one person ahead to tie a rope on the far side and set up a hand-line.

*When fording a creek, use a stick for extra stability.*

Some river crossings should not be attempted until late summer or early fall. If you have questions about a certain crossing, make inquiries when you pick up your wilderness permit. If the person issuing the permit cannot give you an answer, have that person call someone who is familiar with the crossing in question. Remember, river crossings have resulted in the loss of lives in the wilderness.

## HIKING AT HIGH ELEVATION

Hiking in the High Sierra demands a lot more of your body than a low-elevation trip in the coast range. If you simply jump out of your car at the trailhead and head up the trail, chances are you will find yourself moving rather slowly, covering much less ground than you hoped.

It is especially important to figure in the effect of the elevation when you are planning an extended hike through the high country. Do not plan to cover long distances for the first couple of days of your trip. A slow, easy start gives your body time to adjust to the weight of the pack and to the elevation. If the hike begins at high elevation, 7,000 feet or above, spend one or more days near the trailhead acclimating. This is a good time to explore the area with a couple of day hikes before heading out on the long trek.

## EXHAUSTION AND ALTITUDE SICKNESS

Hikers who head straight from their low-elevation homes to the High Sierran trailheads will find that their bodies need time to adjust to the thinner air. Breathing becomes rapid as your lungs try to extract the customary amount of oxygen from the air. Given time, your blood increases the proportion of oxygen-carrying corpuscles to compensate for the lack of oxygen. If you do not give your body enough time to make the necessary adjustment, you can expect to feel fatigue, nausea, weakness, and shortness of breath. These symptoms should be regarded with concern as they may be the early signs of high-altitude pulmonary or cerebral edema and could culminate in loss of life.

If you find yourself suffering from even the slightest symptoms of exhaustion or altitude sickness, slow down, drink more fluids, and eat a high-energy snack. If you wait until you are sick to do something, you have simply compounded the problem. Even if you do not feel any symptoms on the first day of the hike, make a special effort to drink plenty of liquids.

If the symptoms do not improve after a night's rest or if you notice dizziness, shortness of breath, rapid pulse, confusion, loss of memory, or persistent coughing, you should descend to a lower elevation as rapidly as possible. If you have a large party, send someone ahead to alert officials.

## SNAKES

Rattlesnakes are found throughout California and should be a matter of constant concern below 7,000 feet. Along the trail, always check for snakes before you sit down or set your pack down. Make a thorough area check before you set up your tent. Never stick your hand into a crack or under a log or rock without carefully visually inspecting it first.

Snakes tend to strike low, at the foot or ankle level. Protect yourself by wearing boots and long loose pants. Do not walk around camp barefoot in a snake-infested area. In the evening when going for water or firewood, always wear shoes. If camping in a snake area, use a tent and keep the door closed to avoid having one of these warmth-loving reptiles decide to share your sleeping bag with you.

Snakes do not want to see you any more than you want to see them. They will avoid contact with people whenever possible. When contact is unavoidable, the snake will announce its presence by an aggressive rattle that means it is time for you to move away because the snake cannot.

If someone in your party is bitten by a rattlesnake, the best treatment is to immobilize the victim then transport this person out. The victim should move as little as possible.

Like all other living creatures, rattlesnakes are protected by law in national parks. The snakes are a natural part of the wilderness and should be respected.

## TICKS

In the coastal regions, ticks appear after the first good rains of November or December and are annoyingly in evidence until the end of June. In the mountains the season varies with the snow melt, beginning in March. They hang on the ends of grass and brush and wait for a critter, human or otherwise, to come along and brush them off.

Ticks do not dig in immediately, they usually crawl around a bit to find a warm place before attaching themselves. If you feel something crawling under your clothes, stop and check it out. Ticks are hard to get off once they are set.

Ticks prefer tender skin so check under the band of your pants, underwear, collar, and socks frequently. At night do a thorough tick check, which means running your hand through your hair, exploring arm pits, and checking out all the other "you know where" places that can't be mentioned by name in a family book.

Ticks are less in evidence during the middle of the day. The eager-beaver early risers will get the most ticks on the trail. Late starters will find that most of the ticks have been brushed off already. Hikers who are first on the trail may find a tick-stick to be handy. This is a walking stick that can be used to beat any brush that overhangs the trail.

Protective clothing such as long-sleeved shirts and long pants with cuffs or gaiters can help protect you from ticks. Insect repellent that has a heavy dosage of $N, N$-diethyl-meta-toluamide (DEET) is also effective.

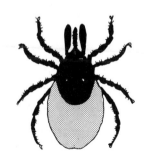

*Western black-legged tick*

Because ticks are known carriers of Lyme disease and Rocky Mountain spotted fever, it is important to remove all ticks as soon as you find them. If the tick has imbedded itself, cover it with heavy oil (carry some in your first-aid kit for this purpose). The oil will close up the tick's breathing pores, forcing it to withdraw. Wait for half an hour; if the tick has not backed out, you must unscrew it by pulling counterclockwise with tweezers. If you can not remove the tick or if part of the tick remains behind, you must see a doctor.

## POISON IVY AND POISON OAK

You should be aware of poison ivy and poison oak when hiking in the coastal regions and in some low-elevation sections of Sequoia and Kings Canyon National Parks.

Poison ivy and poison oak grow leaves in distinctive groups of three. Watch for these plants along creeks and in wooded areas. In the fall the leaves turn bright red. The poison from these plants is an oil that is carried in the sap and may be picked up by brushing the leaves with your legs or by handling the twigs and wood. If you burn these shrubs the toxins become airborne and are very dangerous to breathe.

The best defense against poison ivy and poison oak is not to touch it. Wear protective clothing when hiking, then take it off before you get into your tent at night. Handle your clothing with care. If you should brush up against the poison oak or ivy, wash the affected area thoroughly with soap and water. Be very careful not to get it on your hands and spread it to other parts of your body.

*Poison ivy*

## MOSQUITOS

In the Sierra, mosquitos can descend on you like a thunderstorm on a peaceful day. That beautiful green meadow, that inviting creek, that peaceful lake, that lovely green forest are all home to hoards of mosquitos in midsummer.

Without a little preparation, your carefully planned hike to one of the most beautiful lakes in the entire Sierra can turn into a mosquito-swatting march in Hell. You must be prepared either to don a covering layer of clothing or to dose your exposed skin and some of your unexposed skin with mosquito repellent. A hat with a face netting can be convenient around camp.

## SUN

Sunglasses and sunblock lotions are essential equipment for hiking in the High Sierra, where the atmosphere lacks the ingredients that block out the harmful effects of the sun. A simple overnight hike can result in a tremendous sunburn and blisters. An extended trip can be ruined by a bad sunburn on the first day out. Continual exposure may lead to skin cancer and melanoma.

Wear protective clothing, including a hat, or apply sunscreen with a SPF factor of 15 or greater many times during the day. Don't miss the ears, nose, cheeks, and neck.

## A FINAL WORD

A safe trip is a trip with preparation. Experienced hikers should accompany the inexperienced. Mountain first-aid classes should be taken by all. An accident can turn a pleasant trip into an instant nightmare. It does not do you any good if you are the only one trained in first aid and you are the one who gets hurt.

Let someone responsible know where you are going and when you will return and when they should start to worry. Take the Ten Essentials and be prepared for the worst, even if it means carrying a few extra pounds in your pack. Always remember, the mountains do not care if you come back dead or alive. So plan ahead, be prepared, and then relax and enjoy your hike.

*Vicky Spring and Tom Kirkendall*

# A Note About Safety

Safety is an important concern in all outdoor activities. No guidebook can alert you to every hazard or anticipate the limitations of every reader. Therefore, the descriptions of roads, trails, routes, and natural features in this book are not representations that a particular place or excursion will be safe for your party. When you follow any of the routes described in this book, you assume responsibility for your own safety. Under normal conditions, such excursions require the usual attention to traffic, road and trail conditions, weather, terrain, the capabilities of your party, and other factors. Keeping informed on current conditions and exercising common sense are the keys to a safe, enjoyable outing.

*The Mountaineers*

# 1 COLE CREEK LAKES

**Round trip: 28 miles**
**Hiking time: 2–4 days**
**High point: 8,280 feet**
**Elevation gain: 3,400 feet in;**
    **1,740 feet out**

**Hikable: mid-July through**
    **September**
**Backpack**

**Maps: USFS Mokelumne Wilderness; USGS Bear River Reservoir and
Mokelumne Peak**

Reservations and Information: Amador Ranger Station and Carson
    Pass Information Center (Case 1)

Surprising vistas, pleasant lakes, and scenic campsites are the rewards for this long and difficult trek up the Tanglefoot Trail to Cole
Creek Lakes. Despite an off-highway vehicle (OHV) road that allows
back-door access from the Silver Lake area, early season visitors who
do not mind tramping through a bit of snow will find complete solitude.

**Access.** Drive Highway 88 to the Bear River Lake turnoff, located
30.5 miles east of Jackson, and descend 2 miles toward the lake. When
the road divides, stay right following the signs for Cole Creek Campground. After 2.4 miles the road divides again; go left on Road 8N14 for
5.8 miles. Just before Cole Creek Campground go left, still on Road
8N14, and after another 3.4 miles turn left on Road 8N14E for the final
0.4 mile to the Tanglefoot Trailhead (6,640 feet).

The hike begins on a dusty trail that ascends gradually through the
forest. The trail to Shiner Lake (and most of your fellow hikers) will
head left at 1.5 miles (6,800 feet). Your trail then descends into Tanglefoot Canyon, where the small creek is crossed without much difficulty.

Now you begin a meandering ascent of the east side of Tanglefoot
Canyon to reach, at 4.5 miles, Moraine Lake (7,100 feet), a pleasantly
shaded campsite and the last certain water for the next 7.5 miles.

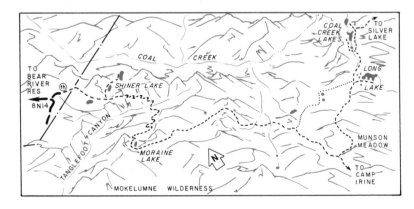

*Hiker overlooking Cole Creek drainage*

Beyond Moraine Lake the trail heads north through forest, skirting flower covered meadows while ascending to a view over the granite maze of Tanglefoot Canyon from a 8,240-foot shoulder of Mokelumne Peak. With your goal in view to the north, the trail makes a heart-breaking descent. After dropping 800 feet, cross two seasonal creeks, pass a couple of small campsites, then begin to climb. The trail, which has been excellent up to this point, now heads steeply up the hillside and virtually disappears in the forest. Follow the blazes on the trees with care.

At 10 miles, reach an open meadow with an old signpost at the center. The trail divides here. Straight ahead is the unmaintained Long Lake Trail which, if you do not get lost, can save a mile of walking and several hundred feet of climbing. The safer choice is the Munson Meadow Trail, which can be found in the upper left-hand corner of the meadow. This trail also has its obscure moments and must be followed with care as it climbs over the forested hillside to a ridge.

From the ridge, descend left to reach the tiny, sloping Munson Meadow at 12 miles. There is an intersection here: water is located to the right, Long Lake and Cole Creek Lakes are to the left. From the meadow, climb briefly then descend to a four-way intersection at 13 miles (7,800 feet). Long Lake and several forested campsites are located 0.5 mile to the right. To the left is the unmaintained Long Lake Trail. Continue straight to reach the first of the three Cole Creek Lakes at 14 miles (8,040 feet).

The first Cole Creek Lake is small and forested. Leave the main trail before it crosses the outlet and follow an unsigned path along the left shore to the second and most scenic of the lakes. Small, secluded campsites with views of Mokelumne Peak may be found along the southwest side of the lake, tucked into folds of the granite hillside.

# 2 SCOUT CARSON LAKE

**Round trip: 11 miles**
**Hiking time: 6 hours**
**High point: 8,950 feet**
**Elevation gain: 1,850 feet**

**Hikable: mid-July through**
**    September**
**Day hike or backpack**

**Maps: USFS Mokelumne Wilderness; USGS Caples Lake**

Reservations and Information: Amador Ranger Station and Carson
    Pass Information Center (Case 1)

Vast alpine meadows, pillars of basaltic rock weathered to exotic
shapes, hillsides bristling with so many rock towers that they look like
pincushions, basins gleaming with granitic rocks, beautiful vistas
framed by old mountain junipers, and a pleasing little subalpine lake
with excellent campsites are just some of reasons to hike up Horse
Canyon Trail to Scout Carson Lake.

**Access**. Drive Highway 88 east from Jackson 45 miles to the Silver
Lake resort. Continue east 0.8 mile and turn right on either the first or
second dirt road after the Oyster Creek Rest Area (7,150 feet). (From
the opposite direction, the trailhead is located 5.8 miles west of the
Caples Lake Resort.) Walk to the north end of the parking area to find
the well-defined trailhead on the right.

The trail ascends past several small meadows, then heads into
mixed-conifer forest. Before long you are winding around pillars of volcanic rock. As the climb continues, watch the hillside to the left for
views of a giant basalt escarpment topped with awesome battlements.

The climb steepens and soon you are scrambling up a rough trail
strewn with granitic boulders. At 2.5 miles pass a spur trail to the Silver Lake Boy Scout Camp on the right and 0.5 mile beyond cross a seasonal creek (8,300 feet), where water flows briskly until midsummer.

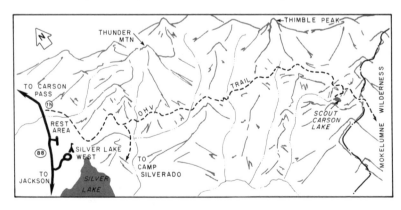

*Mountain juniper*

The trail follows the creek for 0.1 mile, then heads out to open meadows highlighted by a scattering of mountain junipers and views of Silver Lake.

With the majority of the climb completed, the trail traverses an incredible mountain garden with, depending on the season, fields of paintbrush, masses of woolly sunflower, or lupine-covered hillsides. At 5.2 miles, you will arrive at a broad bench below Covered Wagon Peak and an intersection. Go right and cross a lightly forested basin for 0.3 mile on a unmaintained but well-used trail to reach heather-fringed Scout Carson Lake at 5.5 miles (8,950 feet).

If you have extra energy, a 300-foot climb of the hillside above the lake will take you on an OHV (Off-Highway Vehicle) road and views of Fourth of July and Mokelumne Peaks from the top of the ridge.

# 3     EMIGRANT LAKE

**Round trip: 8 miles**
**Hiking time: 4 hours**
**High point: 8,600 feet**
**Elevation gain: 810 feet**

**Hikable: mid-July through**
   **September**
**Day hike or backpack**

**Maps: USFS Mokelumne Wilderness; USGS Caples Lake**

Reservations and Information: Amador Ranger Station and Carson
    Pass Information Center (Case 1)

Emigrant Lake lies on the dividing line between forest and high alpine meadows. At the north end of the lake a few hardy trees provide sheltered campsites, while the remainder of the lake is surrounded by steep cliffs and flower-covered meadows. Easy access makes this a popular destination in midsummer, so plan to arrive early to find a good campsite.

Snow lingers on the forested hillsides below Emigrant Lake long

*Emigrant Lake*

after it has melted from the open slopes above. Early season visitors should be prepared with good footwear for crossing steep, icy snow slopes and for fording flooded creeks.

**Access.** Drive Highway 88 west for 0.8 mile from Caples Lake Resort. Park just below Caples Lake dam (7,790 feet).

The trail begins at the upper right-hand side of the parking area and heads straight up the steep hillside to top of the dam, where it enters the Mokelumne Wilderness. The broad and nearly level trail parallels the lakeshore, passing through a popular fishing area. After the first 0.2 mile you will pass from forest to meadows then back into forest. At the 1 mile point, the Old Emigrant Road Trail branches off on the right. Continue straight ahead on a trail that becomes progressively rougher.

The trail leaves Caples Lake at 1.7 miles and heads up a forested valley, paralleling Emigrant Creek. At 2 miles, you will pass a spur trail to Kirkwood Ski Area on the right, then begin a steady climb. The trail crosses a seasonal stream then Emigrant Creek. Above Emigrant Creek, a switchback brings you up the granite-strewn hillside to meadows where boot-beaten paths to campsites branch off in every direction. Continue straight across the meadow and through a narrow band of trees to Emigrant Lake (8,600 feet).

The lake is in a deep cirque with Covered Wagon Peak towering over the southwest side and a shoulder of Fourth of July Peak dominating the eastern skyline. Both these peaks are easy cross-country destinations for hikers with off-trail experience and a good map. Experienced route finders may make a loop on the return trip by contouring west cross-country from Emigrant Lake to the ski area, then following the Old Emigrant Trail back to Caples Lake. The trail is nearly invisible in the vicinity of the Kirkwood ski runs. The best course is to contour the basin to the first chairlift and then descend. Find the ski area service road and follow it 0.5 mile to a well-marked trail on the right. Head down to rejoin the Emigrant Lake Trail on the shores of Caples Lake.

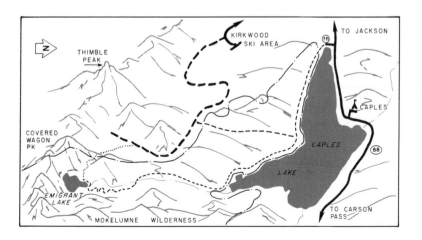

# 4  ROUND LAKE

Round trip: 10.5 miles
Hiking time: 5 hours
High point: 8,760 feet
Elevation gain: 320 feet in;
   740 feet out

Hikable: mid-June through
   September
Day hike or backpack

Maps: USFS Mokelumne Wilderness; USGS Caples Lake, Carson Pass,
   Echo Lake

Information: South Lake Tahoe Forest Service Office and Carson Pass
   Information Station (Case 2)

From sculptured mountain Jeffrey pines to colorful meadows to odd
and fantastic rock formations, this area has a wonderment of diversity.
Even subalpine Round Lake, the destination of this hike, shows amazing diversity with dark volcanic cliffs on one side and sloping granite
hills on the other.

If you can brave the armies of mosquitos that invade the meadows in
early summer, the best time to visit is shortly after the snow melts. At
that time open slopes around Meiss Pass explode with masses of alpine
flowers: lupine, scarlet gilia, mountain pennyroyal, and paintbrush.
Later in the summer, cattle reduce the beautiful meadows to stubble.

**Access.** Drive Highway 88 toward (Kit) Carson Pass. At 0.2 mile
west of the summit turn north into a large parking area (8,480 feet).

Follow the unsigned Pacific Crest Trail (PCT) north from the lower
west end of the parking area and head down-valley, skirting the
stately mountain Jeffrey pines growing on granite outcroppings. After
0.5 mile the trail crosses a small seasonal creek, then begins to climb
through the meadows.

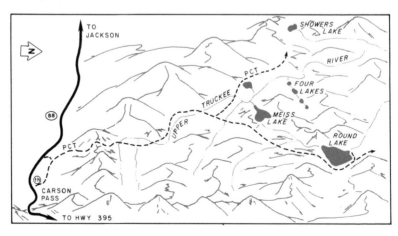

*Balsamroot growing on shore of Round Lake*

At 1.2 miles, pass a junction with the Old Meiss Trail on the left then continue up another 0.3 mile to reach Meiss Pass, the 8,760-foot high point of the hike. The view from the crest demands attention. Across the valley Elephants Back, Round Top, The Sisters, Thimble Peak, Black Butte, and Caples Lake fill the horizon. On clear days, Lake Tahoe is visible to the north. Of more immediate interest are the open slopes to the east and west, ideal for roaming and exploring.

If you can keep your feet on the trail, head across the saddle and descend steeply, dropping 400 feet to the meadows below. At the base of the hill is a seasonal creek, which must be forded in early season. At 2.6 miles you recross that same stream. Shortly beyond the second ford lies the reconstructed Meiss cabin and barn (now used as a skiers' warming hut in the winter) and the intersection where you leave the PCT and go right toward Round Lake on a multiple-use trail that is a popular mountain-bike route.

The Round Lake Trail climbs out of the meadows, then heads over a forested knoll. A short descent leads to yet another meadow. Cross the meadow then descend a forested hillside to reach the shores of Round Lake (8,030 feet) at 5.2 miles. Campsites are located all around the lake. This is a popular destination, so backpackers should arrive early on weekends to secure a scenic campsite. Day hikers can follow the trail until it leaves the lakeshore at the northeast corner of the lake and follow spur trails to picnic sites near the small dam at the outlet.

# 5    GROUSE LAKE

**Round trip: 12 miles**
**Hiking time: 7 hours**
**High point: 9,260 feet**
**Elevation gain: 1,324 feet in;**
   **900 feet out**

**Hikable: August through**
   **September**
**Day hike or backpack**

**Maps: USFS Mokelumne Wilderness; USGS Pacific Valley, Carson**
   **Pass, Caples Lake, and Mokelumne Peak (trail not noted)**

Reservations and Information: Amador Ranger Station, Carson Ranger
   Station, Carson Pass Information Center, Markleeville Guard
   Station (Case 1)

This is a magnificent High Sierran ramble through verdant meadows and across rocky ridges to the shores of a small subalpine tarn
cupped in a granite basin. The relatively minor elevation gain makes
this hike superb for beginning backpackers or an excellent day trip for
ambitious walkers. Campsites can be found at several points along the
trail; however, by midsummer the only certain water is at Granite and
Grouse Lakes.

**Access.** Drive Highway 88 east from Carson Pass 6.4 miles, then
turn right on Blue Lake Road. (From the east the turnoff is located 2.5
miles past the Lake Tahoe intersection.) Follow Blue Lake Road for
11.9 miles (of which 7.2 are on pavement) to an intersection at Lower
Blue Lake. Go right on a signed PG&E road for 1.7 miles to find a
parking area at the base of Upper Blue Lake dam. The hike begins
from the left-hand side of the parking area (8,136 feet).

The trail starts by crossing the overflow channel of Upper Blue
Lake. If the water happens to be flowing, cross on the dam and walk

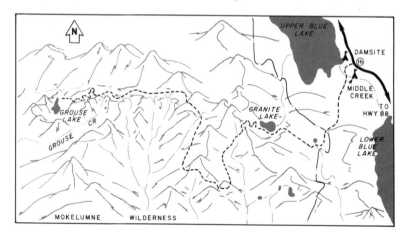

back down the opposite side of the channel to reach the trail. After heading through forest for 1,000 feet, cross a small creek and then pass the first of two spur trails from Middle Creek Campground before beginning a gradual but steady climb. At the 1-mile point, you will arrive at an unmarked intersection. Continue straight and enter the Mokelumne Wilderness.

The meandering climb continues. The trail passes a small lake at 1.3 miles and reaches aptly named Granite Lake at 2 miles (8,700 feet). Traverse along the shore to the southwest corner of the lake then go left and cross a low saddle. The trail then descends into the first and the prettiest of three basins.

At 2.5 miles reach the lower end of the first basin, where the trail abruptly heads uphill on a steep rib of granite. The well-defined tread disappears here and you must follow the tree blazes and ducks (small piles of rocks) to keep on course. The climb is followed by a traverse to the west on a steep hillside overlooking Meadow Lake then a descent through a second basin. The trail climbs steeply again then drops into the third basin.

Cross the third basin and ascend west to a rocky ridge with an excellent view over the Mokelumne Wilderness. The trail heads north along the open ridge crest to reach the trip's 9,260-foot high point, then begins a descending traverse. At the 5-mile point Grouse Lake comes into view and the trail suddenly plunges downhill, dropping 800 feet in the next mile as it descends a steep gully to a small bench. Contour right through grass, brush, then forest to reach Grouse Lake (8,400 feet) at 5.5 miles. The trail ends at the lakeshore. Campsites are located to the right and left.

*Grouse Lake Trail*

# 6 MILK RANCH MEADOW TRAIL

**Round trip: 10 miles**
**Hiking time: 5 hours**
**High point: 9,000 feet**
**Elevation gain: 800 feet**

**Hikable: mid-July through**
  **September**
**Day hike or backpack**

**Maps: USFS Carson-Iceberg Wilderness; USGS Ebbetts Pass and**
  **Dardanelles Cone**

Reservations and Information: Hathaway Pines Ranger Station or Alpine Ranger Station (Case 1)

The lack of crowds makes the beautiful meadows and grand vistas along the Milk Ranch Meadow Trail unique in the Highland Lakes area. This is an excellent day hike all summer; however, the seasonal

*Peep Sight Peak, a landmark along Milk Ranch Meadow Trail*

nature of the creeks and streams puts a mid-August limit on the use of the most scenic campsites. Late-season backpackers must rely on cattle-polluted water in Milk Ranch Meadow or a couple of seeps in the high meadows, or descend along Weiser Creek to camp.

**Access.** Drive Highway 4 to the Highland Lakes turnoff, located 12.7 miles east of Lake Alpine's East Shore Road or 1.3 miles west of Ebbetts Pass Summit. Head south on this rough and very steep dirt road for 4.2 miles to Tryon Meadow and park on the edge of the road. The trail starts at the first spur road on the right (8,430 feet).

Walk up the spur road, passing first a signboard, then a gate. Stay with the road for the first 0.2 mile as it climbs steeply to an intersection. Go right, passing a sign announcing the Carson-Iceberg Wilderness boundary. In 300 feet the road divides again. Go straight on what soon becomes a well-constructed trail and head northwest around Folger Peak. You will cross a small meadow, jump a couple of small seasonal streams, and pass a small man-made pond before descending to Milk Ranch Meadow, the 8,400-foot-high summer home of many cattle.

The trail crosses a small creek, then parallels the meadow. Pay attention to your route here and make an effort to stay with the best trail and avoid the cow paths. At the 2-mile point, pass through a cattle gate then continue up the meadow to a small lake and several campsites, summer home of millions of mosquitos.

After a second cattle gate, the trail becomes narrow, steep, and rough as it heads up a hillside covered with flowers. Rolling meadows and the first grand vistas are reached at 3 miles (8,800 feet). Continue southwest on a traverse around Peep Sight Peak through alternating forest and meadows. At 4 miles the trail reaches its 9,000-foot high point. Here you tread between rounded granite boulders and weathered basaltic spires for 0.5 mile to an open ridge overlooking Weiser Creek. Leave the trail here and walk left along the ridge for views of Henry and Bull Run Peaks to the west, Airola and Iceberg Peaks to the east, and Dardanelles Cone to the south. This is the ideal turnaround point for day hikers. Backpackers may want to descend another 0.5 mile to the Weiser Creek Trail (8,720 feet) for water and off-trail camping.

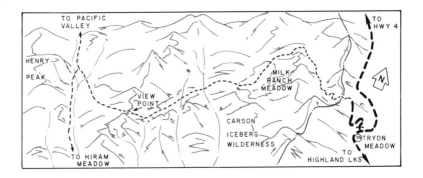

*Upper Gardner Meadow*

# 7 PARADISE VALLEY LOOP

**Loop trip: 15 miles**
**Hiking time: 2–3 days**
**High point: 9,340 feet**
**Elevation gain: 2,170 feet**

**Hikable: mid-July through**
**September**
**Backpack**

**Maps: USFS Carson-Iceberg Wilderness; USGS Dardanelles Cone and Disaster Peak**

Reservations and Information: Hathaway Pines Ranger Station or Alpine Lake Ranger Station (Case 1)

The rugged mountains of the Carson-Iceberg and Emigrant Wilderness form a dramatic backdrop for the miles of rich green meadows traversed on this scenic loop. Your route follows the Pacific Crest Trail south along the ridge crests, then descends through beautiful meadows of Paradise Valley to Adams Camp. The final leg of the loop climbs gradually through alternating forest and meadows to end with a stroll across the enchanting Upper Gardner Meadow.

This hike is at its best between mid-July and early August when snow still lingers on the trail. The snow may make walking harder but it keeps the cattle out and the seasonal creeks still flow with vigor, providing numerous campsites with water.

**Access.** Drive Highway 4 to the Highland Lakes Road turnoff, located 1.3 miles west of Ebbetts Pass summit. Follow the steep Highland Lakes Road south for 5.1 miles. Turn left just before the first lake and park at Gardner Meadow Trailhead (8,575 feet).

The hike begins on a broad trail that crosses (with a long jump) an active little creek, then winds around a steep hillside. At 0.5 mile the trail divides; stay left following the signs to Wolf Creek Pass. The right-hand trail is the return leg of your loop.

The well-used trail weaves across several small, soggy, very over-grazed meadows to reach an intersection at 1.7 miles (8,400 feet). Take the right fork and head south on the Pacific Crest Trail (PCT) toward Sonora Pass.

The PCT climbs steadily to an 8,720-foot forested divide, then descends into upper Wolf Creek basin. After crossing the creek, the trail climbs around the shoulder of a meadow-covered ridge to reach the Murray Canyon Trail intersection at 5.5 miles. About 500 feet beyond, pass the base of a hill composed of columnar basalt, then cross a forested saddle. The trail rolls along the hillside, passing an excellent campsite at the headwaters of Murray Canyon.

At 7 miles the trail crosses a saddle and enters a vast sagebrush-covered amphitheater surrounded by rows of peaks, including Stanislaus and Sonora and White Mountain. From the saddle descend for 0.6 mile to a four-way intersection, where the loop route leaves the PCT and turns right on the Disaster Creek Trail.

Head up the Disaster Creek Trail for 300 feet until it disappears on the dry hillside. Go right and walk straight up the slope to find the trail in the trees. The trail remains well defined as it climbs to the 9,340-foot crest of a broad ridge. At 8 miles, head down into Paradise Valley, passing through rich meadows and by several campsites. The trail parallels tumbling and cascading Paradise Creek throughout the 3-mile descent.

At 11 miles cross Paradise Creek, usually on a log, and enter the popular Adams Camp (7,720 feet). Go right, recross Paradise Creek, and follow Disaster Creek up-valley through a series of well-grazed meadows for the next 2.5 miles. At 13.5 miles pass the Arnot Creek Trail turnoff and continue straight into the nearly level Upper Gardner Meadow. At 14.5 miles your trail intersects the Wolf Creek Pass Trail; go left for the final 0.5 mile back to the Gardner Meadow Trailhead.

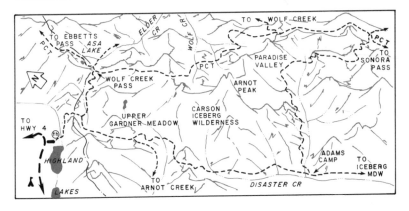

# 8 NOBLE AND ASA LAKES

**Round trip to Noble Lake: 9 miles**
**Hiking time: 5 hours**
**High point: 8,700 feet**
**Elevation gain: 400 feet**

**Hikable: mid-July through**
**September**
**Day hike or backpack**

**Maps: USFS Carson-Iceberg Wilderness; USGS Ebbetts Pass**

**Round trip to Asa Lake: 14 miles**
**Hiking time: 8 hours**
**High point: 9,350 feet**
**Elevation gain: 950 feet**

**Hikable mid-July through**
**September**
**Backpack**

**Maps: USFS Carson-Iceberg Wilderness; USGS Ebbetts Pass**

Reservations and Information: Carson City Ranger Station (Case 3)

Noble and Asa Lakes are popular destinations for day hikes and backpack trips from Ebbetts Pass. It is lucky the lakes are there, otherwise it would be hard to know when to stop walking on this spectacular stretch of trail. Snow lingers on the steep hillsides in the Ebbetts Pass area, often through mid-July. Early season hikers should carry an ice ax.

**Access.** Drive Highway 4 for 0.4 mile east of Ebbetts Pass summit to the large Pacific Crest Trail (PCT) parking area located on the south side of the road (8,700 feet). Trailhead facilities include a rest room but no running water.

From the upper end of the parking area, follow the trail as it climbs at a gradual pace through the forest for 0.2 mile to intersect the PCT. Go left on the PCT South, and continue the well-graded ascent to a saddle between two rounded knolls. Views of weathered ridge crests and a host of unnamed summits can be found by taking a short side trip to the crest of one or both knolls.

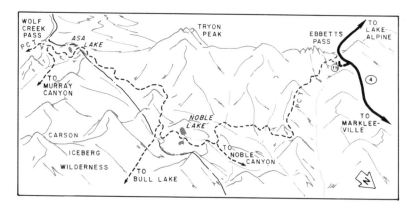

*Pacific Crest Trail south of Ebbetts Pass*

The trail descends, losing 100 feet of elevation, then contours a sloping meadow and crosses a seasonal stream. At 1.2 miles begin an even longer descent, which starts with a switchback down a forested hillside then continues as a sloping traverse over a meadow covered hillside overlooking Noble Canyon. To the east is a magnificent wall of rocky summits dominated by Silver and Highland Peaks. At 2.7 miles, shortly after passing the spur trail to Noble Canyon on the left, the descent ends and the trail resumes its climb.

At 3.2 miles cross Noble Creek on a log, then switchback up a hillside covered with volcanic boulders to reach a broad but somewhat overgrazed meadow below Tryon Peak at 4.5 miles. Shortly after entering the meadow, Noble Lake (8,700 feet) comes into view. Campsites are located around the lake, in the trees surrounding the meadows west of the lake, and at a secondary lakelet on the hill to the east.

To reach Asa Lake, pass Noble Lake and continue up the broad, open basin. The trail passes the Bull Lake intersection to reach a 9,350-foot saddle with views over Bear Tree Meadow and the Highland Lakes at 5.3 miles. You then descend gradually for 1.7 miles to the Asa Lake intersection. Go right and head steeply uphill for 500 feet to the small, forested lake and several campsites at 7 miles (8,580 feet).

# 9 RAYMOND LAKE

**Round trip: 21.2 miles**
**Hiking time: 2–3 days**
**High point: 9,000 feet**
**Elevation gain: 1,200 feet**

**Hikable: August through**
    **September**
**Backpack**

**Maps: USFS Mokelumne Wilderness; USGS Ebbetts Pass**

Reservations and Information: Carson Ranger Station (Case 3)

Keeping your eyes on the trail rather than glued to the scenery is the most difficult challenge of hiking this extraordinary section of the Pacific Crest Trail (PCT). The trail wanders over a meadow-covered plateau skirting the base of weathered ridges and colorful hillsides while passing jagged rock pillars and oddly rounded domes. The objective, Raymond Lake, is an alpine beauty tucked in a rock-bound cirque at the base of Raymond Peak.

**Access.** Drive Highway 4 to the large PCT parking area 0.4 mile east of the Ebbetts Pass summit (8,700 feet).

The hike begins with a gradual climb up a forested hillside to intersect the PCT at 0.2 mile. Continue straight, following the PCT North. At 0.5 mile carefully cross the Ebbetts Pass Highway, then climb with an easy switchback to the crest of a granitic saddle for the first of many sweeping vistas, this one overlooking the highway and Kinney Reservoir. The trail traverses north around Ebbetts Peak, descends, and then climbs, passing several ponds and little Sherrold Lake. At 2.2 miles pass a spur trail to Upper and Lower Kinney Lakes.

The trail follows a high route around Upper Kinney Lake, then begins one of the most exotic traverses on the entire PCT. At this point you leave the granitic landscape behind and enter Raymond Meadows, which lies at the southern end of a broad, meadow-covered bench. On the hills above, volcanic pillars make up the fantastic ramparts of Reynolds Peak.

The trail crosses a seasonal creek, then climbs around an open hill before descending to cross Raymond Meadows Creek at 4.5 miles. You then climb a low hill and descend to Eagle Creek at 5.6 miles. Following the creek, the trail heads down-valley for 0.2 mile, then turns uphill, winding its way among rocky pillars to an 8,500-foot pass before switchbacking down to cross Pennsylvania Creek at 7.4 miles. Campsites are limited here, so continue on, gaining over 600 feet in the next mile, to the crest of a sage-covered saddle.

The trail descends 300 feet into deeply gullied Raymond Canyon, then climbs to the crest of the next ridge and shortly beyond arrives at the Raymond Lake Trail intersection at 9.9 miles (8,660 feet). Go left and spend a final 0.7 mile on a gradual ascent to a well-earned rest at the lake. Campsites here are small but have the advantage of the early morning sunshine.

*Rocky ridge crest north of Eagle Creek*

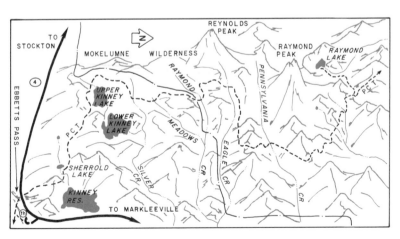

*Wolf Creek*

# 10    WOLF CREEK

**Round trip to Murray Canyon**
**Cutoff: 11 miles**
**Hiking time: 6 hours**
**High point: 7,720 feet**

**Elevation gain: 1,140 feet**
**Hikable: June through**
**mid-October**
**Day hike or backpack**

**Maps: USFS Carson-Iceberg Wilderness; USGS Wolf Creek**

Reservations and Information: Carson Ranger Station (Case 3)

Snow-capped peaks provide an almost surreal backdrop for the dusty green sage and grass-covered meadows at the upper end of Wolf Creek Valley. The low elevation of the meadows means that this area is snow free long before most other hikes in the Ebbetts Pass region, and the relatively low elevation gain ensures a good start to the summer hiking season. Finally, the system of self-registration at the trailhead makes this a great place for spur-of-the moment hikes.

This hike is troubled by some features not usually found in a wilderness. The 1984 California Wilderness Act allows for motorized access by grazing permitees in the Wolf Creek Valley, and a rugged jeep road serves as the trail. Motorized vehicles use this road throughout the summer; however, cattle generally are not grazed in the upper meadows until mid-to-late season.

**Access.** Drive west on Highway 4 for 2.5 miles from the Highway 89 intersection or 11 miles east from Ebbetts Pass. Turn south on Wolf Creek Road and follow it for 2.3 miles on pavement then for 1.4 miles up a steep and very rough gradient. At 3.7 miles from Highway 4 the road divides; go straight for another 1.5 miles to a small campground at the road's end (6,580 feet).

The trail (a 4x4 route) begins at the campground entrance and heads up-valley paralleling the creek. At 0.7 mile climb steeply over a rib of granite, then enter the first of many large meadows. The trail traverses around the edge of the meadow and at 1.2 miles arrives at Dixon Creek, the first obstacle encountered on this otherwise easy trek. For most of the summer this is a shallow but damp crossing. The alternative is to search up the creek for a log.

Beyond Dixon Creek the trail skirts in and out of the forest, passing meadows covered, in early season, by lupine and California sunflowers. As you head up-valley the granite slabs are left behind and gradually replaced by dark reddish volcanic breccia. Except for a climb over one rocky rib, this is a section of easy walking.

At 4.2 miles pass the unsigned Bull Canyon Trail, then descend to an unavoidably wet crossing of Bull Creek at 4.5 miles. Once past the ford, the trail heads straight up a rocky rib then descends to a wide bench dotted with weathered junipers. Pass through a cattle gate, then carefully descend the steep slope below the trail for a view of Wolf Creek Falls. The falls is an ideal turnaround point for day hikers. Backpackers, however, should continue on.

A spur road to the grazers' cabins branches left at 5.2 miles. The trail then rounds a fenced-in field and fords Wolf Creek. Shortly after the trail divides. The Murray Canyon Trail goes left and the Asa Lake Trail goes right. Scenic campsites can be found in both directions.

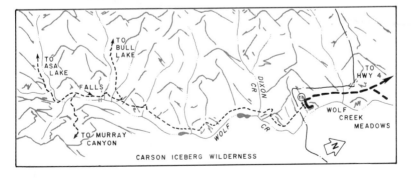

# 11     CRABTREE TRAIL

| | |
|---|---|
| **Loop trip: 13 miles** | **Elevation gain: 1,030 feet** |
| **Hiking time: 6 hours** | **Hikable: July through September** |
| **High point: 7,900 feet** | **Day hike or backpack** |

**Maps: USFS Emigrant Wilderness; USGS Pinecrest and Cooper Peak**

Reservations and Information: Pinecrest Ranger Station (Case 1)

Day hikes, easy weekend backpack trips, and extended adventures all are possible along this unique trail system through the northwest corner of the Emigrant Wilderness. The scenery—from the rounded granitic domes and rock-walled canyons to the sparkling lakes and flower-covered meadows—is addicting, enticing you to explore further into the wilderness.

Two main trails, a ridge route and a valley route, provide the main legs of any loop in this area. The two main trails are joined by several connectors allowing you to create a trip to suit your time and energy.

**Access**. Drive east from Sonora on Highway 108 for 29 miles to the Summit District Ranger Station at the Pinecrest Lake turnoff. Go east on Pinecrest Lake Road 0.3 mile to an intersection, then turn right and head uphill toward the Dodge Ridge Ski Area for 3.1 miles. When the road divides, stay right, following signs to Aspen Meadow for 0.5 mile. At a T intersection, turn left. After 1.6 miles this road divides; continue straight on Road 4N26 and drive through Aspen Meadows. After 2.8 miles the Crabtree Trailhead spur road leaves the main line and descends to a huge parking area. One-night camping is permitted here (7,180 feet).

From the parking lot, cross Bell Creek on a wide bridge then pass the Lake Valley Trail. Stay on the Crabtree Trail as it heads up

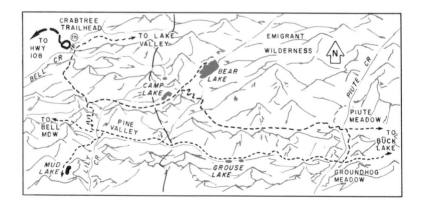

through forest. At 1.3 miles note the Pine Valley Trail on the right; this is the return leg of the loop. Stay left and continue on to Camp Lake (campsites are located south of the lake on the ridge and have a one-night limit). Pass the 1-mile spur trail to Bear Lake, then descend to cross Little Creek, hopefully on a log. The trail then climbs to the crest of a large hump where it levels off and passes a series of small puddles and larger, lily-covered mosquito hatcheries. A steep descent off the hump brings you to Piute Meadow at 6.3 miles.

Hop Piute Creek on the rocks and continue about 200 feet to an intersection. At this point the described loop turns right on Groundhog Meadow Trail and descends 0.5 mile to the lower end of Groundhog Meadow. For campsites go left to the meadow. The loop route heads right (west) and recrosses Piute Creek, then descends a narrow, scenic canyon to reach Grouse Lake at 8.7 miles. Campsites are located to the right of the trail at the edge of the cliffs.

At 9.8 miles scout around to find a log to cross Bear Creek, then head through the forest. The Mud Lake intersection is passed at 10.5 miles and 1,000 feet beyond you will find the Pine Valley Connector on the right. Head uphill past a group of anomalous basaltic towers to reach the Crabtree Trail at 11.5 miles. Go left to complete your 13-mile loop.

For other, longer, trips consider continuing east from Piute Meadow to Gem Lake for a 19.5-mile loop or to Deer Lake for a 21.6-mile loop. If you continue on all the way to Buck Lake, you will have a 24-mile loop adventure.

*Granite stairway on Crabtree Trail*

# 12   WHITESIDES MEADOW

**Round trip: 12 miles**
**Hiking time: 6 hours**
**High point: 9,160 feet**
**Elevation gain: 1,280 feet in;**
    **880 feet out**

**Hikable: August through**
    **September**
**Day hike or backpack**

**Maps: USFS Emigrant Wilderness; USGS Pinecrest and Cooper Peak**

Reservations and Information: Pinecrest Ranger Station (Case 1)

This is a ridge-top ramble to the vast meadows at the northwest corner of Emigrant Wilderness. Whitesides Meadow is just one of many possible destinations for this hike and an ideal location for a base camp for further exploration.

**Access.** Follow the access directions for Hike 11 from Highway 108 for 8.3 miles. Pass the Crabtree Trailhead turnoff and continue straight on Road 4N27 for 4.1 miles to the Gianelli Cabin Trailhead at the top of the ridge (8,570 feet).

The trail starts out with an easy grade, heading north to the edge of a ridge overlooking the South Fork Stanislaus River canyon, then begins a switchbacking ascent of the forested hillside. At the ridge crest the trail heads out over the open summit of Burst Rock (9,161 feet) to views of Castle Rock, the Three Chimneys, and The Dardanelles. A sign tells the story of the emigrants who brought their wagons over the

*Summit of Burst Rock*

trail you will be hiking—something to think about as you head up the next steep hill.

From Burst Rock descend to a broad saddle and the popular Powell Lake, where you will leave most of your fellow hikers. Beyond the saddle the trail climbs up and over a granite-capped ridge, then descends steeply to the upper end of a grassy meadow, where, at the 3-mile point, the Lake Valley Trail branches off to the right. Continue straight, climbing up the next ridge to reach the hike's 9,160-foot high point. As you descend the east side of this ridge you will see Hay Meadow to the northeast and massive Granite Dome to the east.

The trail dips to a saddle and a junction with the Y Meadow Dam Trail, then begins a gradual ascent past several small ponds and a small creek. A dam at 5.3 miles signals your entrance into Whitesides Meadow (8,830 feet). Campsites may be found across the dam or at the upper (northeastern) end of the meadow along the Cooper Meadow Trail.

*Snow plant*

For day excursions from a base camp at Whitesides Meadow, try a 6-mile round trip to Cooper Meadow and its historic cabins, a 5-mile round trip to Upper Relief Meadow, a 4-mile round trip to Toejam Lake, or a 7-mile round trip to Wire Lake or Long Lake.

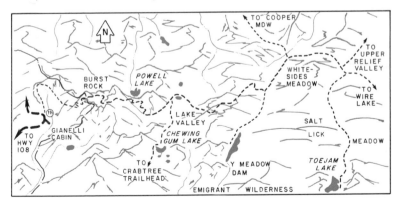

# 13  NEW SPICER MEADOW RESERVOIR

**Round trip: 11.6 miles**
**Hiking time: 6 hours**
**High point: 7,590 feet**
**Elevation gain: 640 feet in;**
  **1,360 feet out**

**Hikable: July through**
  **mid-October**
**Day hike or backpack**

**Maps: USFS Carson-Iceberg Wilderness; USGS Spicer Meadows Reservoir**

Reservations and Information: Hathaway Pines or Pinecrest ranger stations (Case 1)

This sublimely peaceful hike wanders through pine and fir forest to a large campsite at the upper end of New Spicer Meadow Reservoir. Unlike the quiet trail, the campsite, located at the intersection of three popular trails, is bustling with activity. Backpackers use this campsite as a base camp for explorations around the wilderness. Fishermen linger here a day or more to try their luck. Horse packers overnight here. You may even find campers who have come up the lake in kayaks or canoes.

**Access.** Drive Highway 108 east from Sonora 48 miles to the Clark Fork turnoff, or west 17.5 miles from Sonora Pass summit. Head north on Clark Fork Road for 0.9 mile. Cross the Middle Fork Stanislaus River and Clark Fork then take the first left on Road 6N06, which is rough and unpaved. Pass Fence Creek Campground and Wheats Meadow Trail before reaching road's end at the County Line Trailhead at 6.4 miles (7,200 feet).

The small, sloping parking area is remarkably busy on weekends. The main users are hikers; however, the occasional horse party adds their bit to an already dusty trail.

Two trails start from the County Line Trailhead. You should follow the County Line Trail, which begins on the left and immediately heads uphill. The climb lasts for 0.5 mile as the trail gains the 7,590-foot

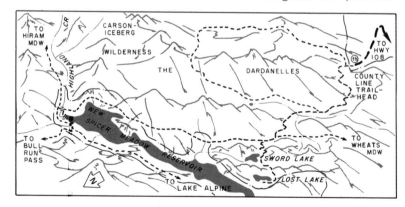

crest of a ridge, where you will pass a viewpoint over Middle Fork Stanislaus River Valley and Donnell Lake.

Pass the Dardanelles Spur Trail on the right, then descend through meadows and then forest for a mile to the valley floor, where the trail levels under the shade of pines and beautiful red and white firs. At 2 miles the Dardanelles Creek Trail branches off to your left and at 2.5 miles the trail divides. Watch carefully for this intersection. The broad, well-used trail to the left goes 0.2 mile out of your way to Sword Lake, a great place for a picnic or a quick dip. The trail you want is the narrow path on the right signed to Gabbott Meadow, a place that is now under the reservoir.

The trail skirts by several swamps, then crosses two seasonal creeks before it begins to climb again. Cross a 7,080-foot saddle at 4 miles, then descend to a singularly unappealing lakeshore dotted with dead trees. Do not be discouraged; the scenery and the lakeshore improve ahead.

The trail climbs over two granite knolls, then descends at 6 miles to an unsigned intersection. To the left are several large campsites frequently used by horse packers. Stay right and cross Highland Creek on a wide bridge to reach a second unmarked intersection. Hiram Meadow and Highland Lakes are to the right. Go left and descend to the camp area situated on a small isthmus between the creek and the lakeshore.

For further exploration try a 4-mile round trip to Hiram Meadow, a 7-mile round trip on the rough Bull Run Trail to the pass, or a 3-mile walk along the North Shore Trail toward Lake Alpine just to enjoy the views.

*Highland Creek*

# 14      KENNEDY LAKE

**Round trip: 15 miles**
**Hiking time: 2 days**
**High point: 7,830 feet**

**Elevation gain: 1,450 feet**
**Hikable: July through September**
**Backpack**

Maps: USFS Emigrant Wilderness; USGS Sonora Pass (High Trail not noted)

Reservations and Information: Pinecrest Ranger Station (Case 1)

The beautiful alpine valley at the end of this relatively easy hike to Kennedy Lake is not the place to go in search of solitude. This delightful area attracts a multitude of hikers and horse packers. Adding to the crowd, a large resident herd of cows spends the summer near the lake.

**Access.** Drive State Route 108 for 9.4 miles west of Sonora Pass summit to the Kennedy Meadows Road. Head south for 0.6 mile, then turn left to the large trailhead parking area (6,380 feet).

The hike begins with a very unexciting paved-road walk from the overnight parking area up-valley for 0.5 mile to Kennedy Meadows Resort. Walk past the resort and around a gate and continue up-valley on a dirt road called the Huckleberry Trail.

After a mile, the road ends and the route jogs left onto a wide, rocky trail. At 1.2 miles, cross a sturdy bridge then head up a narrow canyon along the edge of a roaring creek. The climb is steep and the trail, blasted into the perpendicular hillside, spectacular. At 1.5 miles Kennedy Creek comes into view, thundering down the hillside to the left in an impressive waterfall. When the trail divides, stay to the right; you'll rejoin the horse path a little further up.

At 2.7 miles (7,230 feet) leave the Huckleberry Trail, going left on the Kennedy Lake Trail and continuing the steep climb for another 0.5 mile. The climb eases at 3.2 miles when the trail crosses Kennedy Creek on a horse bridge and enters the Kennedy Creek valley. Head up-valley on a wide and very dusty trail and at 4 miles pass an un-

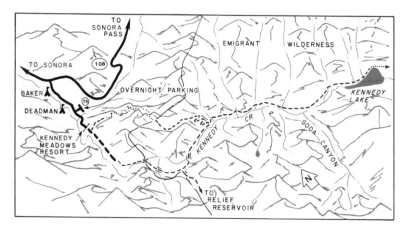

*Cows, permanent summer residents at Kennedy Lake*

signed intersection with the Night Cap Peak Trail. At this point most of the climbing is over and the trail rolls along the nearly level glacier-carved valley floor with views of Soda Canyon and the wide cirque below Relief Peak. As forest gives way to meadows, look for the first of many campsites.

A cattle fence denotes the close proximity of Kennedy Lake. Pass through the gate, then head across a meadow that gets progressively damper as you go. Pass an old cabin then walk to the next bend of the creek, where you will find a shaky log crossing to the large campsites on the opposite side.

To continue to the lake, go left, uphill, to drier meadows where a well-beaten route heads to the lake. Several small campsites are located along the shore.

If time and energy allow, the Night Cap Peak Trail offers a challenging alternative return route. This trail receives only occasional use, requires a good map, and entails some extra climbing. The rewards are solitude and delightful views south over Relief Reservoir.

# 15 EMIGRANT WILDERNESS LOOP

**Round trip: 39.5 miles**
**Hiking time: 4–6 days**
**High point: 12,000 feet**
**Elevation gain: 4,460 feet**

**Hikable: mid-August through**
**September**
**Backpack**

**Maps: USFS-Emigrant Wilderness; USGS Sonora Pass, Emigrant Lake, and Cooper Peak**

Reservations and Information: Pinecrest Ranger Station (Case 1)

This loop travels from the forested valleys to spectacular lakes and broad meadows nestled among the rugged peaks of the Emigrant Wilderness. This is not a trip for novices. The trails are in poor condition, often nothing more than a deep rocky trench churned by years of stock use. In some areas the trails disappear and route-finding skills are required; in other areas the trails are quagmires where cattle have sunk in the soft soil. However, the greatest difficulties are the numerous and occasionally hazardous fords.

**Access.** Drive State Route 108 west 9.4 miles from Sonora Pass summit to Kennedy Meadows Road. Head south for 0.6 mile, then turn left to the large forest service trailhead parking area (6,380 feet). (You may wish to drive the remaining 0.5 mile to the end of the road at Kennedy Meadows Resort and drop off your packs.)

The hike begins with a very unexciting paved-road walk from the parking area up-valley for 0.5 mile to Kennedy Meadows Resort. Walk around a gate and continue on a dirt road called the Huckleberry Trail. The road climbs gradually, skirts around the edge of Kennedy Meadow, and ends 1 mile from the resort. Jog left onto a wide, rocky trail, which enters the wilderness then crosses the Stanislaus River at 1.7 miles.

Beyond the bridge, the trail is blasted into the sides of the cliff as it climbs a narrow canyon. At 2 miles Kennedy Creek comes into view, thundering down the hillside to the left in an impressive waterfall. The trail crosses

*Duckwall Memorial commemorates those who first traveled this trail.*

the river a second time, then climbs to an intersection with the Kennedy Lake Trail at 3.2 miles (7,230 feet). Shortly beyond, pass the PG&E control cabin for Relief Dam. The trail leaves the wilderness at the power company development, then reenters soon after.

Proceeding another mile brings you to a viewpoint over Relief Reservoir. The trail traverses above the east shore of the reservoir, then descends to ford Grouse Creek at 4.2 miles. Water and campsites may be found here before you begin a series of switchbacks that bring you to a Y intersection at 6.2 miles (7,670 feet) and the start of the loop portion of your hike. You will return by the trail on the right. For now, stay left and head up Summit Creek toward Brown Bear Pass and Emigrant Lake.

The trail climbs over a low hill then heads into Saucer Meadow. Before long you are paralleling Summit Creek and passing several inviting campsites. The going is slow as you continue your ascent of the narrow valley on a dusty, boulder-strewn trail that has been pulverized by years of stock overuse. A steep climb leads to Sheep Camp at 10 miles. The trail then heads up to Lunch Meadow to reach an intersection with the Mosquito Pass Trail at 11.5 miles (9,420 feet). Go straight toward Brown Bear Pass.

Most of the stock heads for Mosquito Pass, so the condition of the trail improves significantly after the intersection. The climb to the pass is gradual and is enlivened by views of Granite Dome and Relief Peak. Brown Bear Pass summit is reached at 12.7 miles (9,720 feet). After taking in the view, descend a mile to a large basin where you will find Emigrant Meadow Lake and campsites. Cross the lake's inlet and in 0.2 mile go left and head southwest down Cherry Creek valley. Cross a low ridge, then ford Cherry Creek before reaching Middle Emigrant Lake after 1.2 miles. The trail becomes sporadic as you traverse

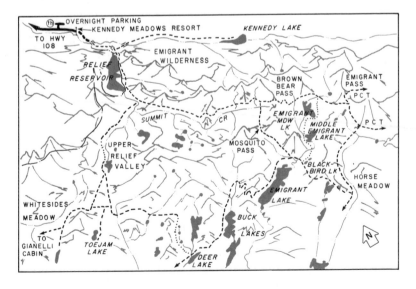

around the west shore of the lake and then make your way downvalley. Eventually the faint tread just disappears in the meadow. When the creek switches from the south to the north side of the valley, ford it and continue down the south side to reach Blackbird Lake at 16.5 miles (9,000 feet).

From Blackbird Lake, head northwest on a good trail 0.5 mile to intersect the Mosquito Pass Trail, then go left to reach Emigrant Lake at 17.5 miles. Good campsites may be found near the lake's inlet and outlet.

Once more you are on stock trail. The tread becomes progressively worse as you traverse the north shore of Emigrant Lake. You must climb over a low ridge then descend to ford Buck Meadow Creek before arriving at Buck Lakes at 20.5 miles (8,300 feet). There are plenty of campsites and lots of people here, many of whom were brought in by horse packers.

Proceeding to Deer Lake you will once again lose the trail among the rocks and verdant, wet meadows. The Forest Service is working on rerouting the trail out of the meadow, so there is hope for improvement. After fording the outlet creek from Long Lake, reach an intersection at 22 miles and go right (north) toward Upper Relief Meadow. The trail is rough to Spring Creek, where there is

another creek to wade. At 26.2 miles, near the upper end of Salt Lick Meadow, the trail divides (8,600 feet). Go right and head northeast for a mile to Upper Relief Valley. This is a marshy area and campsites are best established along the drier edges of the valley.

From the Upper Relief Valley to the Lower Relief Valley the trail is badly eroded and cut by washouts. The descent is steep and difficult. Lower Relief Valley (8,122 feet) has less water than the upper valley and a lot more camping opportunities. Unfortunately the cows also seem to prefer this valley and cow pies decorate the landscape.

From Lower Relief Valley the descent is brisk. The trail parallels

*Granite cliffs near Emigrant Lake*

Relief Creek for a while, then fords it. This is a very dangerous crossing and is not recommended during snowmelt or after a storm. The water runs swift and deep. If you are carrying a stout cord, a hand-line can be very helpful for shorter members of the group to hang on to. You also should wear your boots.

From the ford, the trail heads northeast for 0.3 mile to intersect the Relief Reservoir Trail at 33.3 miles. Go left for the final 6.2 miles back to the trailhead. (The resort offers expensive but good showers. Frogs in the shower stalls are complimentary. Food at the resort is good and not expensive.)

*Forsyth Peak from trail to Chain Lakes*

# 16      CINKO LAKE

**Round trip to Cinko Lake: 30 miles**  **Hikable: mid-July through**
**Hiking time: 3–4 days**            **September**
**High point: 9,400 feet**              **Backpack**
**Elevation gain: 2,200 feet**

**Maps: USFS Hoover Wilderness; USGS Pickle Meadow and Tower
   Peak**

Reservations and Information: Bridgeport Ranger Station or Leavitt
    Meadow Campground (Case 4)

Cinko Lake lies at the upper reaches of the beautiful West Walker
River Basin and is the perfect destination for this idyllic hike, which
wanders from lake to lake through verdant meadows and along thundering creeks to awesome views of the snow- and ice-clad peaks of the
Sierra Crest.

**Access.** Drive east on Highway 108 for 7.9 miles from Sonora Pass
or west 7 miles from the Highway 395 intersection to the Leavitt
Trailhead parking area (7,200 feet). The parking area has running water, toilets, and garbage cans.

From the parking area, walk east on Highway 108 for 500 feet to
Leavitt Meadow Campground. Go through the camp area, staying left
when the road divides, to find the trailhead and day-use parking area
at the river's edge.

The trail begins by crossing the West Walker River on a bridge,
then heading up the dry hillside to a bench and an intersection. Go
right and head through Leavitt Meadow to Roosevelt Lake. (The Secret
Lake Trail, to the left, rejoins your route up-valley, adding an extra
mile to the total.)

Pass two unsigned trails from the horse-packer station on the right in the Leavitt Meadow area, then climb a low ridge to intersect the Secret Lake Trail at 2.5 miles. Continue ahead and descend to Roosevelt Lake at 3 miles (7,290 feet). There are popular campsites here and at adjoining Lane Lake. Beyond Lane Lake you will gain elevation at a steady rate. Pass a good campsite at 4.4 miles where the trail brushes the edge of the West Walker River. At this point the climb becomes serious, pushing up to the crest of a knoll. Enjoy the view from the top, then plunge down to the Hidden Lake Trail junction and campsite at 5.5 miles.

The terrain is exceedingly scenic as the trail traverses granite cliffs along the very edge of the rushing river. At 6.7 miles the trail divides. Your trail fords the river. If the hikers' log is in place, go ahead and cross. If not, take the left fork and continue up-river until you find a safe crossing. Do not try to wade the deep and swift river.

At 7.2 miles the trail divides (7,900 feet). Go right and head up a dusty hillside for 0.8 mile to Fremont Lake (8,220 feet), which has good, though often crowded, campsites. To continue, return to the saddle above Fremont Lake and head toward the Chain of Lakes. This scenic trail climbs to a forested saddle, then descends into a delightful mosquito habitat at the lakes. Stay left at a signed junction to Walker Meadows and left again at an unsigned junction to Fremont Canyon. Descend to the largest lake in the chain, then climb over a granite rib to Lower and Upper Long Lakes and more campsites.

From Upper Long Lake go right (north) for 0.2 mile to intersect the Pacific Crest Trail (PCT) at 11.7 miles (8,960 feet) at the West Fork West Walker River bridge. Go left and walk south on the PCT following signs to Cinko Lake. After 0.2 mile the trail divides. Cinko Lake can be reached by either trail. The Emigrant Pass Trail approach is a mile shorter with one unavoidably wet creek crossing. If you prefer to stay dry, go left and follow the PCT for 2 miles to the second Cinko Lake intersection. From there it is only a 1-mile climb past Bills Lake to reach Cinko Lake (9,230 feet) at 15 miles.

Cinko Lake is a small subalpine gem cupped between Grizzly Peak and a pink granite dome. Campsites are numerous around the lake and among the benches above.

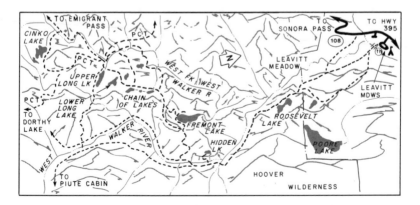

# 17     TAMARACK LAKE

**Round trip: 9 miles**
**Hiking time: 5 hours**
**High point: 9,660 feet**
**Elevation gain: 2,560 feet**

**Hikable: mid-July through**
   **September**
**Day hike or backpack**

**Maps: USFS Hoover Wilderness; USGS Twin Lakes**

Reservations and Information: Bridgeport Ranger Station (Case 5)

Nestled beneath the steep walls of Monument Ridge and Crater Crest in a rocky basin carpeted with high alpine meadows and high-lighted with hardy trees, Tamarack Lake is a true subalpine master-piece. This is a peaceful place, receiving only a fraction of the number of hikers that throng Barney Lake (Hike 18). The trail; however, is steep and can be rather discouraging under the midday sun. Start your hike early and carry plenty of water.

**Access.** Drive Highway 395 to Bridgeport. At the west end of town find Twin Lakes Road and follow it southwest for 10.3 miles. Pass a self-service laundry and showers on the right, then take the first road on the left signed "National Forest Campgrounds." Follow this road for 0.6 mile to the Day Use Area with rest rooms (7,100 feet).

Walk back down the road 400 feet to find the start of the trail opposite a campground entrance. The trail begins by climbing steeply. After ascending 200 feet, cross the powerline road then continue steeply up an old moraine. Before long you will have a view of Lower Twin Lake, Robinson Creek valley, Sawmill Ridge, and Sawtooth Ridge.

After climbing over two false summits, the trail reaches the 7,930-foot moraine crest and an unsigned intersection at 0.7 mile. Go right and head gradually up along the moraine. To the east lies Upper Summer Meadows, a rich pasture and home to many sheep. After a relatively easy 0.5-mile traverse, the climb resumes up flower- and

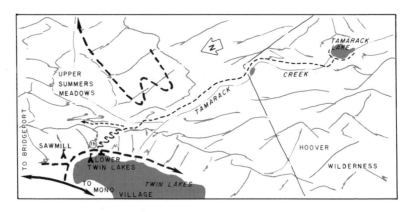

*View of Monument Ridge from meadow near Tamarack Lake*

sage-speckled slopes to Tamarack Creek; cross it with an Olympian long jump.

With the exception of one small grove of aspen trees, the climb is exposed to the hot sun. Watch to the north and east as views of Bridgeport, the reservoir, and the Sweetwater Mountains unfold.

At 3.6 miles the trail reaches the entrance of Tamarack Valley (9,200 feet) and the steep climb subsides a bit. The trail bends left, contouring around an expanding swamp before it can continue up-valley. After a short climb, pass to the left of a lush meadow and reach an unmarked intersection. Go right and cross a small, marshy creek, then head across the wet meadow using tree limbs to guide you over the mud and back onto the well-marked path. The trail heads up through a band of trees to reach Tamarack Lake (9,660 feet) at 4.5 miles. Campsites are spread around the lake; take your pick.

Unlike the steep and impenetrable granitic mountains to the west, the area around Tamarack Lake is of volcanic origin and invites exploration. The cross-country hiker may continue on from the end of the trail at Tamarack Lake to two other lakes or to an 11,100-foot saddle on the Crater Crest.

*Kerrick Meadow*

# 18 CROWN POINT LOOP

**Loop trip: 22.5 miles**
**Hiking time: 3 days**
**High point: 10,150 feet**
**Elevation gain: 3,340 feet**
**Hikable: August through**
**September**
**Backpack**

**Maps: USFS Hoover Wilderness;**
**USGS Buckeye Ridge and**
**Matterhorn Peak**

Reservations and Information:
Bridgeport Ranger Station (Case 5)

Lingering snow fields and a difficult river crossing make it advisable to wait until August before setting out on this elegant loop through the Hoover Wilderness to a remote corner of Yosemite National Park. The suggested itinerary allows three days for the hike with overnight camps at Crown and Peeler Lakes.

**Access.** Drive Highway 395 to the ranger station located 1 mile south of Bridgeport and pick up your wilderness permit. Head north to the center of town and turn west on Twin Lakes Road for 14 miles to road's end at Mono Village Resort. The large resort parking area (fee charged) is to the left (7,070 feet).

Start your hike at the north side of the marina store. Go left and walk as straight as possible through the crowded and dirty campground following occasional Barney Lake signs. At the far end of the campground pass a gate, then walk the road for 30 feet to find the trail on the right. Before long the trees give way to open meadows with Victoria Peak to the right and the incredible Sawtooth Ridge to the left. At 2.9 miles the trail begins to climb with a series of long, lazy switchbacks.

After hopping a couple of creeks, reach Barney Lake (8,300 feet) at 4 miles. Several campsites and a million mosquitos may be found near the outlet. The trail continues up-valley heading toward Crown

Point, climbing then descending granite slopes along the lakeshore.

At 4.5 miles you must cross Robinson Creek. The unavoidable ford is fairly deep but not extremely fast. The trail then heads steeply up the forested hillside for 0.3 mile and fords the creek again. Here the water is deep, fast, and dangerous. Take time to find a good log crossing.

Beyond the fords, the trail zigzags up the granite hillside to an intersection at 6.7 miles (9,100 feet), which marks the start of the loop portion of the hike. Go left and traverse a lake-studded bench below Crown Point to reach Crown Lake (9,030 feet) at 8.2 miles. Tent sites on the granite ledges above the lake have views of Slide Mountain, Kettle Peak, and Sawtooth Ridge.

Beyond Crown Lake the trail climbs 0.7 mile to an intersection with the Mule Pass Trail. Stay right and continue up the open valley, passing Snow Lake to reach Rock Island Pass (10,150 feet) at 10.2 miles.

From the pass, head down a faint and poorly marked trail into Yosemite National Park. At 12.3 miles, cross Rancheria Creek (usually a dry crossing), then go left for 100 feet to intersect the Kerrick Meadow Trail (9,300 feet).

Head to the right and hike up through a classic Sierra meadow where granite boulders pop up like mushrooms in a velvet sea of green. The meadow is wet and the trail crosses numerous little creeks. Reach the next intersection at 13.8 miles, 5.5 miles from Crown Lake. Take the right fork and head toward Peeler and Twin Lakes.

Peeler Lake (9,500 feet) at 14.4 miles has two outlets, one to the east and one to the west. Campsites may be found near the east outlet or halfway around the lake.

From Peeler Lake the trail climbs 100 feet out of the basin, then descends briskly for a mile to close the loop portion of the hike at the Crown Lake intersection. Retrace your steps for the final 6.7 miles back to Twin Lakes.

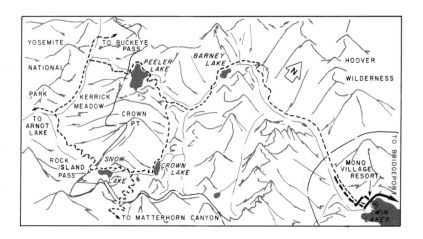

# 19 HOOVER LAKES

| | |
|---|---|
| **Round trip to Hoover Lakes:** 13 miles | **Elevation gain: 1,780 feet** |
| **Hiking time: 2 days** | **Hikable: mid-July through September** |
| **High point: 9,860 feet** | **Backpack** |

**Maps: USFS Hoover Wilderness; USGS Dunderberg Peak**

| | |
|---|---|
| **One-way from Virginia Lakes:** 11.5 miles | **Elevation gain: 1,250 feet** |
| **Hiking time: 2 days** | **Hikable: August through September** |
| **High point: 11,110 feet** | **Backpack** |

**Maps: USFS Hoover Wilderness; USGS Dunderberg Peak**

Reservations and Information: Bridgeport Ranger Station (Case 5)

Except for several difficult creek crossings, the Green Creek Trail to Hoover Lakes is ideal for relaxed backpacking. The numerous lakes, excellent scenery, and low-mileage days make this the kind of hike where you spend more time enjoying the scenery than nursing sore feet up the trail.

**Access.** To reach the Green Creek Trailhead, drive south on Highway 395 for 3.9 miles from the Bridgeport Ranger Station. Go right on gravel-surfaced Green Creek Road for 3.5 miles to the intersection with Virginia Lakes Road. Turn sharply right for another 5.2 miles to a large trailhead with a toilet, running water, and garbage cans (8,080 feet).

The hike begins with a stroll along a forested ridge above Green Creek Campground. After 0.5 mile the trail intersects a gated road; go right and follow the road up-valley for 0.3 mile to the road's end and an old trailhead.

The ascent is steady as the trail heads up-valley through beautiful

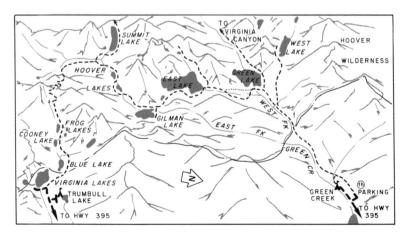

*East Lake*

wildflower gardens along Green Creek. Climb over two granite humps with views up Glines Canyon to Virginia Peak, and at 2.7 miles pass an intersection with the West Lake Trail (an excellent 3-mile side trip). The main trail stays to the left and continues up-valley for 0.3 miles to Green Lake (8,945 feet). Here you must cross the creek, either on the dam or, when the water is high, on a log.

From the forested shores of Green Lake, the trail climbs south making two creek crossings before reaching East Lake (9,458 feet) at 4.5 miles and another creek crossing. If the creek is high, cross on the dam. Campsites are located all around this subalpine lake.

The trail heads around the east side of the lake, then passes little Nutter Lake and more campsites. At 5.5 miles a spur trail branches left to very scenic Gilman Lake, located in a basin below Dunderberg Peak.

Beyond the intersection the trail ascends again, passing a couple of small lakelets before making a mandatory and moderately difficult ford of East Green Creek. At 6.5 miles you will pass through a narrow canyon that soon opens up to a broad 9,819-foot bench and the first Hoover Lake. The trail threads its way between the first and second lakes, fording the creek again. Campsites around these high alpine lakes are open, exposed, and scenic.

**One-way trip.** A one-way hike from Virginia Lakes adds even more enchanting lakes and views to your trip. From the trailhead, climb past Virginia Lake (9,890 feet) to Blue Lake, then on to Cooney Lake. The trail crosses a creek, then ascends past Frog Lake, where the climb steepens. At 3 miles reach the summit of a spectacular 11,110-foot divide. From the divide, follow the trail down 1.3 miles to a junction (10,000 feet) and go right for 0.7 mile to Hoover Lakes.

# 20  KOIP PEAK PASS TRAVERSE

**One way: 23.7 miles**
**Hiking time: 3–4 days**
**High point: 12,263 feet**
**Elevation gain: 3,743 feet**

**Hikable: August through**
  **September**
**Backpack**

**Maps: USFS Ansel Adams Wilderness; USGS Koip Peak**

Reservations and Information: Lee Vining Ranger Station and Rush
    Creek Trailhead Permit Booth (Case 6)

This scenic High Sierran traverse crosses four passes, parallels the
shores of five alpine lakes, traverses numerous flower-covered meadows, and passes so many high vistas you will feel like you are walking
on top of the world. Although extremely scenic, this is a difficult
traverse with steep and rocky trails, lingering snow fields, and high
elevations.

**Access.** Drive south from Lee Vining to the northern June Lake
Loop turnoff and go right for 1.5 miles. At the Parker Lake-Walker
Lake sign go right on a dusty road, then take an immediate left. At 0.4
mile stay right, following the Walker Lake signs. At 1.3 miles from the
June Lake Road take a left on a rough and narrow road for 1.9 miles to
a small trailhead parking area (8,360 feet). Leave your second vehicle
at the Rush Creek Trailhead, 7 miles beyond the Walker Lake turnoff.

Your hike begins with a steep climb, gaining 160 feet of elevation.
Cross a forested ridge, then plunge down the far side toward Walker
Lake (7,940 feet). At 0.5 mile the trail divides, stay left. The trail
gradually levels, then heads around the top of the lake where you cross
Walker Creek on a log jam and battle mosquitos to reach an intersec-
tion at 0.8 mile. Go left and begin the hardest, and hottest, climb of the

*Campsite near Alger Lakes*

traverse up Bloody Canyon to Sardine Lakes. The trail is steep, designed for hardy hikers rather than horses. At 3.5 miles pass Sardine Lake (9,880 feet). Continue up the amazingly steep trail, which takes only 0.5 mile to climb the next 500 feet. At the top of the hill, pass a small tarn. Leave the trail and go left to good campsites at Upper Sardine Lake (10,360 feet).

From Upper Sardine Lake it is an easy 0.5-mile stroll to Mono Pass (10,840 feet). Follow the trail 0.1 mile north from the pass, then go left on the poorly signed, all-but-invisible Parker Pass Trail. Cross the meadow to find a well-defined trail on the far hillside. The trail climbs up the low ridge, then heads south into breathtaking views.

At 6.7 miles the trail crests 11,050-foot Parker Pass, then descends past a couple of small tarns with mediocre campsites. The lowest tarn is at 10,810 feet and beyond this point the trail begins its climb to Koip Peak Pass. The trail is steep and switchbacks relentlessly with unexcelled views east over Mono Lake. Allow at least three hours to reach the 12,263-foot pass. (Consider the possibility of electrical storms before you start up.)

The descent from Koip Peak Pass is rapid and relatively easy to Alger Lakes (10,620 feet), reached at the 13.5 mile mark of the traverse. Campsites are located on the peninsula between the two lakes.

From Alger Lakes the trail climbs briefly past a couple of meadow-fringed tarns, then traverses southeast to forested Gem Pass (10,410 feet) at 15 miles. From this point it is a 4-mile descent to Gem Lake (9,045 feet) and the Rush Creek Trail. Campsites are located at the intersection and to the east along the lakeshore. Go left for the final 4.7 miles of scenic walking along Gem Lake, then Agnew Lake. The traverse ends with a breathtaking descent down the cliffs to the Rush Creek Trailhead at Silver Lake.

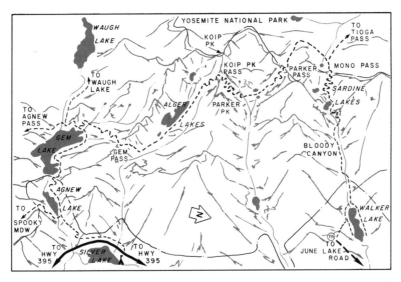

# 21 RUSH CREEK LOOP

**Loop hike: 21 miles**
**Hiking time: 3 days**
**High point: 10,200 feet**
**Elevation gain: 3,477 feet**

**Hikable: mid-July through**
  **September**
**Backpack**

**Maps: USFS Ansel Adams Wilderness; USGS Koip Peak and Mt. Ritter**

Reservations and Information: Mono Lake Ranger Station and Rush
    Creek Trailhead (Case 6)

An endless stream of summer visitors make the long trek up Rush
Creek to fish or sit by the shore of one of four large, sparkling lakes
and contemplate the rugged peaks reflecting in their crystalline waters. Apply for your backpacking permit in early March if you wish to
ensure a time and date for hiking this popular loop route.

**Access.** Drive south from Lee Vining on Highway 395 to the first
June Lake Loop Road turnoff, then go west on Highway 158 for 8.5
miles to the Rush Creek Trailhead (7,223 feet).

The trail crosses Alger Creek on a log bridge, then skirts an RV park
before switchbacking up the cliffs on the hillside above Silver Lake.
You will cross the Cal Edison funicular railroad twice before the con-
crete edifice of the Agnew Lake Dam comes into view. As soon as you
spot the dam, look left for the unsigned Spooky Meadows Trail, which
is the return route for your loop.

Walk past Agnew Lake (8,508 feet) and continue the climb to a second dam, which holds the waters of beautiful Gem Lake (9,045 feet).
The trail makes an up-and-down traverse around the north side of the
lake, passing numerous campsites. At 4.7 miles, pass the Alger Lakes
Trail intersection and the last of the lakeshore campsites. At this point

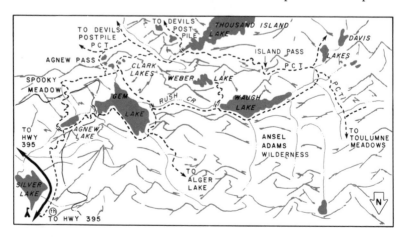

the trail leaves the lake and heads over a ridge to forested Rush Creek and the Agnew Pass/ Clark Lakes Trail intersection. Continue straight, paralleling Rush Creek and passing several large campsites while ascending gradually to the dammed outlet of Waugh Lake (9,424 feet) at 6.5 miles. Pass a spur trail to Weber Lake, then continue straight around Waugh Lake to find campsites at 7 miles. More campsites are located on an unmarked spur trail at the upper end of the lake.

Beyond Waugh Lake the trail climbs gradually to cross Rush Creek (look for a good log), then heads south to intersect the combined John Muir Trail/Pacific Crest Trail (JMT/PCT) at 8.5 miles (9,680 feet). Go left (south) and ford three forks of Rush Creek (wet in early season) in the next 0.4 mile. Shortly beyond the third crossing is the sometimes-obscure Davis Lake Trail intersection. The 1-mile side trip to Davis Lake leads to small but scenic campsites away from the crowds.

At 9.9 miles reach the crest of 10,200-foot Island Pass. Descend past a couple of small but inviting tarns with excellent views, then continue down to reach the outlet

*Gem Lake*

of Thousand Island Lake (9,834 feet) at 11.4 miles where the JMT and PCT split. All camping here must be done at least 0.2 mile away from the outlet.

The loop follows the PCT south for 1.7 miles to the Clark Lakes Trail. Go left and cross the ridge at an unnamed 9,900-foot saddle, then descend to Clark Lakes and several small campsites. Continue descending to reach a three-way junction at 14.8 miles. To the left a well-graded trail descends back to the Rush Creek Trail near Gem Lake. If your knees are not strong or the soles of your shoes are a bit slick, that is the trail to take. The loop route goes to the right, ascending to a small tarn then descending steeply through Spooky Meadow. Below the meadows the trail switchbacks down a slope of loose scree, then crosses Rush Creek just below the Agnew Lake Dam. This ends the loop portion of the hike. Go right for your final descent back to Silver Lake on the Rush Creek Trail.

*Banner Peak and Garnet Creek*

# 22 THOUSAND ISLAND LAKE LOOP

**Loop trip: 18.9 miles**
**Hiking time: 2–4 days**
**High point: 10,160 feet**
**Elevation gain: 2,760 feet**

**Hikable: mid-July through September**
**Backpack**

**Maps: USFS Ansel Adams Wilderness; USGS Mammoth Mountain and Mt. Ritter**

Reservations and Information: Mammoth Ranger Station (Case 6)

The stunningly beautiful Middle Fork of the San Joaquin River Valley has a richly deserved reputation as an excellent hiking area. There are three trails up the Middle Fork Valley that converge near Thousand Island Lake, creating an ideal loop. This hike follows the High Trail north to Thousand Island Lake, allowing you to enjoy exceptional views of the Minarets and the Ritter Range, then returns south along the base of the Ritter Range via the River and John Muir Trails.

**Access.** The loop starts from the first parking lot at the Agnew Meadows Trailhead (8,320 feet). See Hike 23 for directions and shuttle bus information.

Start your loop by following the High Trail north from the first of the two parking areas. After several hundred feet, cross an unsigned trail from the pack station. Go straight and begin a series of switchbacks that will take you 500 feet above the valley floor to meadows and views of Mammoth Mountain, then head northeast on a long, ascending traverse. At 2.7 miles pass an eye-catching viewpoint of Shadow Lake, the Minarets, and Mt. Ritter. Beyond the viewpoint, the trail begins a scenic 4.5 mile-traverse over open meadows covered with waist-high

lupine and corn lilies. The first of three trails to Clark Lakes and
Agnew Pass branches off to the right at 5.2 miles. One mile beyond, go
straight at a four-way intersection with a trail to Agnew Pass on the
right and a connector to the River Trail on the left. Contour around the
head of the valley, passing the swampy Badger Lakes at 6.3 miles.
Campsites are located at the largest Badger Lake, 0.2 mile to the
southeast. The High Trail and River Trail join at 6.8 miles. Continue
straight for 1 more mile to Thousand Island Lake (9,840 feet). No
camping is allowed within a 0.2-mile radius of the lake's outlet. Good
campsites may be found by heading cross-country along the north or
south shore of the lake.

From Thousand Island Lake, head south on the John Muir Trail
(JMT), which climbs to Emerald Lake then to Ruby Lake. Campsites
may be found at either of these two jewels. The trail then climbs to a
10,160-foot pass before descending to Garnet Lake (9,700 feet) at 10.3
miles. With snow-speckled Banner Peak piercing the sky at the upper
end, Garnet Lake is the undeniable gem of this loop. Find your campsite along the north shore, at least 0.2 mile away from the outlet.

Cross the Garnet Lake outlet and pass an unmarked junction with a
River Trail lateral. Head around the lake for another 0.2 mile then
climb to a 10,160-foot saddle with lazy switchbacks. The descent down
the south side of the saddle is rocky and before long the trail enters the
forest. At 14.5 miles the JMT intersects the Shadow Creek Trail and
goes left, down-valley.

At 15.3 miles leave the JMT and go straight on the Shadow Lake
Trail. Weave your way around the day hikers near the lake, then descend along the cascading Shadow Creek to cross the Middle Fork San
Joaquin River on a sturdy bridge (8,000 feet). At 17.3 miles, go right on
the River Trail and climb the 320 feet required to bring you back out of
the valley. At 18.4 miles the River Trail ends. Go left on the PCT following signs to Agnew Meadows. A few feet beyond the intersection,
the trail divides; stay right for the final 0.5 mile back to the trailhead
parking area.

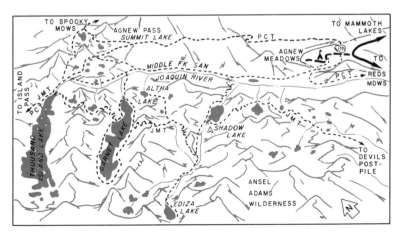

# *23* SHADOW OF THE MINARETS

**Round trip to Ediza Lake: 20 miles**
**Hiking time: 3–4 days**
**High point: 9,630 feet**
**Elevation gain: 2,620 feet**

**Hikable: mid-July through**
  **September**
**Backpack**

**Maps: USFS Ansel Adams Wilderness; USGS Mammoth Mountain and**
  **Mt. Ritter**

**One-way traverse: 16.2 miles**
**Hiking time: 3–4 days**
**High point: 10,300 feet**
**Elevation gain: 3,580 feet**

**Hikable: August through**
  **September**
**Backpack**

**Maps: USFS Ansel Adams Wilderness; USGS Mammoth Mountain, Mt.**
  **Ritter, and Crystal Crag**

Reservations and Information: Mammoth Ranger Station (Case 6)

Let your own abilities determine which of these two hikes you will take into the spectacular country at the base of Mt. Ritter and the Minarets. The Ediza Lake hike follows excellent trails to this beautiful lake. The traverse hike—which continues from Ediza Lake on a steep and sketchy route to Iceberg, Cecile, and Minaret Lakes—requires route-finding skills, a bit of easy scrambling, and for much of the summer an ice ax for crossing the icy slopes around Iceberg Lake. At Minaret Lake the traverse route rejoins well maintained trails for the descent to Devils Postpile National Monument.

**Access.** From the Mammoth Lakes Forest Service Visitor Center,

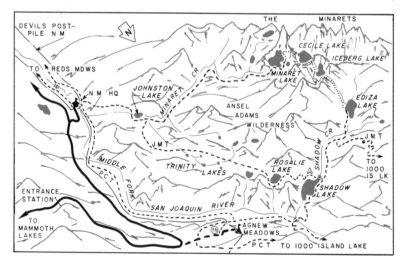

*The Minarets towering above Minaret Lake*

drive up through town on Highway 203. After 1.2 miles, go right on Minaret Road (Highway 203) and continue up for another 4.2 miles to the Mammoth Mountain Ski Area, then take the shuttle bus to Agnew Meadows. From the bus stop, walk the dirt road 0.3 mile to the second trailhead parking lot (8,320 feet). The bus ride is mandatory between the hours of 7:30 A.M. and 5:30 P.M.; if arriving before or after these hours you may drive to the trailhead. See Wilderness Permits, Case 6 for more shuttle-bus information.

From the parking area, walk south on the Pacific Crest Trail (PCT), following signs to Shadow Lake. The trail crosses Agnew Meadow, then traverses the forest. At 0.5 mile, pass an unmarked spur trail to the campground on the right. Continue straight to a major intersection where you will leave the PCT and head right on the River Trail.

The River Trail descends to the San Joaquin River, then heads up-valley. At 1.5 miles leave the River Trail and go left on the Shadow Lake Trail, which crosses the San Joaquin on a sturdy bridge. The trail then climbs, switchbacking up an open hillside along cascading Shadow Creek to Shadow Lake (8,789 feet) and the first close-up view of the Minarets.

Follow the trail around the north shore to the upper end of Shadow Lake, where you will join the John Muir Trail (JMT) at 4.2 miles. The

*View of steep descent route from Cecile Lake and Minaret Lake*

only legal campsites in this overused area are located to the left from the intersection. To continue on to Ediza Lake, go straight following the JMT north up the forested valley, paralleling Shadow Creek. At 5 miles you must leave the JMT as it turns north toward Garnet Lake. Continue up the delightfully scenic valley to reach Ediza Lake (9,340 feet) at 7 miles. Camping here is limited to the east shore or on the benches high above the lake.

Ediza Lake is a true alpine beauty and a satisfying destination for any trip. It can be used as a base camp for day hikes to the lakes above or as an overnight stop before attempting the next stage of the very difficult traverse.

The official trail ends at the north end of Ediza Lake; however, a well-defined path heads around the lake. At the south end, stop and look ahead at your route to Iceberg Lake. The lake is located south of Ediza Lake at the base of the Ritter Range. Look up and spot a granite hump. The good-sized creek that descends from a low saddle on the left side of the hump is the outlet from Iceberg Lake, your destination.

As you start up, the trail fractures into a multitude of bootpaths. You need to find the well-used trail that parallels the creek then climb up and over the saddle to Iceberg Lake (9,840 feet).

Iceberg Lake sits in a granite basin and is the recipient of large amounts of snow, which slides off the Minarets throughout the winter and spring. The snow lingers here for most of the summer and the next stage of your hike to Cecile Lake often requires traversing or climbing icy snow slopes. Campsites that are both comfortable and legal are difficult to find here.

Once again, stop and scope out your route before continuing on from Iceberg to Cecile Lake. Look south across the lake to the waterfall descending from a low saddle 500 feet above. The top of the waterfall is your goal.

Traverse around the left (east) side of Iceberg Lake, then, keeping your goal in sight, ascend the rocky slope on the left side of the waterfall. The final 75 feet are very steep, requiring both hands to hang onto the rocky slope. Cecile Lake (10,300 feet), at the top of the waterfall, has several comfortable and very scenic campsites at either end. The lake is nestled right at the base of Clyde Minaret and the feeling of high-mountain wilderness is all-pervasive.

The next stage of your traverse is a boulder hop around the east side (shorter but more difficult) or west side (longer and slightly easier) of Cecile Lake to a spectacular view of the Ritter Range. Then you must head down the steep, cliffy hillside to idyllic Minaret Lake in the basin below. There is no easy way down. From the southeast end of the lake, walk to the trees at the end of the moraine and look to locate a rugged gully that descends in giant steps. Head down using both hands at the start. Descend slowly and use a great deal of caution.

Minaret Lake (9,820 feet) is reached after an incredibly long, hard, and time-consuming 3-mile hike from Ediza Lake. Excellent campsites are located around the lake on all but the north shore.

Once you reach the base of the cliff below Cecile Lake, you will be on a good trail for the remainder of the traverse. The trail heads around the east shore of Minaret Lake to the outlet, where you should take a last look at the Minarets rising over the lake before descending steeply on well-worn tread to intersect the JMT opposite the marshy shores of Johnston Lake (8,120 feet) 4.5 miles from Minaret Lake (14.5 miles from the Agnew Meadow Trailhead).

Continue down-valley for another 0.2 mile to a ford of Minaret Creek. An unsigned log, located above or below the ford, will save you an annoying wade. About 50 feet beyond the ford, pass the Beck Lakes Trail intersection and shortly after begin to descend into the San Joaquin River valley on a wide and very dusty trail. Your goal is now the headquarters of the Devils Postpile National Monument. Near the floor of the valley, cross the PCT and follow the signs to the monument headquarters on the JMT, which will take you around the meadows to a sturdy bridge over the river. Leave the JMT and go left, heading back up-valley for 0.1 mile to reach the headquarters (7,600 feet) and road at 16.2 miles. From here you simply wait for a shuttle bus for the free ride back to your car.

# 24 BECK MEADOWS LOOP

**Loop hike: 14 miles**
**Hiking time: 2-3 days**
**High point: 9,580 feet**
**Elevation gain: 2,970 feet**

**Hikable: mid-July through**
**September**
**Backpack**

**Maps: USFS Ansel Adams Wilderness; USGS Crystal Crag, Cattle Mtn.,
Mt. Ritter, and Mammoth Mtn.**

Reservations and Information: Mammoth Ranger Station (Case 6)

A strikingly picturesque group of High Sierran lakes is the objective of this long, hot, and very dusty loop hike. Little water will be found along the loop and late-season visitors must rely on the lakes to refill their water bottles.

**Access.** The loop begins at Devils Postpile National Monument Visitor Center. See Hike 23 for driving directions to Mammoth Mountain Ski Area, where you will park your car and ride the shuttle to the monument's small Visitor Center and headquarters (7,560 feet).

Begin your hike at the Visitor Center and head down-valley on the wide trail to the Devils Postpile. After 0.2 mile of level walking, the trail to the Devils Postpile intersects the John Muir Trail (JMT). Go right and follow the JMT north. Cross the San Joaquin River on a bridge, then head uphill for 100 feet to a second intersection and the start of the loop. Go left on the King Creek Trail, which offers a scenic approach and several camping options.

The King Creek Trail climbs, passing a viewpoint of the Devils

*King Creek below Beck Meadows*

Postpile, then heads over a pumicey ridge burned in 1992. At 0.5 mile cross the Pacific Crest Trail (PCT), then continue climbing to the 7,970-foot crest of the ridge. You then descend into Snow Canyon, passing several large campsites, before reaching the King Creek ford. A messy log jam and short bushwhack starting 200 feet below the ford is available to all who prefer dry feet.

Once across the creek, the trail settles into the business of climbing, gaining 1,250 feet in the next 2.5 miles. Views soon include the Silver Divide to the south, Mammoth Mountain to the east, and a range of unnamed peaks to the north. At 5.5 miles the trail divides. Stay right toward Fern Lake.

Reach the Fern Lake Trail intersection 6 miles from the Visitor Center. Fern Lake (8,960 feet) lies in a granite bowl 0.3 mile west of the King Creek Trail and has campsites along the east shore.

From the Fern Lake intersection, the King Creek Trail descends to cross Anona Creek (8,760 feet), then climbs steeply up an open hillside, paralleling the cascading King Creek. The trail is somewhat indistinct on the rocky slope, but the direction is obvious.

At 6.9 miles the trail fords King Creek (a wet crossing for much of the summer) and 0.1 mile beyond arrives at the Beck Meadows intersection (9,000 feet). Ashley and Holcomb Lakes are to the left, reached by recrossing King Creek, usually on a log. Once across, pass several excellent campsites (better then those found near the lakes), then head uphill. Strikingly beautiful Ashley Lake (9,580 feet) is 1.5 miles to the west at the base of Iron Peak. Holcomb Lake, 1 mile from the King Creek ford, lies in a deep granitic cup, surrounded by towering peaks.

To complete the loop, head east passing Becks Cabin and the Beck Lakes Trail at 7.1 miles. Beck Lakes, located 2 miles northwest, are high, rocky, and exotic. The loop trail climbs over a couple of forested ridges and at 10 miles begins an exhausting and somewhat boring descent to intersect the JMT just below Johnston Lake at 13 miles. Go right on the JMT and continue descending, following signs to the Visitor Center and the end of the loop at 14 miles.

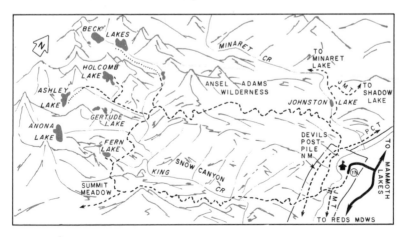

*Duck Lake*

# 25 MAMMOTH CREST TRAVERSE

**One way: 12 miles**
**Hiking time: 7 hours**
**High point: 11,230 feet**
**Elevation gain: 810 feet**

**Hikable: July through**
**   September**
**Day hike or backpack**

**Maps: USFS John Muir Wilderness (Northern Section); USGS Bloody**
**   Mountain (meters) and Crystal Crag**

Reservations and Information: Mammoth Ranger Station (Case 6)

From the popular Mammoth Lakes recreation area the Mammoth Crest appears as a solid wall of impenetrable cliffs, so it may come as a surprise to find that the moderately sloping southwest side of the crest is an excellent place for a scenic hike. Views from the crest are expansive, spanning the High Sierra from Silver Divide, over Fish Valley, across the John Muir Wilderness, down into the Devils Postpile area, then north across the Ansel Adams Wilderness to the Minarets and Mt. Ritter.

This traverse is almost a loop, beginning at Cold Water Campground and ending 2.2 miles northwest at George Lake. Two miles of this traverse between Duck Pass and Deer Lakes are actually more like a route than a trail as you follow a sketchy path over high meadows. (Note: The connection between Duck Pass and Deer Lake is not shown on the John Muir Wilderness map and is marked incorrectly on the Ansel Adams Wilderness map.)

**Access.** From the Mammoth Lakes intersection on Highway 395, follow Highway 203 for 3.7 miles to the Lake Mary Road. Continue straight for another 3.7 miles, then turn left on Forest Road 4S09, signed for Lake Mary and Cold Water Campground. After 0.6 mile go left again and follow Forest Road 4S25 through the campground for 0.6 mile. Park at the second trailhead (9,120 feet).

The first 4 miles of your traverse are spent hiking up the wide and well-traveled Duck Pass Trail, which begins with a moderate climb into an upper valley then levels off to pass Arrowhead Lake, Skeleton Lake, Red Lake, and Barney Lake.

From Barney Lake the trail switchbacks up a steep wall to the 10,800-foot summit of Duck Pass. Go 100 feet past the crest of the pass, then head up the hill on the right. Walk through a grove of hardy trees then over meadows, staying just a bit to the right of the ridge crest. Once you reach the meadows, watch for a well-worn boot path that heads steadily west to an 11,230-foot divide. The path crosses the divide, then descends across a grassy basin to a view of upper Deer Lake.

At the lower end of the basin the trail makes one switchback down a band of rocks, then disappears. Stay to the left and continue down by clambering over the rubble. At the base of the rocks you will find a path that contours around the right side of Upper Deer Lake, then crosses a low saddle before descending along the left side of Middle Deer Lake (10,560 feet). At the base of the middle lake you will pass several large campsites then meet the Mammoth Crest Trail.

The Mammoth Crest Trail climbs steeply to an 11,180-foot point just below the crest, then heads northwest in a rolling traverse. At one point the trail divides; the two paths rejoin shortly after. Before long you will descend to an open plateau sprinkled with lupine. Cross this open area, then walk along the ridge until you reach a point where the soil turns red. The trail divides here. For the best views, stay left and follow the unofficial trail along the ridge crest for 0.5 mile, then go right to rejoin the official route, which spends the next 2.5 miles in a switchbacking descent. At 11 miles, pass the spur trail to Crystal Lake and at 12 miles arrive at the busy Lake George parking area. If you did not come prepared with a shuttle car, you now have a 2-mile road walk back to the Duck Pass Trailhead.

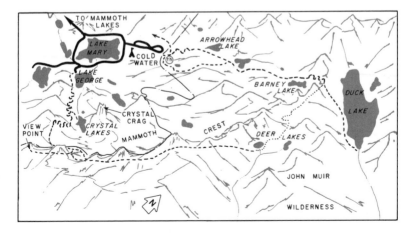

# 26 McGEE CREEK

| | |
|---|---|
| **Round trip to Steelhead Lake:** 11 miles | **Elevation gain: 2,150 feet** |
| **Hiking time: 6 hours** | **Hikable: mid-July through September** |
| **High point: 10,350 feet** | **Day hike or backpack** |

**Maps: USFS John Muir Wilderness (North Section); USGS Convict Lake and Mt. Abbot**

| | |
|---|---|
| **Round trip to Big McGee Lake:** 14 miles | **Elevation gain: 2,280 feet** |
| **Hiking time: 2 days** | **Hikable: mid-July through September** |
| **High point: 10,480** | **Backpack** |

**Maps: USFS John Muir Wilderness (North Section); USGS Convict Lake and Mt. Abbot**

Reservations and Information: White Mountain Ranger Station and Rock Creek Entrance Station (Case 6)

Reds, crimsons, creams, golds, and contrasting blue-grays of the peaks rising straight up from green meadows to the deep blue sky are the first clues of the visual euphoria awaiting those who hike in the McGee Creek Valley. The two destinations listed above are both worth a visit. Steelhead Lake is reached by a side trail off McGee Creek and is a great destination for anglers. The second destination, Big McGee Lake, lies at the base of colorful Red and White Mountain and is fringed with delicate meadows.

Expect lots of dust, horse deposits, and very hazardous creek crossings. The lower valley has little shade, so plan an early start to avoid the heat.

**Access.** Drive Highway 395 to McGee Creek Road, located 6.5 miles north of Tom's Place or 8.5 miles south of Mammoth Junction. Cross Crowley Lake Road, then head up Forest Road 6. Pavement ends at 2.3 miles and the road ends at 3.3 miles at a large parking area with rest rooms (8,200 feet).

From the trailhead sign you may follow either the trail or the old road up-valley. After an easy mile the road and trail join at the wilderness boundary. Continue up the open valley on the old mining road, traversing sage-covered meadows vibrantly highlighted with wildflowers. A couple of seasonal streams are crossed before you reach the first ford of McGee Creek at 2.7 miles.

At 3.2 miles pass a side trail to the left, which descends to a grassy meadow and the first of many campsites. Continuing up-valley, a second and potentially dangerous crossing of McGee Creek is reached at 3.5 miles. A single log has been placed for hikers' use just above the ford.

The road and trail part company soon after the second ford. Stay on the trail and climb steadily through forest to reach the Steelhead Lake intersection at 4.3 miles. If heading to Steelhead Lake, cross rushing McGee Creek on a log; do not attempt to ford. On the south side of the

*The trail crosses several scenic meadows just below Big McGee Lake.*

creek the rocky trail climbs steeply past the turnoff to the forested area around Grass Lake, then on to reach the rocky basin that cradles Steelhead Lake (10,350 feet) at 5.5 miles. Campsites are numerous.

Beyond the Steelhead Lake intersection, the McGee Creek Trail switchbacks over a granite hump, passes Round Lake, then climbs into alpine meadows where it levels a bit before reaching Big McGee Lake (10,480 feet) at 7 miles. The campsites around the lake are small but very scenic.

If you have time to explore, continue on up the trail to Little McGee Lake, then climb steeply to the crest of 11,900-foot McGee Pass at 9 miles. Be prepared to walk over snow, as the pass is rarely clear until September. On the west side of the pass, the trail switchbacks down to more lakes.

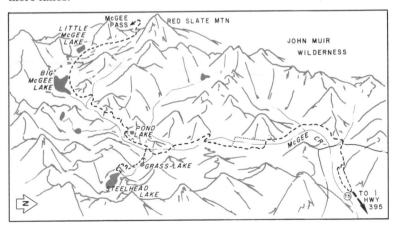

# 27 TAMARACK LAKES

**Round trip: 9.5 miles**
**Hiking time: 5 hours**
**High point: 11,600 feet**
**Elevation gain: 1,900 feet**

**Hikable: mid-July through**
**September**
**Day hike**

**Maps: USFS John Muir Wilderness (North Section); USGS Mt. Morgan**

Reservations and Information: White Mountain Ranger Station and
Rock Creek Entrance Station (Case 6)

Beneath the rugged ramparts of Broken Finger Peak lie the starkly
beautiful Tamarack Lakes. The trail to the lakes is one of the lesser

*Tamarack Lake*

known in the Rock Creek area and you can, at times, find a measure of solitude for quiet contemplation of the High Sierran scene. The low number of visitors stems, in part, from the almost-total lack of comfortable campsites around the rocky, sloping shores of the lakes. Backpackers are advised to camp at one of the lakes below and day-hike up to the Tamaracks.

**Access.** Drive Highway 395 south 15.1 miles from the Mammoth Lakes intersection or 24.2 miles north from the White Mountain Ranger Station in Bishop. Turn west at Tom's Place and follow the Rock Creek Road for 0.2 mile to the entrance station. Check in, then continue up the road another 8.7 miles to the Rock Creek Lake Campground turnoff. Go left and follow the road to the campground, where it divides. Hikers' parking is to the left (9,700 feet).

The trail starts at the end of the second parking bay and heads steeply uphill. At 0.2 mile is an intersection with a trail from Mosquito Flat. Continue straight ahead on a now much wider trail, which climbs for a bit then levels off on a broad bench at 10,170 feet. At 1 mile the trail divides. The left fork goes to Wheeler Crest. Take the right fork and head up a trail that climbs in short, steep spurts, interspersed with level meadows.

The Francis Lake Trail branches off on the right at 1.7 miles and shortly beyond you will pass Kenneth Lake (10,360 feet) and good campsites. At 2.4 miles the trail divides again. The left fork meanders east for 0.5 mile to the marshy shores of Dorothy Lake and more campsites. Stay right and climb over a moraine, then descend into the East Fork Creek Valley where you will cross broad meadows and pass a marshy pond. At 3 miles the trail begins a steep, rough climb up to the rocky world of the High Sierra.

The trail follows the creek up a narrowing valley then, at 11,000 feet, arrives at a marshy meadow beneath a wall of cliffs. Follow a narrow band of vegetation up-valley, then head to your right to avoid the steepest sections of the headwall. At 4.3 miles the climb ends and the final 0.2 mile to the lake is an easy and very scenic traverse along the crest of the headwall to the two Tamarack Lakes. The first lake is tiny. The second lake is much larger and its rich green waters are home to an active population of fish. A rough trail, made more of imagination than form, continues a short 0.2 mile to tiny Buck Lake.

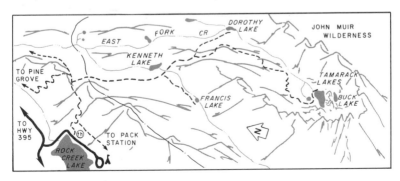

# *28* LITTLE LAKES VALLEY

**Round trip to Lower Morgan
  Lake: 9 miles
Hiking time: 5 hours
High point: 11,104 feet**

**Elevation gain: 804 feet
Hikable: mid-July through
  September
Day hike or backpack**

**Maps: USFS John Muir Wilderness (North Section); USGS Mt. Morgan
  and Mt. Abbot**

Reservations and Information: White Mountain Ranger Station and
  Rock Creek Information Station (Case 6)

You only need to walk a few feet up the Little Lakes Valley to see
that this is a very special place. This is also one of the rare High Sierran hikes where it is not absolutely necessary to acclimate before you
begin your trip, as the relatively low elevation gain makes it an ideal
first hike at high elevation or a great weekend outing for the family.

**Access.** Drive Highway 395 south 15.1 miles from the Mammoth
Lakes intersection or north 24.2 miles from the White Mountain
Ranger Station in Bishop. Turn west at Tom's Place and follow Rock
Creek Road for 0.2 mile to the entrance station. If backpacking, pick
up your permit here. Continue up the paved road until it divides at 9.5
miles. Stay left on a single-lane road for the final 1.2 miles to the road's
end at the Mosquito Flat Trailhead (10,300 feet).

Following signs to Mono and Morgan Passes, head up the Little
Lakes Valley, paralleling Rock Creek on an old road. At 0.2 mile is a
short, steep climb, which should be taken slowly at this elevation. The
trail divides at 0.5 mile with the Mono Pass Trail to Pioneer Basin
heading to the right (see Hike 29). You should stay to the left, following signs to Morgan Pass.

The beautiful scenery crosses over into the realm of the spectacular
as the trail traverses an open meadow with views of four snow- and
ice-clad peaks whose shear walls and serrated ridges tower above the
13,000-foot mark. Watch for climbers with ropes and ice axes heading
up the side valleys to scale the summits.

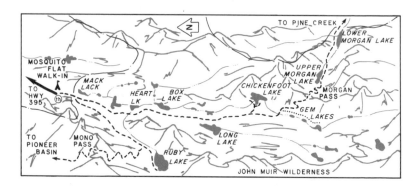

*Hiker following trail up Little Lakes Valley*

At 0.7 mile walk past Mack Lake, somewhat hidden on the left, then head past Heart Lake then Box Lake to reach Long Lake and the first good campsites at 2 miles. At Long Lake the trail follows the route of an old mining road along the lakeshore, then climbs steadily to the Chickenfoot Lake intersection at 2.7 miles. Chickenfoot Lake (10,789 feet) is located 0.2 mile left of the main trail and has excellent camping.

The trail continues its gradual climb through green meadows spotted, in August, with paintbrush and elephants head. At 3.2 miles pass the Gem Lakes spur trail on the right, which leads to a couple of small lakes jammed into a small valley at the toe of the magnificent Bear Creek Spire. Scenic but small campsites can be found around the lakes.

The trail climbs steeply to cross 11,104-foot Morgan Pass at 3.5 miles. Walk between huge chunks of granite, then descend to Upper Morgan Lake (10,940 feet) at 4 miles. The only camping around this boulder-strewn lake is directly below the pass. The trail, which shows signs of use in the 1930s by miners, contours around the upper lake, then drops to Lower Morgan Lake (10,700 feet) at 4.5 miles. This is a friendly lake, lacking the beauty of the Little Lakes Valley but with plenty of large, protected campsites. Beyond the lower lake the trail descends through an unpleasant mess of mining roads and talus to Pine Creek.

# *29* PIONEER BASIN

**Round trip: 20 miles**
**Hiking time: 2–3 days**
**High point: 12,000 feet**
**Elevation gain: 2,581 feet in;**
   **2,000 feet out**

**Hikable: mid-July through**
   **September**
**Backpack**

**Maps: USFS John Muir Wilderness (North Section); USGS Mt. Morgan and Mt. Abbot**

Reservations and Information: White Mountain Ranger Station and
   Rock Creek Entrance Station (Case 6)

Pioneer Basin is one of those places that should be on every hikers "must do" list. This extraordinary hike begins in the beautiful Little Lakes Valley and crosses scenic, 12,000-foot Mono Pass before reaching one of the most enchanting basins in the Sierra.

Your wilderness permit entitles you to one free night at the walk-in campground at the trailhead to acclimate to the thin air at 10,300 feet. The only water available is from the creek; however, you may pick up water at one of the many campgrounds on your drive up. Hikers who do not take time to acclimate should plan on a very short first day.

**Access.** Drive Highway 395 for 25 miles north from Bishop to the Tom's Place exit. Go east on Rock Creek Road for 0.2 mile to the entrance station, where you will pick up your wilderness permit, then continue for 10.1 miles to end of the road at the Mosquito Flat Trailhead (10,300 feet). Parking is a problem; if there are no slots available you must go back down-valley 0.3 mile and find an available space at the picnic area.

The trail parallels Rock Creek as you walk up the Little Lakes Valley toward a wall of 13,000-foot summits. Within a few feet of the trailhead you will pass the walk-in campground. Continue up-valley until the trail divides at 0.5 mile. Stay right following signs to Mono Pass.

At 0.7 mile pass the spur trail from the pack station then continue

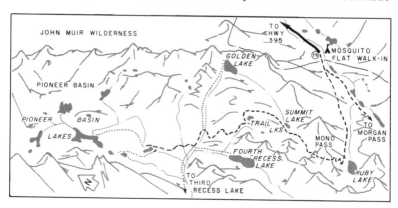

*Snowfields linger for most of the summer on open slopes near Mono Pass and Summit Lake.*

climbing through stunted white bark pines, passing several memorable viewpoints over Little Lakes Valley. At 2 miles, the trail to Ruby Lake branches off to the left (11,300 feet). The lake is 0.3 mile to the west and is well worth the side trip if you are looking for a scenic picnic spot or campsite.

Beyond the Ruby Lake intersection, every step is uphill and with each step the scenery becomes more spectacular. The trail climbs above Ruby Lake with steep switchbacks.

At 3.7 miles you will arrive at the crest of 12,000-foot Mono Pass. This is breathtaking High Sierra country, requiring a mandatory sit-down to catch your breath and enjoy the exhilaration of the high elevation before descending to barren Summit Lake (11,910 feet) at 4.4 miles. The rate of descent increases as the trail nears Trail Lakes at 5.4 miles (11,210 feet). Here you will find the first good campsites below the pass as well as a backcountry ranger station. Needle Lake, located 0.4 mile south of Trail Lakes on a cross-country route, offers a bit more seclusion.

From Trail Lakes, descend steadily for 1.2 miles to ford Golden Creek at 6.6 miles (10,400 feet). The trail parallels the creek as it descends another 0.4 mile to the reach the Pioneer Basin Trail intersection at 10,000 feet. Go right and follow the trail on a steady ascent for the next 2 miles into the basin.

The basin has over twenty lakes with numerous campsites, plentiful views, and an abundance of mosquitos. At 9 miles you will arrive at Lower Basin Lake and the end of the official trail (10,881 feet). Proceed around either side of the lake and continue to climb until you reach the Upper Basin, where you will find some solitude on the lower slopes of Mt. Hopkins, Mt. Crocker, and Mt. Stanford.

If you have several days to spend, plan to take excursions to Golden Lake and the beautiful Fourth Recess Lake.

*The second of the Gable Lakes*

# 30      GABLE LAKES

**Round trip: 9 miles**
**Hiking time: 7 hours**
**High point: 10,740 feet**
**Elevation gain: 3,220 feet**

**Hikable: late July through**
    **September**
**Day hike or backpack**

**Maps: USFS John Muir Wilderness (North Section); USGS Mt. Tom**

Reservations and Information: White River Ranger Station or Rock
    Creek Entrance Station (Case 6)

    The four Gable Lakes in a rocky basin below Four Gables Mountain
are the scenic objective of this difficult hike. Few people make the trek
to these relatively unknown lakes and those who do will find solitude,
fishing, and many photographic opportunities around the old mines
and rocky lakeshores.

**Access.** Drive to the Pine Creek Trailhead (7,520 feet). See Hike 31 for directions.

To find the Gable Lakes Trail, walk to the archway at the entrance to the Pine Creek Pack Station, then go left and head up through the living area for the pack-station employees. After 100 feet the road divides; stay left. When the road bends sharply left, leave it and continue straight on a well-defined trail.

After climbing a few feet, the trail begins the first of many switchbacks. At switchback No. 10 the trail heads into a slightly descending traverse toward the deep Gable Creek Gorge. By switchback No. 16 you will have climbed to an excellent view over the beautiful Pine Creek Valley as well as the pack station and the messy Tungsten Mine with its large settling pond. At the nineteenth switchback pass a couple of old tramway towers and an old phone box (without phone) left by miners. After one more switchback the climb abates at 8,380 feet and the trail heads up-valley on a long ascending traverse. Near 2 miles pass a spur trail heading off to the left, which crosses the valley and climbs to an abandoned mine on the east side.

A second group of switchbacks signals a change of pace. These moderately graded switchbacks climb to the crest of a 9,420-foot bench. The trail then descends to the West Fork Gable Creek and becomes indistinct in the tall grass. It reappears as it heads into the rocks at the upper end of the meadow. The trail again becomes difficult to follow as it crosses a second meadow, where it has been badly eroded by two streams. Once you reach the cliffy slopes beyond you will have well-defined switchbacks to follow.

At the summit of the hill the trail descends to the creek and fords the raging torrent. A couple of mining shacks can be seen on the far side. Do not cross here unless the creek is nearly dry. Most of the summer it is best to stay on the right side of the creek and head uphill on a narrow, boot-beaten path. Climb to a band of rocks and parallel them for 200 feet until you intersect a well-graded trail. To the right the trail climbs over a rocky knoll to the second Gable Lake and several small campsites. To the left, the trail descends to the lowest Gable Lake (9,940 feet) and a relatively easy creek crossing at the outlet. A steep trail then climbs past an immense amount of mining debris to the third Gable Lake (10,740 feet). The fourth Gable Lake is reached by an easy cross-country hike from the third lake.

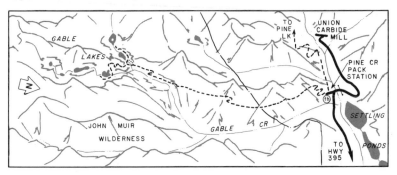

# 31 MOON LAKE

**Round trip: 22 miles**
**Hiking time: 2–4 days**
**High point: 11,110 feet**
**Elevation gain: 4,010 feet**

**Hikable: mid-July through**
  **September**
**Backpack**

**Maps: USFS John Muir Wilderness (North Section); USGS Mount Tom**

Reservations and Information: White Mountain Ranger Station and
  Rock Creek Entrance Station (Case 6)

Ascend to a high, lake-dotted plateau and find a small tent site to be
your temporary home. The view from this new address will be a show-
case of nature's best work. Creeks lace this area, tripping from lake to
lake with spirited little waterfalls. All this scenery makes returning to
a more permanent address rather difficult.

**Access.** Drive Highway 395 north from the White Mountain Ranger
Station in downtown Bishop 10.4 miles or south from Tom's Place 13.9
miles. Turn west on Pine Creek Road for 9.7 miles then go left into a
large dirt parking lot at Pine Creek Pack Station (7,520 feet). Try to
start your hike in the early morning to avoid the heat, which turns this
valley into an oven by midday.

Walk through the pack station, passing the horse corral and tack
rack to find the trailhead on the far side, then shift your body into low
gear and start the long grind up past a large mining operation.

After the first mile the trail ends and you continue your climb with
long hot switchbacks on an old mining road. The trail begins again at
the base of the old Brownstone Mine and heads over a steep, rocky
slope overlooking the Pine Creek waterfalls. By 3.3 miles the trail has
gained the crest of the hill and enters the cool shade of the upper valley forests, where it crosses Pine Creek on a sturdy footbridge. At 4.8
miles from the valley floor, the trail arrives at Pine Lake (9,942 feet).

Head around Pine Lake, then up a small rise to Upper Pine Lake
and the first of many campsites. The trail contours around the lake,
then fords the creek from Honeymoon Lake (a wet crossing until
midsummer). Continue to climb through thinning forest to reach an

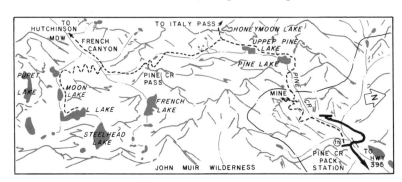

intersection at 6 miles (10,440 feet). Just 0.1 mile to the right are excellent campsites overlooking Honeymoon Lake. Stay left on the Pine Creek Trail and climb past several small, seasonal ponds.

At 8 miles the trail reaches the crest of 11,120-foot Pine Creek Pass. Snow lingers here; however horse packers usually create a safe path by midsummer.

Descend gradually down a wide valley for 1.5 miles to an intersection at the head of French Canyon (10,640 feet). Go left on a trail that is no longer maintained. The trail will cross a small creek then climb past small Elba Lake.

From Elba Lake follow the inlet stream up to Moon Lake (10,998 feet), reached at 11 miles from the pack station. Campsites are found along the south and east sides of this high alpine lake.

The larger L Lake is located just 0.5 mile away on an upper bench. The trail ends there; however, it is easy to continue over this open landscape to find the eight other lakes spread around the basin. Views are excellent, topped with a thundering waterfall across the valley descending from Royce Lake.

*Hiker's camp at Elba Lake*

# *32*      LAKE ITALY

**Round trip: 24 miles**
**Hiking time: 4 days**
**High point: 12,350 feet**
**Elevation gain: 4,850 feet in;**
   **1,160 feet out**

**Hikable: August through**
   **September**
**Backpack**

**Maps: USFS John Muir Wilderness; USGS Mount Tom and Mt. Hilgard**

Reservations and Information: White Mountain Ranger Station and
   Rock Creek Entrance Station (Case 6)

Adventure and beautiful scenery await all who make this difficult
trek from the Pine Creek Trailhead to Lake Italy. The adventure
comes when navigating the well-traveled but only vaguely marked
route from Honeymoon Lake up and over the granite-strewn slopes of
Italy Pass to Lake Italy. Beautiful scenery surrounds you from start to
finish, varying from knife-edged ridges and thundering waterfalls to
exquisite alpine lakes and lush green meadows.

This is not a hike for everyone. The well-maintained trail to Honeymoon Lake is rough and very steep. Beyond the lake the trail gradually
disappears. In theory the route is marked by ducks; in reality the
ducks are nearly impossible to follow and you must rely on your in-
stincts and your map. Carry a compass and wear stout boots in antici-
pation of encountering snow.

**Access.** Following the directions in Hike 31, drive to the Pine Creek
Trailhead (7,520 feet).

Follow the Pine Creek Trail for 6 miles to an intersection marked by
a large rock cairn, located 0.2 mile above Upper Pine Lake (see Hike 31
for details). Go right and walk a few feet to Honeymoon Lake (10,350
feet). Paths, which branch off in every direction, lead to campsites.

At Honeymoon Lake you leave the dust, the horse manure, and the
good trail. From the lakeshore, climb straight up sloping granite slabs,
then hop a creek near the top to find an improved trail that climbs to a
beautiful meadow. Here you must cross another creek before continuing the steep climb. At the crest of a rocky rib, the trail perversely de-

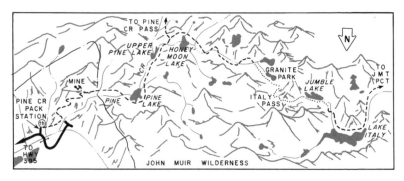

*Royce Peak is just one of the many beautiful High Sierra mountains along the route to Italy Pass.*

scends to ford yet another creek. Once across, head uphill, crossing and recrossing the same creek two more times. (If you stay on the west side of the creek to avoid the next two crossings, be prepared for a bit of scrambling on a steep slope.)

The trail now disappears as it climbs over slabs of rock into an area of little vegetation and numerous lakes (more than the map shows) called Granite Park. Watch closely for the ducks and lines of pebbles defining the route.

At the lower end of Granite Park the trail splinters. Stay low, paralleling the shores of the first two lakes. At the head of the second large lake the trail crosses a creek, then climbs out of the meadows and into the moonscape atmosphere of the upper valley. If you lose the trail now, simply stay to the right side of the valley and hike northwest toward a low divide at the head of the rocky cirque. The 12,350-foot summit of Italy Pass is reached 4 miles from Honeymoon Lake.

From the pass, head down on a trail that is even less defined than the one you came up on. Stay just a little north of center and descend the rocky basin to a small, grassy bench overlooking Jumble Lake, where you will find the trail. This deep blue lake suits its name: the hillsides are a jumble of boulders and campsites are very limited.

The trail contours north above Jumble Lake, then drops steeply to Lake Italy (11,202 feet). Campsites are located on the south shore to the right of the trail and near the outlet. The lack of vegetation around the lake allows for a wealth of views of 13,000-foot peaks. Feast your eyes on Mt. Hilgard, Mt. Gabb, Mt. Abbott, Mt. Dade, Bear Creek Spire, and Mt. Julius Caesar—a line-up that could keep a mountain climber busy for a week.

*Blue Lake*

# 33　SABRINA BASIN

**Round trip to Hungry Packer:**
　**14 miles**
**Hiking time: 7 hours**
**High point: 11,100 feet**

**Elevation gain: 2,020 feet**
**Hikable: mid-July through**
　**September**
**Day hike or backpack**

**Maps: USFS John Muir Wilderness (Central Section); USGS Mt.**
　**Thompson and Mt. Darwin**

Reservations and Information: White Mtn. Ranger Station and Bishop
　Creek Entrance Station (Case 6)

　Sabrina Basin is dotted with lakes, large and small, blue, aqua,
green, and gray. The lakes are nestled below massive granite peaks,
with cliffs and sloping granitic blocks forming the shorelines. If you are
not lucky enough to obtain a wilderness permit for an overnight stay in
Sabrina Basin, plan to day-hike this trail. The long hike is worth the
price of sore toes and tired legs. The trail into the basin is not without
its challenges. From its high-elevation start, the trail climbs to even
thinner air, making for slow going on the steep and rocky ground.
When crossing granite slabs, the trail disappears and some route finding skills are required. Streams must be forded, which is a wet proposition in early summer.

　**Access.** From the center of Bishop, drive west on Highway 168 following signs to Sabrina and South Lakes for 10.1 miles to the Bishop
Creek Entrance Station where you must pick up wilderness permits or

select a campground before continuing up. At 15.4 miles the road divides; take the right fork and continue to Lake Sabrina. The backpackers' parking area is located at the North Lake turnoff, 18.5 miles from Bishop. Day hikers may continue another 0.7 mile and park near the trailhead or at the north side of the dam (9,080 feet).

The trail climbs above the dam, then traverses open slopes above the southeast shore of Lake Sabrina. At 1.2 miles a lateral trail to George Lake climbs steeply off to the left. Shortly after this intersection, cross two creeks where, if you are very lucky, you may be able to keep your feet dry. The trail then heads into the trees and makes several dusty, dry, horse-churned switchbacks to an overlook of the valley and ruby-colored Mt. Emerson. Up-valley, Mt. Wallace, Mt. Haeckel, and a roaring falls of the Middle Fork Bishop Creek dominate the scene.

The climb is steady as the trail bends into a side valley to reach extremely popular Blue Lake (10,390 feet) at 3 miles. Campsites and mosquitos may be found on granite benches all around this rocky lake.

To continue on you must make a challenging crossing of the deep outlet creek on skinny logs. The trail then heads around the west side of the lake for 0.2 mile to an intersection. Go right on the Dingleberry Lake Trail.

Follow the trail as it works its way around a series of granite ridges and passes the marshy Emerald Lakes in an elegant setting at 4 miles. At 5 miles descend to the attractive Dingleberry Lake and more campsites (10,480 feet).

Shortly after Dingleberry Lake, the trail divides. Stay right and walk over a granite slab to a ford of Middle Fork Bishop Creek. Stepping stones help to keep feet dry in the late season; however, early-season hikers are advised to take their boots off and wade.

The horse and hiker trails rejoin after the ford and cross a meadow before climbing more granite. At 5.7 miles a 1-mile spur trail branches right to Midnight Lake (11,060 feet) and several nice campsites. At 6.2 miles the Hungry Packer Lake Trail branches off on the right for a 0.7-mile trek to the lake and campsites (11,100 feet). The Sabrina Basin Trail ends at 7 miles in the midst of sloping granite slabs at the edge of Moonlight Lake (11,070 feet).

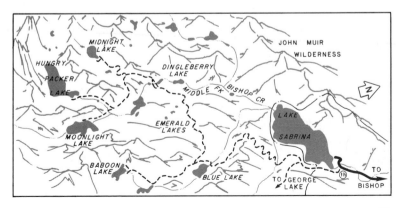

# 34 HUMPHREYS BASIN

**Round trip: 16.8 miles**
**Hiking time: 2–3 days**
**High point: 11,827 feet**
**Elevation gain in: 2,507 feet**

**Hikable: mid-July through**
**September**
**Backpack**

**Maps: USFS John Muir Wilderness (North Section); USGS Mt. Darwin and Mount Tom**

Reservations and Information: White Mountain Ranger Station and Bishop Creek Entrance Station (Case 6)

Reserve your wilderness permits early for a trek to this popular High Sierran basin. Part of the hike is on the busy Piute Pass Trail and part of the hike is on sketchy boot-beaten paths or on unmarked cross-country routes over the open hills. Walk softly, staying on rocks whenever possible, and carry a detailed map to help you navigate between the many lakes and vistas scattered through Humphreys Basin.

This is a high-elevation hike and it is best to spend the night before the hike either at North Lake Campground or at Sabrina Campground. Thunderstorms come up very quickly and Piute Pass and the basin are very exposed. Be prepared at all times for changing weather; it may even snow!

**Access.** From Highway 395 in Bishop, turn west on Highway 168 (called Line Street) and follow it toward Lake Sabrina. At 10.1 miles pass the Bishop Creek Entrance Station, where wilderness permits and campground assignments are issued. At 15.2 miles the road divides; stay left for 3.2 miles before turning right on North Lake Road.

*Horse packers in Humphreys Basin*

Head up for 2.1 miles to North Lake Campground, where you will want to drop your packs before driving back down-valley 0.7 mile to the hikers' parking area (9,360 feet).

From the parking area, walk the road back to the campground to find the Piute Pass Trailhead at the far end of the walk-in campsites. Two trails start here; take the one on the right and begin a gradual climb. At 1.3 miles the trail proves that it was designed for horses rather than people by fording the North Fork and shortly beyond recrossing the creek (wet crossings in early season). Near the 2-mile point, arrive at the headwall of Piute Crags and Mt. Emerson. With a series of steep switchbacks, the trail works its way up to Lock Laven Lake (10,740 feet) at 3.1 miles. Campsites and picnic spots are located all around this rock-bound lake.

The trail continues its ascent through delightful meadows covered with wildflowers. Stumbling feet will remind you to watch the trail rather than the scenery. Windblown Piute Lake (10,950 feet) and more campsites are passed at 4.2 miles. At 5.4 miles the trail crosses a small snowfield. Stop here for a final view over Piute and Lock Laven Lakes, then head up to the crest of 11,423-foot Piute Pass and a spectacular view of Humphreys Basin, Muriel Peak, Goethe Cirque, and Pilots Knob.

At this point you have a myriad of possible destinations, some reached by well-traveled routes and others found by cross-country trekking. Good campsites may be found by an easy 2-mile cross-country walk from the pass to Marmot Lakes, Humphreys Lakes, and Muriel Lakes. Reach Upper and Lower Golden Trout Lakes by descending 1.5 miles west from Piute Pass to an unsigned but heavily used intersection. Go left for 1 mile to the lakes (10,800 feet). Camping is prohibited within 500 feet of the lower lake.

For a less-overused destination, go right at the Golden Trout Lake intersection and head north toward the Desolation Lakes. The boot-trail swings around the east side of Lower Desolation Lake (11,157 feet) then divides. For the most seclusion go left (west) to Mesa Lake and Wedge Lake. To the right is Desolation Lake (11,381 feet), the largest of the Humphreys Basin lakes, where you will find numerous campsites at 8.6 miles from the trailhead.

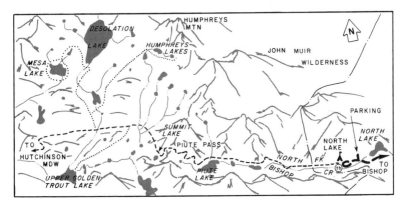

# 35 EVOLUTION VALLEY

**One-way hike: 53 miles**
**Hiking time: 5–7 days**
**High point: 11,980 feet**
**Elevation gain in: 8,958 feet**

**Hikable: August through**
**September**
**Backpack**

**Maps: USFS-John Muir Wilderness (North and Central Sections);**
**USGS Mt. Darwin, Mount Tom, Mt. Hilgrad, Mt. Henry, Mt.**
**Goddard, North Palisade, Mt. Thompson**

Reservations and Information: White Mountain Ranger Station and
Rock Creek Entrance Station (Case 6)

Three High Sierran passes, fields of alpine flowers that are more
like gardens than meadows, crystalline lakes, glacier-scoured canyons,
dancing creeks, lofty peaks that cleave the sky well over the 13,000-
foot mark, and ideal mountain weather make the semi-loop hike of the
Evolution Valley from North Lake to South Lake one of the best extended treks found anywhere.

By map, North Lake and South Lake are close together. However, no
trail link exists between the two lakes, so a two-car shuttle is the best
system for traveling between trailheads. If you do not have two cars at
your disposal, try the Backpackers Shuttle Service in Bishop (contact
the White Mountain Ranger District Office for details).

This long hike follows well-maintained trails for the entire distance.
However, many of the river and creek crossings do not have bridges, so
expect to wade at the fords. Even in early August some of the crossings

*Muir Pass Hut*

will be deep and fast. A pair of
water shoes are a good idea for
saving feet from cuts and bruises.

Snow slopes linger at the upper
elevations through much of August. July hikers are well advised
to carry an ice ax. By August, falling through a thin area on a snow
bank is the main hazard. When
possible it is best to walk around
snow patches.

Thunderstorms are an ever-
present hazard in August and
September. Your best defense is
to try to cross the high passes before midday, as storms are most
common in the afternoons. However, watch the weather and do
not approach a pass if the clouds
are building at any time of day.

The trails starting from North
Lake and South Lake are both

very popular and you should apply for wilderness permits in early March. For experienced route finders, there is a third option when daily quotas are filled on the Piute Pass or Bishop Trails. From North Lake you may take the trail to Lower and Upper Lamarck Lakes. Just before Upper Lamarck Lake, a well-used but unmaintained trail branches left and climbs to the ridge above the lake. This trail ultimately crosses Lamarck Col. You then work your way down to Darwin Lakes and Darwin Canyon under Mt. Mendel and follow a trail to the meadow near the Evolution Lake outlet. This trail is not shown on new maps, but old books and old maps show it clearly.

As North Lake and South Lake trailheads are above 9,000 feet, it is advisable to acclimate by spending the night before your trip in a campground as close to 9,000 feet as possible.

**Access.** This hike begins at North Lake (see Hike 34 for directions) and ends at South Lake (see Hike 36 for directions). Hiking direction should be contingent on permit availability.

Begin your hike at 9,320 feet at the North Lake hikers' parking area and follow Hike 34 for 5.5 miles to Piute Pass (11,423 feet). The trail then heads down, descending gradually past Summit Lake and through Humphreys Basin. The trail continues down, paralleling Piute Creek through parklike meadows.

At 10.9 miles the trail levels, then crosses the French Canyon Creek delta. Even in August you will find the crossing to be a challenge. There are at least six knee-deep fords in about 200 yards. Do not put your shoes back on until you have crossed all of them. At 11 miles reach the French Canyon Trail junction and campsites in an area known as Hutchinson Meadow (9,440 feet).

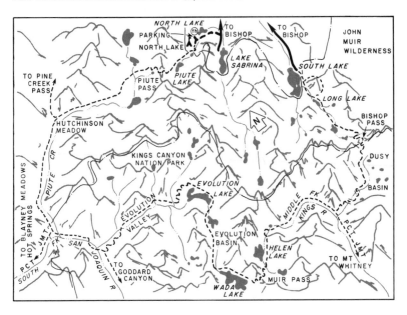

Below the meadow the descent is gradual through lodgepole forest for the next mile to East Pinnacles Creek (a moderately easy crossing). The rate of descent increases and the valley walls close in as the trail descends across the steep walls of The Pinnacles while Piute Creek roars and froths below. At 13.4 miles ford West Pinnacles Creek and at 14.6 miles ford Turret Creek. Piute Canyon Trail ends near the bottom of the canyon when it intersects the combined John Muir Trail/Pacific Crest Trail (JMT/PCT) at 15.8 miles (8,800 feet). At this point many hikers take a side trip down-valley to soak in Blayney Meadows Hot Springs, located near the John Muir Trail Ranch, adding 6.4 miles to your trip.

From the intersection with the JMT/PCT go left and cross Piute Creek on a steel bridge, then enter Kings Canyon National Park. Passing several campsites, the trail heads southeast up the narrow South Fork San Joaquin River valley toward Evolution Valley. At 18.2 miles the trail crosses the river on a solid bridge and passes several good campsites. Reach the Goddard Canyon Trail intersection at 19.1 miles, then recross the river on another strong bridge (8,470 feet).

Beyond the bridge the trail climbs a steep, sunbaked hillside where the spectacular waterfalls on Evolution Creek keep you interested even when feet seem to drag. A deep and wide ford of Evolution Creek, especially difficult on the fast-running south side, marks your entrance to Evolution Valley at 20.4 miles (9,210 feet). The trail then climbs gradually as you wander through alternating trees and meadows as you head up-valley from Evolution Meadow for 2.2 miles to McClure Meadow (where a ranger station is located), fording several tributary streams as

*Wanda Lake*

you go. Cross a couple more small tributary creeks on logs and rocks before reaching Colby Meadow at 24.4 miles (9,840 feet).

A mile beyond Colby Meadow the trail nears the end of Evolution Valley and heads steeply up, gaining 1,000 feet in a 1.5-mile climb to high country in Evolution Basin. At the last switchback, pass an unsigned trail to Darwin Canyon. The trail reaches Evolution Lake (10,850 feet) at 26.9 miles. Head around the west side of the lake along the flanks of Mt. Darwin for 1.4 miles to a ford of Evolution Creek at the inlet. The climb is gradual as the trail passes several tarns before reaching Sapphire Lake, then steepens a bit to switchback up and recross Evolution Creek near Wanda Lake (11,452 feet). Campsites are numerous.

From Wanda Lake the trail swings southwest to Lake McDermand. Snow patches are frequent, advice from the ranger or north-bound hikers can be helpful in choosing your route. Above Lake McDermand, the trail climbs steadily to reach 11,955-foot Muir Pass on the crest of the Goddard Divide at 32.9 miles. Scenery at the pass is spectacular, with views north over Evolution Basin and south to the Black Giant. Take time for a visit to the Muir Pass Hut, a well-known landmark. Careful hikers have kept it clean and in good shape for sixty years. Do your part and at least close the door when you leave.

From Muir Pass the trail descends quickly past Helen Lake, which tends to be snow-covered until late summer. You may prefer to hike cross-country along the higher, exposed rock ribs running up the valley and avoid the snow.

Beyond Helen Lake the trail passes several campsites as it descends to Le Conte Canyon and Middle Fork Kings River. The best campsites are found at Big and Little Pete Meadow and further sites are located near the Le Conte Ranger Station (8,700 feet). Leave the JMT/PCT at the 40-mile point of your hike and go left to begin your ascent of Bishop Pass. The trail climbs relentlessly, gaining 2,000 feet in the next 4.5 miles to lower Dusy Basin. The grade eases as you climb from the lower to the middle basin, then steepens as you head up to reach the crest of 11,980-foot Bishop Pass at 47 miles. The final 6 miles are an easy descent through a beautiful, lake-dotted valley, which brings you to the South Lake Trailhead at 53 miles.

# 36 THE CHOCOLATE PEAK LOOP

**Loop hike: 7 miles**
**Hiking time: 4 hours**
**High point: 11,300 feet**
**Elevation gain: 1,500 feet**

**Hikable: mid-July through**
**September**
**Day hike or backpack**

**Maps: USFS John Muir Wilderness (Central Section); USGS Mt. Thompson**

Reservations and Information: White Mountain Ranger Station and Bishop Creek Entrance Station (Case 6)

The circumnavigation of Chocolate Peak promises maximum scenic rewards for a moderate expenditure of energy, a very important consideration when hiking at 10,000 feet and above. Wandering from lake to lake and vista to vista makes this an excellent day hike or backpack trip. The loop is short but not easy. The trail has several steep and very rough sections, and between Ruwau Lake and the upper Chocolate Lake it disappears entirely.

**Access.** From Bishop, drive west on Highway 168 following signs to South Lake. At 10.1 miles reach the Bishop Creek Entrance Station, where you can pick up your wilderness permit if backpacking or camping permit if car camping. Continue up the road another 5.3 miles, then go left up the South Fork Bishop Creek valley for 7.2 miles to road's end at South Lake (9,768 feet). Parking is limited, especially for backpackers. If the upper lot is full, backpackers must go back down the road 1.3 miles to park.

Start your loop by following the Bishop Pass Trail from the lower end of the backpacker parking area. The trail descends briefly to meet the horse packer's trail, then goes right and heads around South Lake. Although the elevation may make the climb seem steep, the ascent is gradual and steady.

Pass a branch trail to Treasure Lakes on the right at 0.7 mile and continue up-valley, winding around granite outcropping and small meadows. At 1.5 miles a short trail to Marie Louise Lake branches off on the left. Just 0.2 mile beyond you will pass a trail to Bull and

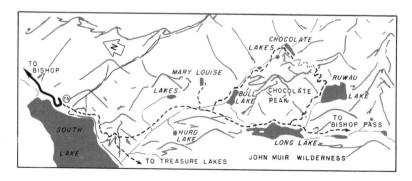

*Ruwau Lake*

Chocolate Lakes, used on the return leg of your loop. For now, continue on the Bishop Pass Trail.

To the left, 11,685-foot Chocolate Peak dominates the skyline as you climb over a low divide to reach the shores of beautiful Long Lake at 2 miles. Follow the trail along the shore of Long Lake to find a branch trail to Ruwau Lake on the left at 2.7 miles. At this point, leave the Bishop Pass Trail and head steeply uphill on a rough and rocky path. Ruwau Lake (11,044 feet) lies in an open basin surrounded by knife-edged ridges. As with all lakes passed on this loop, there are plenty of small campsites.

To continue, follow the sketchy trail about three-quarters of the way around the north shore of the lake, then go left and head steeply uphill. The trail climbs almost to the crest of a ridge then suddenly descends. This is followed by a short climb to an 11,300-foot saddle, where you may look down on upper Chocolate Lake and up at the dark and impenetrable wall of Inconsolable Ridge.

From the saddle the trail begins its descent with a well-defined switchback, then disappears on the rocky slope. Boot-beaten trails continue, making a rough descent to the lake below. Once at the shore of this lake (11,100 feet), go left to find a sketchy path along its steep west side. The trail improves as you go. You must cross the outlet of upper Chocolate Lake (usually on a shaky log) before you head down the right-hand side of the middle Chocolate Lake.

At the lower end of the middle lake, cross the outlet at the base of a small cascade. Follow the trail through meadows around the left side of lower Chocolate Lake, then descend and cross the outlet stream. Walk around the right-hand side of Bull Lake (10,760 feet), then follow a well-maintained trail to intersect the Bishop Pass Trail at 5.2 miles. Go right to return to the South Lake Trailhead at 7 miles.

*Route-finding through Dusy Basin*

# 37 DUSY BASIN

**Round trip: 16 miles**
**Hiking time: 3 days**
**High point: 11,980 feet**
**Elevation gain: 2,180 feet in;**
  **600 feet out**

**Hikable: mid-July through**
  **September**
**Backpack**

**Maps: USFS John Muir Wilderness (Central Section); USGS Mt.**
  **Thompson and North Palisade**

Reservations and Information: White Mountain Ranger Station and
  Rock Creek Entrance Station (Case 6)

Bring lots of film for this hike over Bishop Pass to renowned Dusy
Basin. The scenery along the trail is outstanding and the basin is
unbelievable. Do not expect solitude on the trail or in the basin. Day-
of-hike permits are difficult to get; plan ahead and reserve your wilderness permit early.

**Access.** See Hike 36 for driving instructions. The South Lake
Trailhead is located at 9,800 feet, a high-elevation start by any stan-
dards. Plan to spend a night in one of the Bishop Creek area campsites to acclimate.

From the parking area the trail heads through the brush for 10 feet
to join the horse packer's trail, then heads around the east shore of

South Lake for 0.5 mile before climbing a ravine filled with shooting stars and willows. Pace yourself, breathe steadily, walk with measured steps, and enjoy the scenery as you get used to the elevation.

Pass the Treasure Lakes Trail junction at 0.8 mile. Stay left and continue the well-graded ascent by small flower-covered meadows under the welcome shade of trees. The Marie Louise Lake spur trail branches right at 1.4 miles and at 1.9 miles pass a trail to Bull and Chocolate Lakes (see Hike 36). Continue up through a garden of wildflowers for another 0.2 mile to reach Long Lake (10,710 feet) at 2.1 miles. With its backdrop of knife-edged mountains and the appealing foreground of green meadows, granite boulders, and a sprinkling of trees, you may have to force yourself to continue.

Head around Long Lake, passing the spur trail to Ruwau Lake at 2.8 miles. The trail climbs to Spearhead Lake then to the Timberline Tarns to reach island-studded Saddlerock Lake at 4 miles (11,180 feet). At this point you leave the meadows and trees behind and head up into the rocky world of the High Sierra.

After passing unsigned spur trails to Bishop Lake at 4.5 miles, your trail begins its final push to the pass. At 5.7 miles cross a notch in the ridge crest, then head over a broad open plateau for the final 0.3 mile to the 11,980-foot high point of Bishop Pass.

At the pass the trail enters Kings Canyon National Park, then descends with an occasional switchback into Dusy Basin. The sandy trail contours southwest dropping from one rocky bench to the next. Leave the trail at the small inlet creek at 11,360 feet and walk over the granite and delicate meadows to the northernmost of the middle basin lakes. At this point your options are as vast as the basin. You may camp at this lake or head east and climb over a low ridge to more secluded campsites and lakes in the upper basin (11,393 feet).

Once you have set up camp it is time to explore. The easiest trip is to head back to the trail and descend 0.5 mile below the basin's outlet to a bridge over a spectacular waterfall. Strong hikers with considerable cross-country experience can follow a rough route from the lower lakes over Knapsack Pass to Palisades Basin or to Rainbow Lakes.

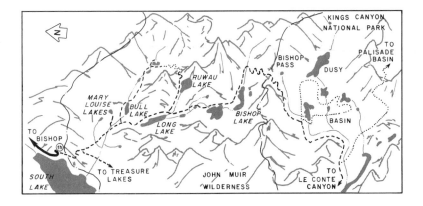

# 38 SOUTH LAKE TO WHITNEY PORTAL

One way: 92.8 miles
Hiking time: 10–12 days
High point: 14,495 feet
Elevation gain: 20,353 feet

Hikable: August through
  September
Backpack

Maps: USFS John Muir Wilderness (Central and South Sections);
  USGS Mt. Thompson, North Palisade, Split Mtn., Mt. Pinchot, Mt.
  Clarence King, Mt. Brewer, Mt. Williamson, Mt. Kaweah, Mt.
  Whitney, and Mt. Langley

Reservations and Information: White Mountain Ranger Station and
  Bishop Creek Entrance Station (Case 6)

Walk along the very crest of the Sierra on one of the finest hikes in
the United States. Along the route you will scale six major passes,
climb to dizzying heights and breathless views, and end your traverse
by ascending to the highest point in the lower 48 states. Your feet will
follow a trail that crosses through flower-covered meadows, skirts
around crystalline lakes, passes bubbling cascades and thundering torrents, and scales cliffs of sparkling granidiorite while your mind feasts
on endless vistas and the enchanting aspects of the High Sierra.

The main portion of the hike from South Lake to Whitney Portal follows the combined John Muir Trail/Pacific Crest Trail (JMT/PCT). The
trail is well maintained; however, you must be prepared to face numerous challenges along the route that require resourcefulness as well as
considerable hiking experience. The major challenges include unbridged river crossings, snow and ice that may cover the trail at the
passes for most of the summer, heavy packs, high elevations, and sudden storms. You must also be prepared for route finding, as trail signs
are often not replaced for several years after they are stolen or damaged.

The best way to deal with the unbridged river crossings and the
snowfields is to plan your hike for August and September (see the Introduction for more suggestions). Check with the Forest Service and
National Park Service concerning river and snow conditions before you
start.

Transportation between trailheads is also a challenge for hiking
groups that do not have two cars. From Whitney Portal at the end of
the trail to Lone Pine, 12 miles below on the valley floor, you must use
your charm to gain a ride. Once in Lone Pine, Greyhound provides
once-a-day service north to Bishop. In Bishop you may call the Backpackers Shuttle Service (phone 619-872-2721) to arrange transportation back to the South Lake.

**Access.** The hike begins at the Bishop Pass Trailhead (9,780 feet)
located at the end of South Lake Road (see Hike 37 for details).

The first 6 miles are spent climbing to the summit of Bishop Pass
(see Hike 37). Although at 11,972 feet this is the lowest major pass
crossed on the hike, it may feel like the hardest. Take it slow; the high

*John Muir Trail / Pacific Crest Trail near Forester Pass*

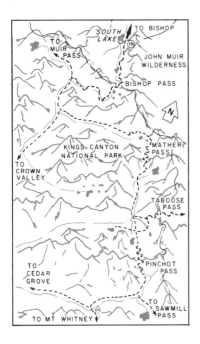

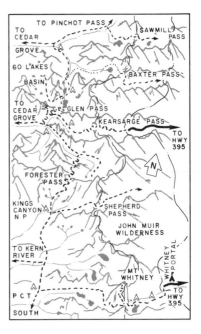

*John Muir Trail/Pacific Crest Trail south of Vedette Meadow*

elevation will drain your strength until you acclimate, and your pack, with its 10-day supply of food, will get lighter each day.

One of the best ways to face this first pass is to plan a short first day and camp either near Long Lake, about halfway up to the pass, or just over the crest in Dusy Basin.

From Bishop Pass the trail descends past lakes, meadows, and waterfalls to reach the Middle Fork Kings River and an intersection with the JMT/PCT at 12 miles from South Lake. Go left (south) and descend gradually through Grouse Meadows.

At 15 miles (8,000 feet) the trail begins to climb again. The elevation gain is gradual as you head up through Deer Meadow, then increases as you climb past Palisade Lakes to reach 12,100-foot Mather Pass at 25.2 miles.

From Mather Pass the trail descends nearly 2,000 feet through lake-studded Upper Basin to a challenging crossing of the South Fork Kings River (5.2 miles below the pass), before heading back up to cross the 12,000-foot crest of Pinchot Pass at 33.7 miles.

From Pinchot Pass, the trail descends gradually for 7 miles through meadows and forest to cross Woods Creek at 8,492 feet on a delightful suspension bridge. After Woods Creek you can expect a lot of company as you hike the most scenic portion of the famous Rae Lakes Loop (see Hike 61). The campsite on the south side of Woods Creek is well used and has a food-storage box. From Woods Creek the trail climbs to Dollar Lake and beautiful Rae Lakes at the base of Fin Dome and the Painted Lady. There is a one-night limit at the campsites in this area. At mile 49, cross 11,978-foot Glen Pass.

From Glen Pass the trail descends briskly to the Kearsarge Plateau, passing spur trails to Charlotte Lake and Kearsarge Lakes (these beautiful and popular lakes also have a one-night camping limit). Continuing down, the trail relentlessly descends a sparsely forested hillside to reach Vedette Meadow at 54.2 miles (9,510 feet). This extremely popular camp area is known for the bears that pillage food and packs. Be sure to use the food-storage boxes provided.

At Vedette Meadow, the Rae Lakes Loop and many of your fellow hikers will head west down Bubbs Creek. However, there is little solitude as numerous Whitney-bound hikers from Onion Valley join you for a breathtaking climb over 13,180-foot Forester Pass. On this difficult section of trail you will gain 3,670 feet of elevation in just 7.3 miles. Snow may linger on the north side of the pass for the entire summer. Descend 6 miles down the cliff walls on stony switchbacks then cross a high open plain to reach Tyndall Creek and a popular, overused campsite (10,880 feet) at 67.5 miles.

The Tyndall Creek crossing can be dangerous and is best done in the early morning. Beyond the creek, the trail rolls over the forested Bighorn Plateau to Wallace Creek, then climbs over Stony Meadow to the Crabtree Ranger Station and an intersection at which the John Muir Trail and Pacific Crest Trail part company at 73.5 miles from South Lake. Go left on the John Muir Trail and follow it past several excellent campsites before beginning the climb to the 13,480-foot Trail Crest reached at 78.9 miles.

At Trail Crest there is an intersection. Unless weather conditions prohibit continuing the ascent, go left and climb for another 1.8 miles to the summit of Mt. Whitney (14,495 feet). Do not linger at the summit too long; it is still an 11-mile descent down the famous 97 switchbacks to Whitney Portal. There are two campsites along the descent, at 5 and 7 miles below the summit. Walk-in campsites are available at Whitney Portal.

*Fording Tyndall Creek, difficult even in late summer*

# 39 THUNDER AND LIGHTNING

**Round trip to pass: 10 miles**    **Elevation gain: 2,320 feet**
**Hiking time: 6 hours**    **Hikable: July through September**
**High point: 11,800 feet**    **Day hike or backpack**

**Maps: USFS John Muir Wilderness (Central Section); USGS Mt. Thompson**

Reservations and Information: White Mountain Ranger Station and Bishop Creek Entrance Station (Case 6)

Quiet and solitude, with plenty of views and High Sierra scenery, are the best reasons for exploring the often ignored Green Lake drainage. Day hikers will find the pass above the lake to be a scenic destination. However, if you are full of energy, you may roam the open hills and ridges and even find a secluded lake for camping.

**Access.** From the center of Bishop, drive west on Highway 168 following the signs to South Lake. After climbing steeply for 10.1 miles, reach the Bishop Creek Entrance Station where you will arrange for your permit if you are backpacking or a campsite if car camping. Continue on up the road for another 5.3 miles, then go left on the South

*Hiker near pass area*

Lake Road for 7.2 miles to road's end at the Bishop Pass Trailhead at South Lake (9,755 feet).

Walk to the upper end of the backpackers' parking area, then continue up on an old road. Stay with this road until it starts to descend, then turn left and head uphill, without a trail, for 25 feet to the water pipeline. Go left and follow the pipeline for 1 mile until it intercepts a trail from the pack station. The pipeline requires steady footing. Avoid it when wet or during an electrical storm.

Leave the pipeline and follow the Green Lake Trail as it switchbacks uphill, rapidly gaining elevation for the next 0.2 mile. At 1.2 miles, cross an energetic creek on slippery logs, then follow a newly cut trail around a recent avalanche. The climb abates as the trail enters the first of several wet meadows, where a great deal of ingenuity must be employed to avoid getting your feet wet.

At 1.5 miles the trail fords the outlet stream from Brown Lake; however, if you stay right on a boot-beaten path you can make a dry crossing at the lake's edge (10,770 feet). Only fishermen find anything exciting about Brown Lake and most hikers continue on, crossing another wet meadow and passing a few campsites before climbing up the rocky ridge to reach the 11,100-foot Green Lake basin at 3 miles. The green color of the lake is striking amidst green meadows, wildflowers, and steep, rocky hillsides.

From the lake, the trail makes a steep switchbacking climb to a dry High Sierran plateau below a rounded ridge called The Hunchback. Once on top, the climb slackens and the trail heads south across a rock-strewn high alpine meadow. Look closely to find the miniature flowers that bloom in this harsh environment. The trail, haphazardly marked by wood posts or small ducks, reaches the 11,800-foot pass above Green Lake at 4.5 miles. The view is enormous. Thunderclouds tend to form here, hence the name Thunder and Lightning.

Backpackers heading on the additional 2 miles to Thunder and Lightning Lake should cross the pass and descend to an 11,400-foot bench, then leave the trail and head to the right. Before long the sketchy route becomes a well-defined trail that lasts all the way to the lake.

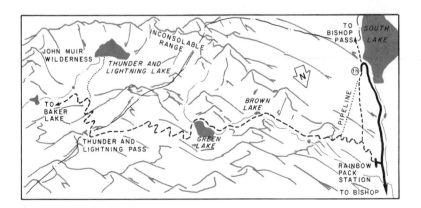

*Temple Crag viewed from First Lake*

# 40  BIG PINE LAKES BASIN

**Loop hike to Summit Lake: 16 miles**
**Hiking time: 2 days**
**High point: 10,920 feet**
**Elevation gain: 3,160 feet**
**Hikable: mid-July through September**
**Backpack**

**Maps: USFS John Muir Wilderness (Central Section); USGS Coyote Flat, Mt. Thompson, and Split Mountain**

Reservations and Information: White Mountain Ranger Station and Upper Sage Flat Campground (Case 6)

Big Pine Lakes Basin lies at the base of a wall of glaciated peaks whose summits pierce the sky at over 14,000 feet. The basin has nine lakes, each in its own granite bowl, exquisitely sculptured by ancient glaciers. The destination of this hike is Summit Lake, although every lake in the basin is worth visiting. Make the basic hike as described here, then plan to spend several days exploring.

**Access.** Drive Highway 395 to the town of Big Pine then go west on Crocker Street, which soon becomes Glacier Lodge Road. Reach Upper Sage Flat Campground at 9.9 miles and pick up your wilderness permit from the camp host. The backpackers' trailhead is located at 0.2 mile further on at 7,750 feet. Day hikers can drive another 0.6 mile and park at the end of the road.

From the backpackers' parking area the trail heads up-valley, traversing a sage-covered hillside for 1.2 miles. As you round the hill and enter the North Fork Big Pine Creek valley, pass a trail on the left that descends to First Falls Walk-In Campground and the day-hikers' parking lot. At 1.7 miles the Baker Lake Trail branches off on the right.

The trail switchbacks up a narrow gorge at the edge of Second Falls, then enters a verdant valley covered with forest and meadows. Near the 3-mile point pass a beautiful old cabin that was once the property of actor Lon Chaney and is now the wilderness ranger's camp. The rate of climb increases as you continue and an unbelievable wall of summits comes into view.

At 4.3 miles the trail divides and the loop portion of the hike begins. Go left and explore the dazzling spectacle of Big Pine Lakes 1 through 7 in numerical order. With the towering mass of Temple Crag reflecting in its waters, First Lake (9,900 feet), passed at 4.5 miles, is an awesome sight. Just 0.2 mile beyond lies equally beautiful Second Lake. Third Lake at 5.2 miles is smaller and has several secluded campsites.

Beyond Third Lake the trail climbs steadily to an intersection at 5.7 miles. To the left, a rough trail scrambles over granite ledges and grassy meadows to the base of Palisade Glacier, an interesting side trip. For now stay right for another 0.3 mile to the Fourth Lake intersection. The right-hand trail is your route back to the Big Pine Creek Trailhead, so go left and head toward Fourth and Fifth Lakes. Skirt the west shore of Fourth Lake and at 6.2 miles pass the trail to Sixth and Seventh Lakes on the left. Continue straight, crossing a small creek to reach Glacier Camp, a popular camp area for horse packers.

Continue uphill. After 100 yards the horse trail to Sixth and Seventh Lakes branches off to the left. Stay to the right and continue climbing until you reach Summit Lake (10,920 feet), 8 miles from the start. This delicate lake has a granite fringe of some of the most impressive summits in the Sierra: the Inconsolable Range, North Palisade (14,242 feet), Mt. Sill (14,162 feet), Mt. Agassiz (13,891 feet), and Mt. Winchell (13,768 feet). Camping is limited to a few sites along the west shore.

To return to your car, descend to the intersection below Fourth Lake and go left to Black Lake. Switchback down a very dry hillside to return to the North Fork Big Pine Trail to complete the loop portion of the hike.

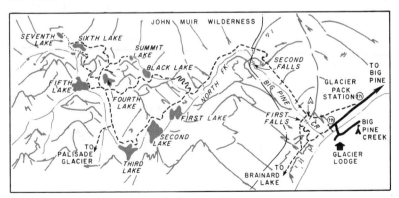

# 41 BRAINARD LAKE

**Round trip: 12 miles**
**Hiking time: 7 hours**
**High point: 10,650 feet**
**Elevation gain: 2,900 feet**

**Hikable: mid-July through**
   **September**
**Day hike or backpack**

**Maps: USFS John Muir Wilderness (Central Section); USGS Coyote Mountain and Split Peak**

Reservations and Information: White Mountain Ranger Station and Upper Sage Flat Campground (Case 6)

Brainard Lake lies in a deep bowl of granite, surrounded by glacier-clad summits towering over 13,000 feet. Massive cliffs create a vertical shoreline for the icy blue waters. This scenic lake is located high up the South Fork Big Pine Creek valley. The trail to Brainard Lake is rough, steep, and hard to follow in some sections. Campsites are small and limited in number.

**Access.** Drive Highway 395 to Big Pine then go west on Crocker Street, which soon becomes Glacier Lodge Road. At 9.9 miles reach Up-

*Palisade Crest*

per Sage Flat Campground where wilderness permits are obtained. The backpackers' parking area (7,750 feet) is located 0.2 mile beyond. Day hikers may continue up the road another 0.7 mile to the small parking area at road's end (7,800 feet).

If starting from the backpackers' parking lot, walk up the road to its end at the upper trailhead. Head around the gate then follow the South Fork Big Pine Creek Trail on an old road past several cabins. After a short 0.1 mile, you will arrive at the confluence of the North and South Forks of Big Pine Creek. The trail goes right and climbs uphill to a sturdy bridge.

At 0.2 mile the trail divides; stay left on the South Fork Trail and follow it across a sage-covered hillside. The climb is gradual but steady with the river rumbling below and the glaciated Palisade Crest and Norman Clyde Peak above. The trail crosses the old roadbed, then continues up-valley. Watch for prickly pear cactus as you walk. After 1.7 miles of easy going, cross the South Fork Big Pine Creek on a couple of broken planks. (If these are water-covered or missing, don't even think of crossing.)

The trail then heads up a talus-covered slope to the base of the valley headwall and begins a series of steep switchbacks, which wind around boulders and scramble across ledges to reach the 9,800-foot ridge crest where a spectacular view of mountains and glaciers bursts forth at 3.4 miles.

Descend across small meadows, losing 180 feet of elevation, before arriving at the Willow Lake intersection at 4.2 miles. Here you go left and cross a small creek with a long jump, then start uphill, paralleling a deep gorge.

The trail passes a small pond then dips to cross a marshy meadow. On the far side of the meadow the trail climbs past a second pond, then swings around a granite ledge to reach the shores of Brainard Lake (10,650 feet) at 5.7 miles.

Backpackers will find tent sites to the left or right of the trail. Day hikers and anglers can scamper along the rocks to find the perfect combination of sun and wind. Cross-country hikers can work their way up the talus to Finger Lake on the bench above, then wander on to several small tarns with close-up views of the glaciers along the Palisade Crest.

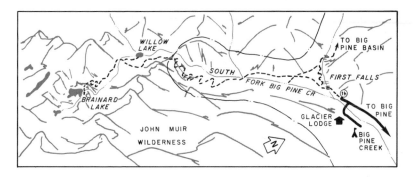

# 42  SAWMILL LAKE

**Round trip: 16 miles**
**Hiking time: 2 days**
**High point: 10,040 feet**
**Elevation gain: 5,400 feet**

**Hikable: mid-June through**
   **September**
**Backpack**

**Maps: USFS John Muir Wilderness (Central Section); USGS Aberdeen Peak**

Reservations and Information: Mt. Whitney Ranger Station (Case 6)

This trail begins in near-desert conditions in the Owens Valley and climbs to a deep blue lake in the High Sierra. Along the way you will pass through a variety of ecosystems as well as sampling some history as you pass beneath the ruins of a mill that supplied lumber to miners in the 1860s. Besides being a challenging weekend backpack, this trail offers an entry or exit from the combined John Muir Trail/Pacific Crest Trail (JMT/PCT) between Pinchot Pass and Glen Pass.

A word of warning, and please consider this very seriously. The Sawmill Trail is hot, dry, and exposed to the sun for the first 2,510 feet of this very strenuous 5,400-foot climb. Get an early morning or late afternoon start, and carry at least two quarts of water per person. Also note that this is a bighorn sheep preservation area; dogs and cross-country hiking are not allowed.

**Access.** From Independence, drive north on Highway 395 for 8 miles to Black Rock Spring Road. Go left, west, for 0.8 mile to a T intersection, then go right on Old Highway 395 for 1.3 miles. At Division Creek Road turn left and head uphill for 2 miles to the trailhead (4,640 feet).

The trail begins by meandering up a sage-covered hillside. At 0.5 mile you will arrive at the base of a steep hillside and begin the business of climbing. The grade is relentless as feet churn up dust on the soft soil of the trail. You climb past a couple of volcanic cones then, enter the bighorn sheep preservation area. Chances of seeing one of these animals are slim but keep your eyes open nevertheless.

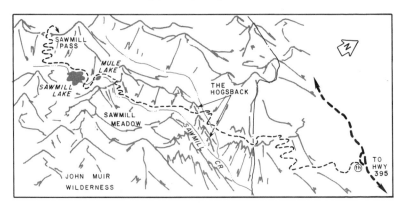

The trail climbs to a sharp ridge (6,831 feet) crested with weathered columns of granite, then makes a long, descending traverse, losing 150 feet of elevation in the next 0.5 mile. Ahead at the center of this imposing valley is a ridge called The Hogsback. As you get closer you will see the old sawmill.

The descent ends when the trail reaches Sawmill Creek, the first water encountered on this hike. Climb along the creek, passing several small, illegal campsites. You will cross the creek three times before you reach the 8,125-foot crest of The Hogsback. The climb continues to the 8,400-foot point, then the trail levels and traverses south to grassy Sawmill Meadow and a couple of nice (if you can ignore the mosquitos) campsites.

Beyond Sawmill Meadow the trail climbs again, switchbacking up a talus-strewn headwall to little Mule Lake and more campsites, then up a lava-covered hillside to reach Sawmill Lake (10,040 feet) at 8 miles. Numerous scenic campsites are scattered around the lake among the foxtail pine.

If time allows, plan an extra day for exploring. From the lake it is only 2 miles to the top of 11,347-foot Sawmill Pass. On the west side of this open pass lies a beautiful high alpine basin where Mt. Cedric Wright towers over lake-dotted meadows. If you descend all the way down the basin you will encounter the combined JMT/PCT (10,346 feet) 5 miles beyond Sawmill Lake.

*Wilderness sign on trail to Sawmill Lake*

# 43 KEARSARGE LAKES TRAIL

**Round trip: 13 miles**
**Hiking time: 8 hours**
**High point: 11,823 feet**
**Elevation gain: 2,623 feet in;**
  **923 feet out**

**Hikable: mid-June through**
  **September**
**Day hike or backpack**

**Maps: USFS John Muir Wilderness (South Section); USGS Kearsarge Peak and Mt. Clarence King**

Reservations and Information: Mt. Whitney Ranger Station and Onion Valley Trailhead (Case 6)

Nature has achieved near perfection in the Kearsarge Lakes area with its arrangement of crystal blue lakes, sculptured trees, and towering peaks.

**Access.** Drive Highway 395 north from Lone Pine 16.7 miles to the town of Independence. Go left (west) on Market Street for 13.6 steep and twisting miles to the large Onion Valley Trailhead parking area (9,200 feet).

Walk past the rest rooms to find the start of the trail, which begins with long, moderately graded switchbacks—suitable for hikers starting out with heavy packs at high elevations. The climb is steady and before long you will be rewarded with views east to the White Mountains.

The first lake, Little Pothole (10,020 feet), is reached after just 1.5 miles of steady climbing. This small lake has a couple of campsites and views. Continue up another series of switchbacks to reach beautiful Gilbert Lake at 2.2 miles. Numerous campsites are located along the north side and at the upper end of the lake on a spur trail to the left. At 2.6 miles pass a signed junction with the Matlock Lake Trail (a 0.7-mile side trip) and shortly after pass several campsites on the shores of Flower Lake. The climb continues with more switchbacks overlooking aptly named Heart Lake in a secluded basin.

At 3.7 miles you will arrive at the edge of a desolate plateau with a view of Kearsarge Pass. The pass is near; however, the trail extends the distance with a couple of long, well-graded switchbacks with views of Big Pothole Lake (very poor campsites). The trail crests the knife edged Kearsarge Pass (11,823 feet) at 5.5 miles. Grab a seat on a rock and sit down to enjoy the magnificent panorama spread out below your feet. Kearsarge Lakes and Kearsarge Pinnacles dominate the scene below. To the left is University Peak, and to the right Mt. Gould dominates the skyline.

With your goal in sight, descend into Kings Canyon National Park. After 0.5 mile, leave the main trail and go left on the spur trail to Kearsarge Lakes. Bear boxes and campsites are spread out around the lakes. Due to the popularity of the area, there is a one-night camping limit.

*The rocky summit of Kearsarge Pass is a popular rest stop for hikers.*

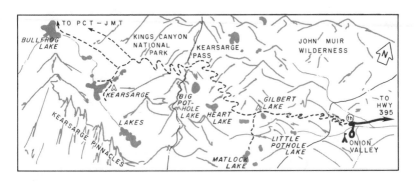

# 44 MEYSAN LAKE

**Round trip: 10 miles**
**Hiking time: 8 hours**
**High point: 11,460 feet**
**Elevation gain: 3,760 feet**

**Hikable: mid-June through**
**September**
**Day hike or backpack**

**Maps: USFS John Muir Wilderness (South Section); USGS Mt. Langley**

Reservations and Information: Mt. Whitney Ranger Station (Case 6)

The Mt. Whitney Trail is the focus of most hikers at Whitney Portal, so anyone looking for a bit of solitude, as well as spectacular scenery, can escape the crowds on this arduous trek to Meysan Lake. Hikers who wisely spend a day acclimating before attempting Mt. Whitney will find this hike a challenging test of strength while bodies adjust to the oxygen-deficient air.

**Access.** From the Mt. Whitney Ranger Station in Lone Pine, drive north on Highway 395 for 0.3 mile. Turn left (west) on Whitney Portal Road and follow it for 11.6 miles to the Meysan Lake Trailhead parking area, which is a dirt turnout on the left side of the road (7,900 feet).

From the parking area, drop down into the Whitney Portal Campground, then go left on the paved campground loop road. Cross Lone Pine Creek on a car bridge, then go left at the first intersection for 200

*Hikers near Grass Lake*

feet to find the trail on the right and head steeply up. After gasping for breath a few times, hikers are relieved to find that the trail levels into a traverse, which ends at a paved road. Walk past several summer homes, then stay right when the road divides. The trail soon reappears on the right.

Climb steeply up a dry slope, switchbacking to the base of an impressive wall of granite, then head up-valley. There is a short section of extremely narrow trail on a precipitous slope where you must watch your step and not the extraordinary view; ahead is a massive headwall which must be climbed, to the south is Lone Pine Peak, and to the northeast are the Alabama Hills and the Owens Valley.

The trail climbs steadily, moving up-valley with each well-graded switchback. At 3.5 miles descend, briefly, to a small forested bench (10,250 feet), then almost immediately turn to head back up. At the bench the wide, well-graded thoroughfare ends. From that point the trail is steep, rough, narrow, and sometimes overgrown with brush as it shoots uphill, gaining elevation rapidly. The route is faint in places as you climb over a rocky rib then up a sandy slope. At 4.7 miles the headlong rush uphill abates and you enter a grassy meadow dotted with rounded granitic ribs where the trail divides. George Lake and some campsites lie straight ahead. Meysan Lake is to the right.

The trail climbs, descends, then climbs again to reach meadow and Camp Lake (11,200 feet) at 5 miles. If backpacking, you may want to take advantage of the campsites in this area and save Meysan Lake with its rocky shores for a day hike.

No officially constructed trail exists between Camp Lake and Meysan Lake. Instead, you must follow one of several boot-beaten paths marked with ducks. Stay to the right as you round the large meadow that surrounds Camp Lake until you reach a green gully and a seasonal creek bed. Follow the creek up past one small bench, then on to a second. At this point go left and head up the hillside on a well-beaten path. The track angles right to a rocky 11,660-foot draw above Meysan Lake. From this vantage point you have the best view of the lake and its imposing headwall, comprised of Mt. Mallory and La Conte. From the saddle, descend the loose, rocky slope to the lakeshore, where a profusion of shooting star grows in tiny pocket meadows.

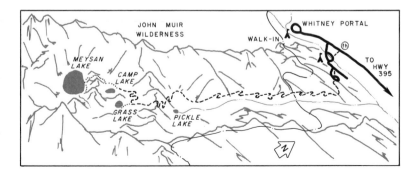

# 45 MOUNT WHITNEY

**Round trip: 22 miles**
**Hiking time: 12–15 hours**
**High point: 14,495 feet**
**Elevation gain: 6,131 feet**

**Hikable: mid-July through**
    **September**
**Day hike or backpack**

**Maps: USFS John Muir Wilder-**
    **ness (South Section); USGS Mt.**
    **Langley and Mt. Whitney**

Reservations and Information:
Mt. Whitney Ranger Station
(Case 6)

People come from all over the world to hike this seriously over-used trail to the highest point in the lower 48 states. However, it is the scenery that brings people back to do this hike time and again.

Before your feet ever touch the trail, you have numerous difficulties to surmount. For most hikers the length of the hike and the elevation require a minimum of one night spent at the trailhead to acclimate and one or more nights spent on the trail. Unfortunately, getting a backpacking permit is difficult (see Case 6 and groan). Hikers without permits walk the entire 21.4 miles in a single day, which requires being in excellent physical condition and having a willingness to start early, by 4:00 A.M. at the very latest.

All Mt. Whitney hikers should carry a wide assortment of clothes to deal with adverse conditions, such as thunder and lightning, heavy rains, arctic winds, snow, and ice. Always wear sunglasses and reapply sunscreen every hour

*Mount Whitney trail at base of the famous ninety-seven switchbacks*

or so. Carry lots of water: day hikers should drink two to three quarts to avoid becoming dehydrated and sick. A large quantity of food is also a must.

Sudden electrical storms are common during the summer months and can be deadly on the exposed slopes and summits of the mountain. When thunderclouds appear, turn back immediately. If you are on the summit, wait out the entire storm in the cabin, even if it lasts for several hours.

Altitude sickness, dehydration, and acute fatigue are major factors

on the trail. Read the Introduction to learn about these problems. If you feel ill, do not be afraid to turn back. You will be charged for the expense of the rescue if you cannot make it down.

**Access.** From the Mt. Whitney Ranger Station in Lone Pine, drive north on Highway 395 for 0.3 mile. Turn left (west) on Whitney Portal Road and head up for 12.6 miles to Whitney Portal. Park in the hikers' area next to the walk-in campsite (8,365 feet).

The trail begins with a long switchback, then heads up the Lone Pine Creek Valley. Vertical walls of granite seem to surround you as you climb. Ahead, Thor Peak dominates the skyline. The climb is steady but never steep, and views expand as you go. To the east the Owens Valley and the amazing Alabama Hills soon become visible.

The trail crosses two small creeks. Near the second creek crossing, at 0.7 mile, pass the first of several unsigned climbers' trails branching off to the right. Beyond the creeks, the trail switchbacks up the headwall of the valley. At 2.7 miles cross Lone Pine Creek and 0.1 mile beyond pass a spur trail to Lone Pine Lake (9,850 feet). The trail continues to climb, heading up a boulder-filled valley then ascending granite walls on superbly engineered switchbacks. A short descent at 3.8 miles marks your entrance into a beautiful oasis of green known as Bighorn Park. At the upper end is Outpost Camp (10,365 feet), one of the two legal camping areas on the trail. The camp has a composting toilet. Be sure to hang your food; rodents are a major problem.

Beyond the camp, the trail climbs again (no big surprise), switchbacking up a granite-covered slope for 0.5 mile to Mirror Lake (10,640 feet). More switchbacks follow, heading up a granite stairway, leaving the trees and shade behind. At 5.3 miles feast your rock-weary eyes on a tiny swath of green known as Trailside Meadow (11,395 feet).

The switchbacks continue, views expand, and the oxygen-rich air is left behind. The next mile goes slowly, as the trail heads over the crest of a ridge to views of Consultation Lake and the summits of Mt. Irvine and Mt. McAdie. Follow the trail through one of nature's most glorious rock gardens to 12,000-foot Trail Camp reached at 6.2 miles. The camp

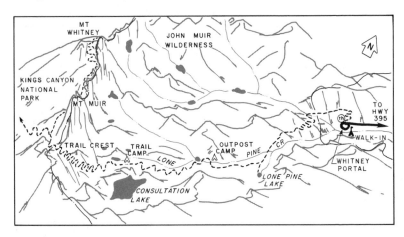

*Hiker on summit of Mount Whitney*

is located by a small lake and has a solar toilet and a ravenous population of marmots. Protect your food by suspending it over the edge of overhanging rocks.

Beyond Trail Camp the fun begins. Head through a boulder field then start up the infamous ninety-seven switchbacks. Early-morning hikers need to watch for ice on the trail in this section. At 8.5 miles you will complete the ninety-seventh switchback and arrive at Trail Crest (13,777 feet) where the trail enters Sequoia National Park and descends, briefly, to meet the John Muir Trail at 8.7 miles. Stay right at this intersection and follow the trail up along the ridge crest. Watch your feet and not the amazing panorama around you.

In the next 1.9 miles you will pass some of the most expansive views found in the Sierra. At the end of the 1.9 miles the trail arrives at a hillside covered with blocks of rock. The trail disappears; however, the route is obvious. Head up the hillside and before long you will reach the crest of the broad plateau that is the summit of Mt. Whitney. Head over to the hut, built by the Smithsonian Institute in 1909, and sign the register. Then wander over to the highest and most scenic toilet in America. Finally, relax and enjoy the natural high that comes from hiking to 14,495 feet.

Remember to keep an eye on the weather and be prepared to head down in a hurry. Clouds can build up suddenly and rapidly.

# 46 NEW ARMY PASS LOOP

**Loop hike: 19.7 miles**
**Hiking time: 2–4 days**
**High point: 12,340 feet**
**Elevation gain: 2,920 feet**

**Hikable: August through**
**September**
**Backpack**

**Maps: USFS John Muir Wilderness (South Section); USGS Cirque
Peak, Johnson Peak, and Mt. Kaweah**

Reservations and Information: Mt. Whitney Ranger Station (Case 6)

This loop has all the trappings that you expect from a trip in the High Sierra: beautiful lakes, verdant meadows, and incredible views.

**Access.** From the Mt. Whitney Ranger Station in Lone Pine, drive north on Highway 395 for 0.3 mile, then go left on Whitney Portal Road. At 3.2 miles turn right on Horseshoe Meadow Road. After 19.3 miles the road divides; stay right for 0.3 mile to the Cottonwood Lakes Basin Trailhead and walk-in campground (10,060 feet).

Begin your loop by following the Cottonwood Lakes/New Army Pass Trail over a low ridge, then descending gradually to cross Cottonwood Creek for the first time at 1.5 miles. At 3 miles pass the Golden Trout horse camp. The trail then climbs at a gradual pace to an intersection at 3.7 miles. Stay left here and follow a trail signed to South Fork Lakes and New Army Pass.

Recross Cottonwood Creek, then climb steadily to reach the South Fork Lakes Trail intersection at 5 miles. Stay right and follow the trail over a low ridge to Cottonwood Lake 1 and views of the basin at 5.2 miles. This is a beautiful area, dotted with lakes and scenic campsites.

Following signs for New Army Pass, walk along the south shore of Cottonwood Lakes 1 and 2 then climb over a boulder-covered ridge to

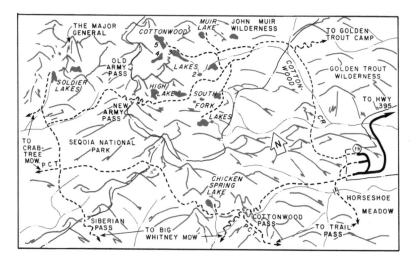

*Rock-covered summit of New Army Pass*

the South Fork drainage. The trail takes you past a small lake with an excellent campsite at the upper end, then up through meadows to Long Lake (11,440 feet). (Campsites are situated at the upper end of the lake.)

Above Long Lake the trail ascends a boulder-strewn basin to New Army Pass. Using long, moderately graded switchbacks, climb with a slow and steady pace to reach the crest of 12,340-foot New Army Pass at 8 miles. The snowbank that lingers just below the crest may cause problems until mid-August. Follow the directions about how to get around the snowbank posted at the trailhead.

From the pass, descend into Kings Canyon/Sequoia National Park for 2.3 miles to an intersection with the Siberian Pass Trail (10,800 feet). Go right here for a 0.6-mile side trip to spend the night at Lower Military Lake.

The loop route heads south (left) on the Siberian Pass Trail and the next 1.1 miles are spent crossing a forested ridge. At 11.4 miles leave the Siberian Pass Trail and go left on the Pacific Crest Trail (PCT). The trail climbs with occasional views west to Siberian Outpost through the pines and reenters the wilderness at 12.3 miles. At this point the trail becomes annoyingly sandy as it swings around a horse-shoe basin where some maps show a lake, though the only water is a seasonal spring. At 15 miles, crest a rocky rib with views of Big Whitney Meadow to the west and Chicken Spring Lake to the east then descend to the lake (11,260 feet) to find a multitude of hikers and fellow campers.

From Chicken Spring Lake, continue south on the PCT for 0.2 mile to Cottonwood Pass (11,160 feet). Leave the PCT here and go left, descending first through forest then along the edge of Horseshoe Meadow to reach the Horseshoe Meadow Trailhead at 19.2 miles. Walk the road for the final 0.5 mile back to your car at the Cottonwood Lakes Basin Trailhead.

*One of the beautiful Rocky Basin Lakes*

# 47 ROCKY BASIN LAKES

**Round trip: 26 miles**
**Hiking time: 2–4 days**
**High point: 11,160 feet**
**Elevation gain: 2,200 feet in;**
   **1,160 feet out**

**Hikable: July through September**
**Backpack**

**Maps: USFS Golden Trout Wilderness; USGS Cirque Peak and**
   **Johnson Peak**

Reservations and Information: Mt. Whitney Ranger Station (Case 6)

Tucked away in a rocky basin (hence the name) is a chain of secluded lakes. The 13-mile trail access route includes two major climbs and usually is hiked in two days with an overnight stop at Chicken Spring Lake or Big Whitney Meadow.

**Access.** From Mt. Whitney Ranger Station in Lone Pine, drive north on Highway 395 for 0.3 mile, then go left on Whitney Portal Road. After 3.2 miles turn left on Horseshoe Meadow Road and follow it for 19.6

miles to its end at the Horseshoe Meadow Trailhead and a walk-in campground (9,960 feet).

Begin your hike on the Cottonwood Pass Trail, passing at 0.2 mile a spur to Trail Pass on the left followed by a horse trail to the Cottonwood Lakes Basin Trailhead that branches right. Continue straight along the north side of Horseshoe Meadow for the remainder of the first mile.

At the upper end of the meadows the trail begins a gradual climb, which ends at 11,160-foot Cottonwood Pass, 4 miles from the trailhead. From the summit you can preview the rest of the trip down to Big Whitney Meadows then up over a forested ridge to Rocky Basin.

At the crest, Cottonwood Pass is a four-way intersection with the Pacific Crest Trail (PCT). Just 0.6 mile north is Chicken Spring Lake, which has excellent though usually crowded camping. To reach Rocky Basin Lakes you must go west and descend the sloping meadow below the pass, then head down gradual switchbacks along Stokes Stringer to the first meadow. Cross this open and often damp area, then walk over a wooded knoll to reach Big Whitney Meadow (9,720 feet). The meadow is a combination of marsh, meadow, sand, and cow-churned mire and the trail cuts straight through all of it. At the center of the meadow is an island of trees and an intersection with the first of two trails to Siberian Pass. The trail then crosses Golden Trout Creek, the last certain water before you reach the basin.

At 8 miles the trail leaves Big Whitney Meadow and passes the second trail to Siberian Pass. A good campsite with a spring is located just 500 feet to the north in a fringe of trees at the edge of the meadow. (This is good water until the cows arrive, usually in mid-August.)

At 8.2 miles the trail divides. Stay to the right and immediately head up a forested hillside, gaining 640 feet in the next 1.7 miles. The trail crosses the crest of a low saddle, then drops 200 feet to an intersection at 10.1 miles in the Barigan Stringer drainage. Campsites are located to the left and straight ahead along the banks of the seasonal creek. Go right for the final gradual climb to the lakes. At 11.5 miles the trail divides. The horse trail goes left and crosses the creek, and foot traffic should stay to the right. A small bug-infested pond at 12.2 miles marks the entrance to Rocky Lakes Basin, and soon after the trail reaches the first lake (10,745 feet). Follow the path along the south shore to reach the second and third lakes at 13 miles. Johnson Lake, located just over the hill from the third lake, is a popular cross-country trip from the basin.

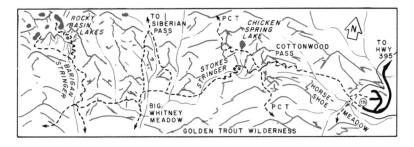

HIGHWAY 198

# *48* COBALT AND CRYSTAL LAKES

| | |
|---|---|
| **Round trip to Crystal Lakes:** 9.8 miles | **Elevation gain: 2,988 feet** |
| **Hiking time: 6 hours** | **Hikable: mid-July through** |
| **High point: 10,788 feet** | **September** |
| | **Day hike or backpack** |

**Day hike or backpack**
**Maps: USFS John Muir Wilderness (South Section); USGS Mineral King**

Reservations and Information: Sequoia National Park and Mineral King Ranger Station (Case 7)

Just a few miles by trail from the extremely popular and overused Monarch Lakes lie four scenic and often overlooked lakes in a basin on a shoulder of the Great Western Divide. Due to a steep and rough access trail, these lakes are somewhat isolated, making them ideal destinations for day hikes and backpack trips.

**Access.** Drive north from Visalia on Highway 198. At the town of Three Rivers, check your odometer, then continue on for another 3.6 miles before turning right on Mineral King Road. The next 24 miles are slow going up a narrow, twisting, partly dirt-surfaced road to the Mineral King Ranger Station, where backpackers must pick up their permits before continuing the final 0.9 mile to the Sawtooth Parking Area (7,800 feet).

The trail begins on the north side of the road at the upper end of the parking area and heads nearly straight up the sage-covered hillside. This initial hot, steep climb does not last long. As you approach the trees, the trail takes off into a long switchback. The first intersection is reached at 0.5 mile. The left fork heads up to Timber Gap (see Hike 49). Stay right and continue the long, traversing switchback.

At 0.9 mile the trail changes character again, heading nearly straight uphill along the edge of Monarch Canyon. After a difficult 0.1

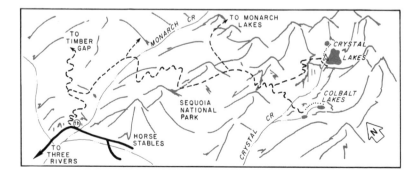

130

*Lower Crystal Lake*

mile, you will enter Groundhog Meadow (8,540 feet). Pass the abandoned trail to Glacier Pass on the left, then cross Monarch Creek with a running long jump. The trail then heads up a forested hillside with well-graded switchbacks.

At 3.2 miles (9,850 feet), arrive at the Cobalt and Crystal Lakes junction. Go right, leaving the wide thoroughfare with its crowds of horses and hikers and head south on a rough, narrow track. Traverse the open hillside into Chihuahua Bowl, where the trail begins to climb, heading past an old mine to a narrow, tree-fringed gap (10,340 feet).

From the gap, you will descend steeply for 0.1 mile to the Cobalt Lakes junction. To reach the Cobalts, go right and continue down to the floor of a 10,000-foot basin. The trail heads across meadows to granite slabs where it disappears. Continue straight to reach lower Cobalt Lake, sandwiched between cliffs and a narrow band of rock, at 4.4 miles. Campsites here have views west to the San Joaquin Valley. Upper Cobalt Lake is reached by a cross-country trek on a boot path that climbs the left side of the band of rocks above the lower lake. Mosquitos plague these two lakes until the first frost.

To reach the Crystal Lakes, continue on from the Cobalt Lakes junction, traversing the open basin to Crystal Creek. The trail climbs steeply over talus and bands of weathered rock to Southern California Edison-enhanced Lower Crystal Lake at 4.9 miles (10,788 feet). Campsites are located on a narrow ledge at the base of the dam (don't sleepwalk), or at the upper lake, reached by a rough trail which branches off 200 feet below the dam.

# 49 FIVE LAKES, LITTLE AND BIG

**Loop hike: 28.4 miles**
**Hiking time: 3–4 days**
**High point: 11,600 feet**
**Elevation gain: 9,310 feet**

**Hikable: mid-July through**
**September**
**Backpack**

**Maps: USFS John Muir Wilderness (South Section); USGS Mineral King and Chagoopa Falls**

Reservations and Information: Sequoia National Park and Mineral King Ranger Station (Case 7)

Three passes with unbelievable views and fourteen outstanding lakes make this the kind of hike you do not want to rush through. (Note: This loop is best hiked in a clockwise direction to avoid an exhausting ascent of the sandy west side of Sawtooth Pass.)

**Access.** The loop begins at the Sawtooth parking area (7,800 feet). See Hike 48 for driving directions.

The trail climbs the steep sage-covered hillside for 0.5 mile to a junction. Take the left fork to Timber Gap; you will return by the trail on the right. A steady climb leads to forested Timber Gap (9,400 feet) at 2.2 miles. This is the first legal (though waterless) camp area on the loop. From the gap descend to Timber Gap Creek, then parallel it through forest and flower-filled meadows. At 4.4 miles the trail leaves the creek, then heads over a ridge and drops into Cliff Creek Canyon. Cross Cliff Creek on rocks or logs, then go right to a camp area and intersection at 5.5 miles (7,040 feet).

Next is a grueling 4,560-foot ascent of Black Rock Pass. Climb from forest, through flower-covered meadows, and into rock gardens to reach the Pinto Lake food locker (8,690 feet) at 8.4 miles where the trail divides. Campsites are to the right and the trail to the pass heads left, crossing the basin to begin the final ascent to Black Rock Pass. There is little shade on this steep trail, which reaches 11,600-foot Black Rock Pass at the 12-mile point of your loop. On a clear day, views from the pass extend east over Little Five Lakes to Mt. Whitney.

From the pass it is a relatively easy descent to Little Five Lakes and campsites. At 13.8 miles the trail crosses the outlet of the second lake (10,480 feet) and divides. The loop route goes straight (east) to reach a junction with the Big Five Lakes Trail at 15.7 miles. The upmost of the Big Five Lakes is located just 1.3 miles to the right. The loop trail continues straight, descending 1 mile to the lowest of the Big Five Lakes. All the lakes have excellent campsites.

From the lowest Big Five Lake the trail heads to Lost Canyon Creek and a junction at 17.7 miles (9,600 feet). Stay right and cross the creek twice as you head up-valley. At the head of the valley the trail makes a short climb to Columbine Lake (11,040 feet) at 22.4 miles. For the most spectacular views of this very scenic loop, ascend the hills near the outlet; Cyclamen and Spring Lakes sparkle below. If you camp in this delicate area, stay off the surviving grass.

From Columbine Lake to Sawtooth Pass the trail is a sketchy route that frequently disappears on the rocky hillside. Consult your map and look for a low notch in the ridge above; Sawtooth Pass is to the right of the notch and slightly higher. The summit of Sawtooth Pass (11,600 feet) is reached at 23.9 miles.

From Sawtooth Pass head down slippery rock and loose scree on an unmaintained trail. At the base of the long open slope is an unsigned intersection; go left and traverse the open hillside to Monarch Lake (10,380 feet), a popular destination for day hikers and backpackers from the Mineral King area. From this point there is a wide, overused trail for the final 4.7 miles back to the Sawtooth Trailhead.

*Hiker resting on food locker at Columbine Lake*

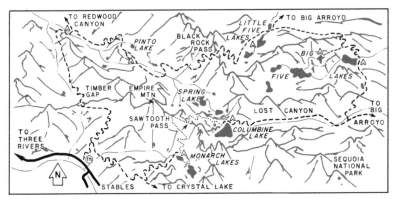

**FRANKLIN LAKES**

**Round trip: 10.8 miles**
**Hiking time: 6 hours**
**High point: 10,337 feet**
**Elevation gain: 2,527 feet**

**Hikable: mid-July through**
**September**
**Day hike or backpack**

**Maps: USFS John Muir Wilderness (South Section); USGS Mineral King**

Reservations and Information: Sequoia National Park and Mineral King Ranger Station (Case 7)

Enclosed in a snow-dappled cirque below Mt. Franklin and Tulare Peak, Lower Franklin Lake is as beautiful as nature and man could make it. Nature did an excellent job sculpting the scene, leaving sand-covered ledges on the granite slopes for scenic campsites. Man, in the form of Southern California Edison, created the large, deep lake. The Upper Franklin Lake was left as nature intended, wild and beautiful.

**Access.** From Visalia, drive northeast on Highway 198. At 3.6 miles beyond Three Forks turn right on narrow and winding Mineral King Road. At 24 miles pass the Mineral King Ranger Station, where back-packers must stop and pick up permits, and continue on another 1.3 miles to the road's end at Eagle Crest Trailhead (7,800 feet).

From the parking area walk back down the road 0.1 mile, crossing the creek to an intersection. Go right and follow a dirt road up-valley to the Mineral King Pack Station. Walk past the corral to find the start of the trail.

Just over the hill from the pack station at an unmarked intersection, stay left. At 0.7 mile cross Crystal Creek, which, like all creek cross-ings on this trail, will be a very damp experience in early season. Be-yond the creek, the trail begins to climb, steeply at first, then moder-ately through a series of well-graded switchbacks. Franklin Creek of-

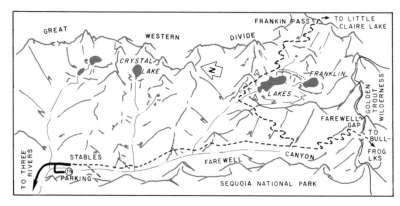

*Lower Franklin Lake*

fers a pleasant place to take a break and catch your breath at 1.5 miles.

After a couple more switchbacks the trail enters Farewell Canyon, where the rich meadows support a beautiful display of wildflowers throughout the summer. At 3.5 miles the trail divides (9,200 feet). To the right the Farewell Gap Trail continues its climb for another 2.7 miles over open meadows. The Franklin Lakes Trail goes left for a long, climbing traverse back into the Franklin Creek drainage.

In the middle of a damp meadow, the trail recrosses Franklin Creek then heads past the old Lady Franklin Mine. Before long the dam comes into view, and at 5.4 miles the trail reaches a rocky promontory overlooking Lower Franklin Lake (10,337 feet). This is a great picnic spot for day hikers. Backpackers should continue on climbing about halfway up the next hill, then descend to a scenic campsite and food locker overlooking the lake.

If you would like to escape the crowds, continue on to a saddle above Lower Franklin Lake to find an unsigned, boot-beaten path on the right. Follow this brush-covered path to the peaceful seclusion of the upper lake.

# 51     EAGLE CREST

**Round trip to Upper White Chief Basin: 8 miles**
**Hiking time: 4 hours**
**High point: 9,980 feet**

**Elevation gain: 2,180 feet**
**Hikable: mid-July through September**
**Day hike or backpack**

**Maps: USFS John Muir Wilderness (South Section); USGS Mineral King**

Reservations and Information: Sequoia National Park and Mineral King Ranger Station (Case 7)

The Eagle Crest Trail offers you a perplexing choice of three beautiful and very different valleys: White Chief Canyon, Eagle Creek, and Mosquito Creek.

In White Chief Canyon the rocks on the hillsides will dazzle you with their varying shades of white, red, and gray. The hillsides, which appear to have oozed down from somewhere above, end abruptly at the edge of the rich green meadows that coat the valley floor. Eagle Lake Trail leads to an enchanting, man-enhanced (dammed) lake and is the most popular of the three destinations. The Mosquito Creek Valley lives up to its name with plenty of the plaguey critters at each of the five lakes and countless ponds. This is the most difficult of the three areas to access.

**Access.** Drive to the Eagle Crest Trailhead (see Hike 50 for details).

Begin your hike at the upper end of the parking lot and walk past a private cabin. The trail plows its way through fields of corn lilies as it climbs above the Kaweah River. At 1 mile the White Chief Basin Trail forks off to the left.

**Upper White Chief Basin.** From the intersection you will climb steadily for 1 mile, then enter a narrow valley (9,169 feet) at 2 miles from the trailhead. Follow the trail across the meadow to White Chief Creek, where the trail divides. Go right and cross the creek then head

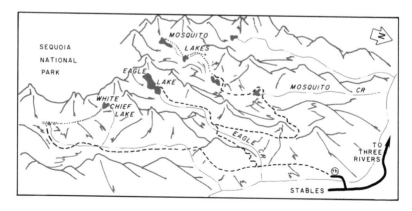

up the hill, passing several old mine shafts and a couple of sinkholes. The trail crosses the bare rock, dividing then rejoining as it climbs to the top of the rock band. Recross the creek, then walk through meadows toward a rocky basin ringed with cliffs. At 4 miles the trail divides; the right fork goes to a camping area and the left fork to a small pothole. Anglers with cross-country experience can head northwest up a rising shelf to reach White Chief Lake in about a mile.

**Eagle Lake.** Although the trail to the lake is short and well marked, this is not an easy hike. The trail gains 2,240 feet of elevation in the 3.4 miles from the trailhead to the lake. From the White Chief Basin Trail intersection, go right and spend the next mile switchbacking uphill. The trail divides a second time at 2 miles (9,500 feet). Go left, climbing steadily for the final 1.4 miles to Eagle Lake (10,000 feet). Campsites may be found on the right (west) side of the lake.

**Mosquito Lakes.** From the Eagle Lake intersection at 2 miles, stay right and follow the trail over a low ridge and then descend, losing 300 feet of elevation, before arriving at First Mosquito Lake (9,100 feet) at 3.6 miles. Cross the outlet creek and follow the best-looking of several paths around the west side of the lake, up the forested valley, then over a steep, rocky headwall to Second Mosquito Lake (9,590 feet).

Cross the outlet creek and follow a chain of ducks and your map up the forested hillside to the next bench. Once you reach this point, the remainder of the hike is easy. If you find the trail, follow it. If not, just head up-valley, passing east of Third Mosquito Lake and west of Fourth Mosquito Lake. The fourth lake has the best campsites and Fifth Mosquito Lake (10,440 feet), reached at 5.1 miles from the trailhead, has the best scenery.

*White Chief Lake*

# 52   GIANT FOREST LOOP

**Loop hike: 9.5 miles**
**Hiking time: 6 hours**
**High point: 7,300 feet**

**Elevation gain: 960 feet**
**Hikable: May through mid-October**
**Day hike**

**Maps: Sequoia National Park—Giant Forest; USGS Giant Forest and Lodgepole**

Information: Lodgepole Ranger Station

With meadows, Indian grinding holes, tree houses, and some of the largest trees on earth to look at, an entire day is needed to walk the 9.5-mile long Giant Forest Loop. You may even wish to plan a little extra time for side trips, intentional or otherwise.

The best way to negotiate the maze of trails in this area is to buy the Giant Forest map issued by the Sequoia Natural History Association and sold at all park visitors centers.

**Access.** Drive to the General Sherman Tree parking lot (6,840 feet), located 2.1 miles east of Giant Forest Village or 2.5 miles south of Lodgepole Village. Begin your hike with a short stroll over to the General Sherman Tree to get a feel for the size and history of the largest living thing on earth, then walk east on the Congress Trail. At 0.4 mile

*The Senate Group*

go left and cross over to the western leg of the Congress Trail, then go left to the McKinley Tree. Continue left at all intersections to General Lee Tree, the House Group, and the Senate Group (a short side trip is required to see the whole grove). Stay on the Congress Trail until you reach a signed trail to the President Tree, then go right for 100 feet to Chief Sequoyah Tree. Go right again on to the Trail of the Sequoias for the next 2.8 miles through lodgepole forest to Tharps Log.

Located at the edge of Log Meadow, Tharps Log was used as summer quarters for Hale Tharp from 1861 to 1890 while he grazed his cattle in the meadow. From the log cabin, leave the Trail of the Sequoias and head west on a paved trail that parallels the meadow for 0.5 mile to a T junction, then go right for 0.3 mile to the Chimney Tree.

From the very charred Chimney Tree, go left following signs to Huckleberry Meadows. Take the second left at 0.2 mile and continue another 0.3 mile to the Squatters Cabin. Take a right here and walk the Huckleberry Meadow Trail for the next mile. At the Alta Trail junction go right for the next 0.6 mile, watching for bedrock mortars where native people ground acorns into flour.

Shortly beyond the bedrock mortars, the trail divides. To the right a 0.3-mile side trip leads to Washington Tree, a giant nearly 30 feet in diameter and almost 250 feet high. The loop route follows the left fork, staying right at two junctions to reach Bears Bathtub. This area along the edge of Circle Meadow has some amazing trees. After passing Bears Bathtub, go left at the next intersection and head toward Crescent Meadow for the next 0.3 mile. At the next junction go left and in 100 yards go left again and follow signs to Cattle Cabin. Cut through Circle Meadow and in the next 0.8 mile walk pass the Black Arch, the Pillars of Hercules, Cattle Cabin, the Founders Group, and the Room Tree to reach an intersection at the McKinley Tree. From this point it is a straight shot along the Congress Trail for 0.7 mile back to the General Sherman Tree.

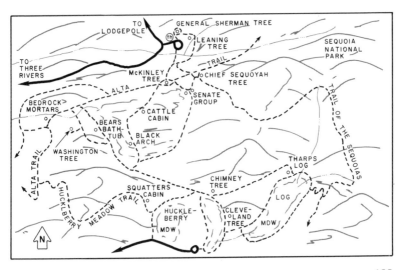

# 53  ALTA MEADOW AND ALTA PEAK

**Alta Meadow**
Round trip: 11.4 miles
Hiking time: 6 hours
High point: 9,300 feet

Elevation gain: 2,060 feet
Hikable: mid-June through
  September
Day hike backpack

**Maps: Sequoia National Park Lodgepole/Wolverton; USGS Lodgepole**

**Alta Peak**
Round trip: 13.8 miles
Hiking time: 8 hours
High point: 11,204 feet

Elevation gain: 3,936 feet
Hikable: July through September
Day hike backpack

**Maps: Sequoia National Park Lodgepole/Wolverton; USGS Lodgepole**

Reservations and Information: Sequoia National Park and Lodgepole
    Ranger Station (Case 7)

There are two destinations in this area, one a green meadow fringed
by the magnificent summits of the Great Western Divide and the other
a peak with views so expansive you may want to sit down and applaud
Mother Nature for the successful creation of one of her greatest pan-
oramas. Either destination can be reached by a long day hike. However, if you can spare an entire weekend, treat yourself to an overnight
hike to the meadows and from there head to the summit of Alta Peak
for an inspirational sunset.

**Access.** Drive the Generals Highway 1.6 miles southeast from
Lodgepole Village. Take the Wolverton turnoff and head uphill, passing a spur road to the corral. Continue for 1.5 miles to the winter
sports area at the road's end, and take the first left to find the trailhead in the upper parking area (7,240 feet).

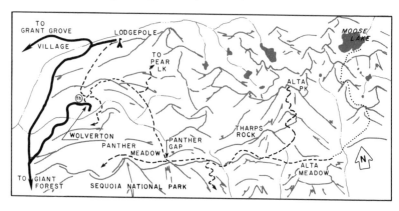

Head uphill 0.1 mile on the Lakes Trail to the ridge crest and junction with a trail from Lodgepole Campground. Go right and in a few feet pass the Long Meadow Trail on the right. Continue straight, following the wide and dusty forested ridge crest. As you climb, the forest gives way to flower meadows. At 1.8 miles the trail crosses a creek and shortly after arrives at the Lakes Trail junction (8,000 feet). Continue straight, heading up through a red fir forest to reach Panther Gap (8,450 feet) at 2.7 miles. Here you meet the official Alta Trail, which begins in the Giant Forest. Go left, climbing along the crest of the gap to views of the Kaweah River 5,000 feet below, and west (depending on the clarity of the atmosphere) to the green orchards of the San Joaquin Valley and the coast mountains.

The views improve as the trail crosses a steep, open hillside to include the peaks of the Mineral King area and the Great Western Divide. At 3.7 miles the Seven-Mile Trail branches off on the right and 0.3 mile beyond you will walk through little Mehrtern Meadow, a small but popular camp area.

The next 0.8 mile is spent in a nearly level traverse to the base of Alta Peak where, at 4.8 miles, the trail divides. To the right, Alta Meadow is an easy 1-mile walk from the junction. Campsites may be found at either end of the meadows; however, water is scarce by mid-September. A hikers' route continues on from the meadow for another 4 miles to Moose Lake.

If Alta Peak is your destination, go left and begin the steep ascent to the summit. Plan at least 2 hours for this hot, dry climb. At the top all your efforts seem minor compared to the rewarding view. The High Sierra surrounds you; the mighty peaks of the Great Western Divide, Mt. Whitney, and the Kaweah Peaks are visible. To the north Mt. Silliman stands alone, while below your feet are the deep blue waters of Emerald and Pear Lakes. The summit of Alta Peak is a rocky mound with a register box at its precipitous crest. To reach the register you must scramble up the rocks. Be very careful; a misstep could be fatal.

*Alta Meadow and Great Western Divide range*

# 54     PEAR LAKE

**Round trip: 13.4 miles**
**Hiking time: 8 hours**
**High point: 9,510 feet**
**Elevation gain: 2,290 feet**

**Hikable: June through**
   **mid-October**
**Day hike or backpack**

**Maps: Sequoia National Park Lodgepole/Wolverton; USGS Lodgepole**

Reservations and Information: Sequoia National Park and Lodgepole
    Ranger Station (Case 7)

The Lakes Trail to Heather, Emerald, and Pear Lakes is the most
popular hike in the Lodgepole/Wolverton area of Sequoia National
Park. With an early start, day hikers will have time to visit all three
lakes; however, to fully experience this beautiful area requires an overnight stay. (Plan ahead; day-of-hike permits are very difficult to get for
this busy trail.)

**Access.** The Lakes Trail begins from the winter sports area at
Wolverton (see Hike 53 for details).

A food locker and large sign mark the start of the Lakes Trail. Head
uphill for 0.1 mile to an intersection with a trail from Lodgepole Campground, then go right along the ridge crest. Just 100 feet after the first
intersection, the Long Meadow Trail branches off on the right. Continue straight and ascend the forested ridge.

At 1.8 miles the trail divides. To the right lies Panther Gap (see
Hike 53). Go left on the Lakes Trail, which heads up the forested hillside for 0.2 mile before splitting in two. Both trails go to Heather and
Pear Lakes and both are about the same length. To make optimum use
of shade and views, take the left fork past The Watchtower on the way
up and return via The Hump Trail.

The trail climbs gradually for the next mile to The Watchtower, a

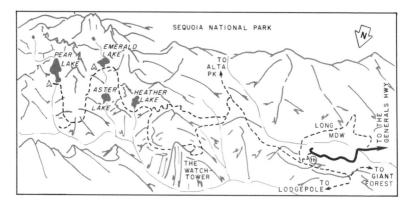

*Solar toilet at Pear Lake*

large wing of granite that juts out of the hillside. Beyond The Watchtower the trail has been etched into the nearly vertical granite hillside and there are breath-grabbing views every step of the way.

At 3.8 miles The Watchtower Trail rejoins The Hump Trail. The combined trail continues on for a nearly level 0.3 mile to reach Heather Lake (9,180 feet) at 4.1 miles. This quaint lake has been trampled by enthusiastic visitors for many years and is open for day use only.

The trail continues over gently rolling terrain for 1.1 miles to Emerald Lake (9,170 feet). Ten numbered campsites and a solar toilet are located near the lake.

It will take a great deal of willpower to pull yourself away from beautiful Emerald Lake and continue the gradual climb. Before long you will have a view of the Tokopan Valley and The Watchtower. At 5.9 miles a trail to the backcountry ranger station branches off to the left. Stay right and complete the final ascent to reach Pear Lake (9,510 feet) and the end of the trail at 6.2 miles.

The lake is surrounded by towering peaks and granite spires that bristle into the sky. The most notable is Alta Peak, which towers over the south end of the lake. There are twelve numbered campsites at the lake and the most scenic solar toilet for miles around.

*Twin Peaks on Silliman Crest above Twin Lakes*

# 55    TWIN LAKES

**Round trip: 13.6 miles**
**Hiking time: 8 hours**
**High point: 9,500 feet**
**Elevation gain: 2,975 feet**

**Hikable: June through**
   **mid-October**
**Day hike or backpack**

**Maps: Sequoia National Park Lodgepole/Wolverton; USGS Mt.**
  **Silliman**

Reservations and Information: Sequoia National Park and Lodgepole
    Visitor Center (Case 7)

Fraternal rather than identical is the best way to describe these two
Twin Lakes located on a small basin below the Silliman Crest. The
smaller twin is surrounded by a marsh beautifully highlighted by
masses of shooting stars, in season, and an abundance of grass. The
larger twin is partially forested with heather and lupine meadows and

giant white granite boulders covering the open spaces.

**Access.** Follow the Generals Highway to Lodgepole Village and Visitor Center, then drive east into the campground. Park in the large open area between the Nature Center and the Amphitheater (6,760 feet).

Walk to the upper end of the parking area, then go left and cross the Middle Fork Kaweah River on a car bridge. Pass the Tokopan Trail and continue on another 100 feet to a large signboard that designates the beginning of the Twin Lakes Trail.

The trail contours along the edge of the campground, then heads west up the forested hillside. The climb is brisk as the trail gains 500 feet in the first 0.8 mile before it bends north on a large sloping bench above Silliman Creek. The trail descends a bit then begins a gradual climb through lodgepole forest.

The climb intensifies as you approach Silliman Creek at 2.1 miles, where great dexterity is required to keep your feet dry when crossing in early season. Just 0.5 mile beyond the creek, you will find the first campsites at the edge of Cahoon Meadow (7,740 feet). As the damp meadows are breeding grounds for a healthy population of ambitious mosquitos, it is best to pass these campsites by and continue the steady climb to reach the forested crest of 8,645-foot Cahoon Gap at 4.2 miles.

From the gap, the trail descends, losing 250 feet of elevation in the next 0.6 mile before arriving at East Fork Clover Creek. After crossing the creek on a log or with a mighty long jump, you will pass a popular forested camp area, complete with a food locker. The trail then traverses the nearly level valley for 0.3 mile to an intersection with the JO Pass Trail (see Hike 56). Stay right and begin a 2-mile climb, which ends 1,000 feet above at the lakes. The forest thins and soon you are climbing through flower gardens interspersed with large slopes of granite. At 6.8 miles trail arrives at Twin Lakes (9,500 feet) on a forested bench surrounded by the towering cliffs of the Silliman Crest. Campsites are numerous and you will find food lockers and a backcountry toilet as well. From the lakes it is an easy hike over 10,100-foot Silliman Pass to Ranger and Beville Lakes.

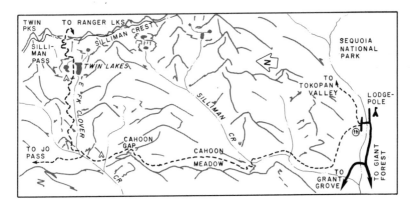

# *56* SILLIMAN CREST LOOP

**Loop hike:** 23 miles
**Hiking time:** 3–4 days
**High point:** 10,100 feet
**Elevation gain:** 2,410 feet

**Hikable: mid-June through mid-October**
**Backpack**

Maps: USFS John Muir Wilderness (South Section); USGS Muir Grove and Mt. Silliman

Information: Hume Lake Ranger District
Permits: Lodgepole Visitor Center, and Grants Forest Visitor Center (Case 7)

This loop explores the Jennie Lakes Wilderness as well as the backcountry of Sequoia National Park. Meadows, forests, lakes, sweeping granite ridges, and fascinating domes are all part of this excellent hike.

**Access.** Drive the Generals Highway south from Giant Village 8.3 miles, then turn left on Forest Service Road 14S11 signed to Big Meadow and Horse Corral. (From the south, this turnoff is located 18.1 miles northwest of Lodgepole Visitor Center.) Follow Road 14S11 for 9.6 miles, then turn right on Road 13S14 signed to the Rowell Meadow Trailhead. Pass the pack station then continue up for 2.1 rough miles to the trailhead, which has campsites, a pit toilet, and running water (7,935 feet).

The trail begins at the lower end of the parking lot and climbs at a steady pace up the forested hillside for 500 feet to an unmarked intersection with the trail from the pack station. Go right and at 2 miles reach an important intersection and the start of the loop portion of the hike (8,770 feet). For now take the left fork; you will return to this point on the trail to the right.

The trail swings around the east side of Rowell Meadow, passing a ranger's cabin at 2.2 miles. Cross Rowell Creek at 2.4 miles. Campsites

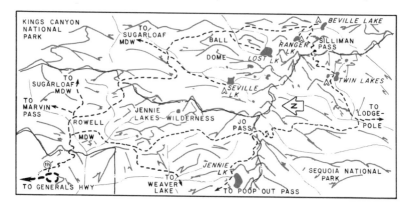

can be found along the trail in this area; however, they are well trampled by cows in late summer. Shortly beyond the creek is a four-way intersection with the Marvin Pass and Roaring River and Seville Lake Trails. Go right and head through the forest to Seville Lake.

The trail climbs gradually through mats of lupine to reach the crest of a low saddle (9,100 feet) at 3.7 miles then drops steeply for the next 1.8 miles into the Sugarloaf drainage of Sequoia National Park. Reach the Seville Lake intersection at 5.5 miles (8,275 feet). The lake, located 1.2 miles to the southwest, is an excellent spot for the first night's camp.

From the Seville Lake intersection the loop route parallels Sugarloaf Creek for 0.2 mile before crossing it on a log. Climb the forested flanks of Ball Dome, passing the Lost Lake Trail at 7.3 miles. (Lost Lake lies in a granite basin below Twin Peaks and has several nice campsites.) The trail crosses two spurs of Lost Lake Creek, then climbs to an intersection with the Ranger Lakes and the Beville Lake Trails at 10.5 miles. Campsites can be found at either lake. The trail continues to climb for another 1.3 miles to the 10,100-foot crest of Silliman Pass, then descends to reach the popular campsites at Twin Lakes (9,500 feet) at 12.8 miles.

From Twin Lakes the trail drops 1,000 feet in the next 2 miles to the JO Pass junction. Go right here for 1.9 miles of steady climbing to reach 9,414-foot JO Pass at 3.9 miles from Twin Lakes.

At JO Pass the trail reenters Jennie Lake Wilderness and meets the Jennie Lake Trail. The loop route goes right and descends 5.5 miles back to the Rowell Meadow Trailhead. To the left is a 1.5-mile side trip to granite-bound Jennie Lake (9,012 feet).

*Jennie Lake*

# 57 REDWOOD CANYON LOOP

**Loop hike: 9.5 miles**
**Hiking time: 5 hours**
**High point: 6,240 feet**
**Elevation gain: 500 feet**

**Hikable: mid-May through**
   **October**
**Day hike or backpack**

**Map: USGS General Grants Grove**

Reservations and Information: Kings Canyon National Park and
   Grants Grove Visitor Center (Case 7)

Explore one of the world's largest groves of the world's largest trees
on this walk through some of the least-visited sequoias in Kings Canyon National Park. Although the trees are the undoubted stars of this
hike, you will find numerous other delights, such as a small waterfall,
a well-shaded creek, meadows, vistas, delightful picnic sights, and
even a place to camp.

This is an excellent early or late season hike. However, no matter
when you walk it do not underestimate the time required to complete
the loop. The trees command your attention and the pace slows frequently as eyes are lifted to the tree tops.

**Access.** From Grants Village, drive south along the General Grants
Highway for 5 miles. The turnoff is not marked, so look for the Quail
Flat sign on the east side of the road. Your turnoff is just opposite this
sign on the right (west) side of the highway. Head downhill on a narrow dirt road for 1.8 miles to Redwood Saddle, then turn left into the
large parking area (6,080 feet).

The loop hike begins on the right-hand side of the parking lot and
follows the Sugar Bowl Grove Trail south. Walk the forested ridge
crest to reach, at 1 mile, Burnt Grove. This group of giant sequoias
looks very healthy even though it has been subjected to terrible fires.

You will gain only 250 feet of elevation in the first 2.5 miles of ridge
walking to Sugar Bowl Grove, where the trail meanders through the
giants then leaves the ridge crest and descends into Redwood Canyon
through a forest of cedars, ponderosa pines, sugar pines, and oaks.
Near the end of the 2.5-mile descent the trail crosses an old burn
where young sequoias are growing as thick as grass.

At 5 miles (5,720 feet), the Sugar Bowl Trail intersects the Redwood
Creek Trail and ends in a grove of giant sequoias. Go right on the Redwood Creek Trail for 0.1 mile to a second intersection then take a left
on the Hart Tree Trail. (Backpackers will continue straight at this intersection to campsites down the canyon.)

The Hart Tree Trail immediately crosses Redwood Creek (not an
easy task in early season), then climbs out of the canyon through a
mixed conifer forest. At 5.6 miles the trail divides; to the left is the
Fallen Goliath, a once-mighty tree that is now rather tired looking.
Continue climbing and at 7.2 miles you will arrive at the turnoff to
Hart Tree, which is located 100 yards to the right. This great tree
ranks as the seventh tallest and sixteenth most massive in the world.

*Hiking in the shadows of giant sequoias on Redwood Creek Trail*

Beyond the Hart Tree the trail crosses the East Fork of Redwood Creek just below a small waterfall then heads northwest, climbing over a couple of low ridges. On the way you may walk through a burnt log and look over Redwood Canyon from a rocky overlook viewpoint. The trail then descends, passing an old log house near Burton's Post Camp (an old sequoia logging site remarkable for its high stumps with deep springboard notches). At 9 miles the Hart Tree Trail intersects the Redwood Creek Trail and ends. Go right for the final 0.5-mile climb to the parking lot at Redwood Saddle.

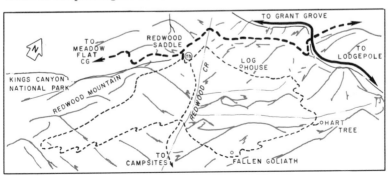

# 58 EAST KENNEDY LAKE

**Round trip: 23 miles**
**Hiking time: 2–4 days**
**High point: 10,800 feet**
**Elevation gain: 6,100 feet**

**Hikable: mid-July through**
**September**
**Backpack**

**Maps: USFS John Muir Wilderness (Central Section); USGS Cedar Grove and Slide Bluffs**

Reservations and Information: Kings Canyon National Park; Cedar Grove Ranger Station or Roads End Information Station (Case 7)

The trail up the Lewis Creek drainage to East Kennedy Lake is long, steep, and blazing hot in the midday sun. This 6,100-foot climb is a daunting proposition; however, hikers who go the entire distance will be rewarded with tremendous views. This area also boasts a great deal more solitude and wilderness feeling than the other, more accessible trails from Cedar Grove.

**Access.** After picking up your backcountry permit, drive west, back down-valley, for 1.4 miles from Cedar Grove Village Junction to the Lewis Creek Trailhead. Park on the south side of the road (4,720 feet).

Your long ascent begins with your first step. By 1.9 miles you will have already gained 1,030 feet of elevation when you reach a junction with the Hotel Creek Trail from Cedar Grove Village.

The trail dodges in and out of the forest, trading shade for sweltering heat on the open hillsides. The heat can be so intense that you may actually welcome the ford of Comb Creek at 3.3 miles (a difficult crossing in early season) and the ford of East Fork Lewis Creek at 4.2 miles (also difficult in early season).

The unmaintained trail to Wildman Meadow, which branches off to the left at 6 miles, marks your entrance to the Frypan Meadow area (7,480 feet). Here the climb eases and at 6.1 miles you will pass the first campsites. Continue on, crossing a creek and a swampy meadow, to more campsites. At this point you will have gained nearly half the elevation needed to reach the pass, making it a reasonable, though not very scenic, place to spend the first night.

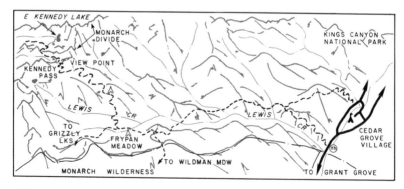

Just above the camp area pass the unmaintained trail to Grizzly Lakes, then settle into the long ascent to the pass. The climb begins in forest, where you ford two small unnamed creeks then Lewis Creek. Before long you will reach an open, manzanita-covered slope and continue the climb with views of the Great Western Divide. You will trade off between open slopes and shady groves of trees for the rest of the way to the top.

Reach the 10,800-foot summit of Kennedy Pass at 10 miles. There is a treasure chest of views over the Middle Fork of the Kings River and ridge line after ridge line of rugged High Sierra peaks. Before leaving the pass, walk east 100 feet to an overlook of East Kennedy Lake, your destination.

From the pass, follow the trail north passing several tarns, where with a bit of searching you can find several nice campsites. Continue down to the second set of tarns 0.5 mile below the summit. Here the trail makes a turn to the right and heads into the Kennedy Creek drainage. After dropping for another 0.5 mile to reach 10,280 feet, look for a small tarn below you to the right. Leave the trail and drop down a wide, grassy gully to the tarn, then follow its left shore to a rocky hillside where you will make your final ascent to East Kennedy Lake (10,250 feet) at 11.5 miles. Small campsites are located along the west shore. Above you to the south is the impressive wall of the Monarch Divide and the view to the north is almost as good as from the pass. If you are lucky enough to have this place to yourself, the solitude is almost deafening.

*View of East Kennedy Lake from overlook near Kennedy Pass*

# 59 GRANITE LAKE AND GRANITE PASS

**Round trip to lake: 21 miles**
**Hiking time: 2–4 days**
**High point: 10,100 feet**
**Elevation gain: 5,392 feet**

**Hikable: mid-July through**
**September**
**Backpack**

**Maps: USFS John Muir Wilderness (Central Section); USGS The Sphinx and Marion Peak**

Reservations and Information: Kings Canyon National Park, Cedar Grove Ranger Station, or Roads End Information Station (Case 7)

Nestled between sweeping meadows and the base of skyscraping mountains, Granite Lake attracts many visitors for reasons that need no further explanation. However, the often overlooked crown jewel of this area is the glorious ascent to Granite Pass, an easy morning stroll from the lake. (Note: The ascent to the lake and pass is long and hot. Even hikers who are in good physical shape should plan an early start to avoid the midday heat and carry at least two quarts of water per person.)

**Access.** From Grant Village drive 32 miles northeast to Cedar Village, where you may pick up your permit at the ranger station before continuing up-valley another 6 miles. At Roads End are a huge parking area, rest rooms, running water, and an information station (5,035 feet).

The trail begins at the far north end of the parking area and soon begins to climb. You will start off with a long series of switchbacks that take you up the first 1,400 feet of your climb. The trail then swings into Copper Creek Canyon and continues to climb with the occasional welcome shade of a Sugar pine, Jeffrey pine, or white fir.

Reach Lower Tent Meadow (7,600 feet) at 3.5 miles. This is the first

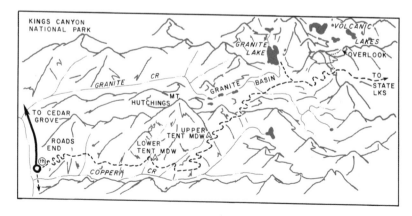

*View south over Granite Basin from Granite Pass*

comfortable campsite on this trail that has a year-round water source and several almost-level campsites. Upper Tent Meadow (8,160 feet), located 1.5 miles on up the trail, has more campsites and a food locker.

At 7 miles the trail switchbacks up a 10,347-foot saddle between the Copper Creek and the Granite Creek drainages. At this point you must convince your aching legs to change modes and descend, losing 348 feet of hard-gained elevation, before reaching the floor of aptly named Granite Basin. The next 2 miles are an agreeable climb through forest and meadows to the Granite Lake Trail intersection at 9.5 miles. Go west for 1 mile to Granite Lake (10,080 feet), where you will find a campsite with a view. If you continue west you will find more campsites at the upper lake.

After you have settled in and explored the immediate neighborhood, it is time for a trip to the pass. Head back 1 mile to the main trail, then go left for a 1.5-mile ascent to 10,673-foot Granite Pass. After taking in the deluxe view from the pass, head west (uphill), skirting a large flaking dome of granite. Just beyond a low saddle you will find a panoramic view of the Volcanic Lakes.

*The Sphinx*

# 60 SPHINX CREEK FORD

**Round trip: 14 miles**
**Hiking time: 7 hours**
**High point: 8,700 feet**
**Elevation gain: 3,665 feet**

**Hikable: mid-July through**
**September**
**Day hike or backpack**

**Maps: USFS John Muir Wilderness (South Section); USGS The Sphinx
and Sphinx Lakes**

Reservations and Information: Kings Canyon National Park, Cedar
Grove Ranger Station, and Roads End Permit Station (Case 7)

Relatively unknown and usually passed by in the rush to high country, the Sphinx Creek Trail is the perfect day hike or weekend hideaway. This spectacular trail scales the granite walls of Bubbs Creek valley to find forest, hidden meadows, and a small creek above. Skilled hikers can continue from the ford on a roughly marked route to the beautiful Sphinx Lakes.

The trail to Sphinx Creek Ford is steep and exposed. If you have a fear of heights, the trail can be unnerving. Heat is a real problem by mid-afternoon, so start early and carry plenty of water.

**Access.** From Grants Village, drive Highway 180 east, passing Cedar Grove Ranger Station before reaching Roads End at 38 miles (5,035 feet).

Begin your hike by following the popular Rae Lakes Loop and Mist Falls Trail. Walk past the Information Station and head up the Kings Creek Valley on a wide, dusty, and nearly level trail. After 2 miles the trail divides (5,098 feet). Mist Falls and Paradise Valley are to the left, so stay right and follow the Bubbs Creek Trail, crossing the South Fork Kings River on a sturdy bridge. In 0.2 mile the trail will divide again; stay left and cross abraded and meandering Bubbs Creek.

After the bridges the trail begins to climb, heading steadily up the granite hillside on well-graded switchbacks. The Sphinx (you will recognize it by its distinctive shape) can be seen on the skyline to the south. The trail climbs over the granite wall and into the Bubbs Creek Valley. At 4 miles reach Sphinx Creek Junction Camp and a trail intersection (6,300 feet). The camp has a one-night stay limit.

At Sphinx Creek Junction Camp, leave the Bubbs Creek Trail and go right, crossing Bubbs Creek on a sturdy bridge. Walk past several more campsites, then begin the climb out of the valley. In the next 3 miles you will climb 2,400 feet in 39 switchbacks on a trail that was etched into the granite cliffs with a generous amount of blasting powder. It is a relentless climb that is made bearable by the incredible view. At switchback No. 23 the trail crests the granite wall and heads into the Sphinx Creek valley and after four more switchbacks you will enter the forest and find some relief from the glare of the sun.

At switchback No. 39, the trail fords a small creek (a dry crossing if you climb above the trail) then climbs to an 8,700-foot high point and begins a very gradual descent. On this very relaxing portion of the hike, the trail passes through forest and meadows before arriving at Sphinx Creek at 7 miles (8,507 feet). Cross the creek, usually a dry operation, to reach the forested camp area and trail intersection on the far side. The Sphinx Creek Trail stays to the right and continues its climb for another 3 miles to the forested crest of 10,058-foot Avalanche Pass. If you go left from the intersection at the ford you may follow an unmaintained route up Sphinx Creek valley for another very difficult 2.2 miles to Sphinx Lakes (10,520 feet), where you will find scenic campsites, excellent views, and good fishing.

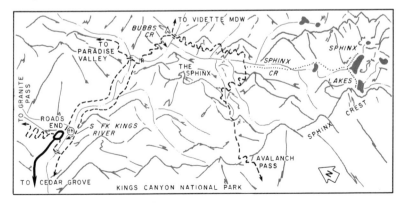

# 61 RAE LAKES LOOP

**Loop hike: 46 miles**
**Hiking time: 5 days**
**High point: 11,978 feet**
**Elevation gain: 6,943 feet**

**Hikable: August through**
**September**
**Backpack**

**Maps: USFS Kings Canyon National Park—Rae Lakes Loop; USGS The Sphinx and Mt. Clarence King**

Reservations and Information: Kings Canyon National Park; Cedar Grove Ranger Station and Roads End Information Station (Case 7)

Besides being a perfect loop with excellent campsites, good trails, and ideally located campsites, the Rae Lakes Loop embodies the spirit of Kings Canyon National Park: the granite-walled valleys, the cascading creeks and rivers, the green meadows brilliant with wildflowers, and the stark beauty of the high mountain lakes and the euphoric views from the crest of one of the lofty mountain passes of the High Sierra.

This is a popular loop and you will have lots of company on your long trek. To keep hikers from congregating at scenic points, a one-night camping limit has been established at Kearsarge Lakes, Charlotte Lake, and Rae Lakes. In Paradise Valley you must stay in a numbered campsite and abide by a two-night limit. Bullfrog Lake is closed to

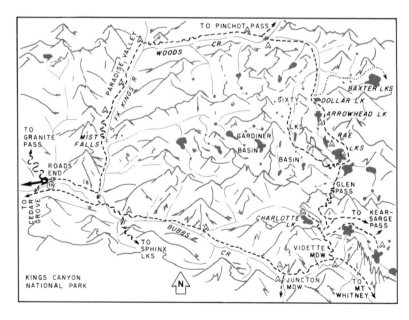

*Mist Falls*

camping. Food lockers have been installed at all major camping areas along the loop and are significantly helping to reduce the bear problem. If you camp away from the food lockers to avoid the crowds, you must either hang your food or store it in bear-proof canisters, which may be rented at the Cedar Grove Store.

Clockwise is the most popular direction for hiking the Rae Lakes Loop. The standard five-day itinerary places camps in Paradise Valley, Woods Creek Crossing, Rae Lakes, and Junction Meadow. If you have extra time, plan side trips to Sixty Lakes Basin, Charlotte Lake, Kearsarge Lakes, and Lake Reflection. If the clockwise direction is full, reverse the itinerary and head up Bubbs Creek. When hiking counter-clockwise, make a special effort to start your hike early to avoid the oppressive afternoon heat in the Bubbs Creek valley.

*Fin Dome reflecting in still waters of middle Rae Lake*

**Access.** From Grants Grove drive Highway 180 east for 32 miles to Cedar Grove, where you will pick up your reserved permit. Continue for another 6 miles to Roads End. Park in the backpackers' area located beyond the Information Station (5,035 feet).

Walk past the Information Station and head up-valley on a wide, dusty, and poorly signed trail. After 2 miles of nearly level hiking the trail divides. This is the start of the loop portion of the hike. If hiking in a clockwise direction, go left and head up Paradise Valley. You will return by the trail on the right.

The Paradise Valley Trail parallels the South Fork Kings River, climbing gradually for the next 2 miles to Mist Falls (5,663 feet). At this point you leave most of the day hikers behind and the trail begins switchbacking up the steep hillside. The trail climbs to the cliffs then traverses along the sandy base of the granite wall. The ascent is steady until the trail enters Paradise Valley at 6.9 miles. Just 0.1 mile beyond, you will reach Lower Paradise Valley Camp (6,586 feet).

From the first camp, the trail heads up the nearly level valley, climbing and descending over forested ribs. At 9 miles pass Middle Camp (unsigned at the time of this writing) and at 10 miles reach Upper Paradise Valley Camp (6,879 feet).

Above the upper camp the trail crosses the South Fork Kings River on a large log then heads east up Woods Creek Valley. The trail steepens and before long climbs out of the forest onto the brushy avalanche slopes of the upper valley. It is a long, hot ascent beneath giant granite walls and domes that tower above on both sides of the valley. Try to complete this portion of the hike in the cool of the morning.

Pass a stock fence, then make a short descent into Castle Domes Meadow at 14.5 miles. A camp area with a food locker is located at the upper end of the meadow (8,200 feet).

Beyond the meadow the climb is gradual for the final 1.5 miles to the combined John Muir Trail/Pacific Crest Trail (JMT/PCT) intersection. Stay right and head south on the JMT/PCT, which immediately crosses Woods Creek on a swaying, swinging suspension bridge. On the south side of the creek is the popular Woods Creek Crossing Camp (8,492 feet), at the 16-mile point of your loop.

From Woods Creek the trail climbs constantly, paralleling the South Fork Woods Creek up the open valley. You will gain 1,748 feet of elevation in the next 5 miles to Dollar Lake (10,240 feet), where you will get your first view of Fin Dome. There are campsites near the lake but no food lockers.

Follow the trail around the west shore of Dollar Lake then make a short climb to a large bench just above. Here you will find the lowest Rae Lake and the first of three official Rae Lakes campsites (10,300 feet). The most popular campsites as well as the best views of the famous Fin Dome and the Painted Lady are found at the upper two camp areas located on the middle lake (10,560 feet).

From Rae Lakes the trail climbs at a steady pace leaving vegetation and heading across a moonscape spotted with deep blue tarns. It then switchbacks up to a dark ridge that marks the crest of 11,978-foot Glen Pass at 26.5 miles. The remainder of the loop is all downhill.

The trail descends past a small lake with a couple of campsites at the south end, then crosses over a saddle to contour above a smaller lake, with limited camping, before swinging west then south for a high traverse of Charlotte Lake. At 2.5 miles below Glen Pass, the horse trail to Kearsarge Pass branches off to the left and shortly beyond you will reach the Charlotte Lake intersection (10,800 feet). Charlotte Lake, a backcountry ranger station, and a camp area with food lockers are reached by a 1.5-mile side trail.

Follow the JMT/PCT past the second Kearsarge Pass intersection and after another 0.5 mile pass a third trail to Kearsarge Pass that passes by Bullfrog Lake, Kearsarge Lakes, and a backcountry camp area. At this point you are 29 miles into the loop. Continue down a seemingly endless descent with views of East and West Vidette Peaks and Vidette Meadow. At 31 miles you will arrive at the Vidette Meadow camp area (9,520 feet). The campsite here has been a favorite of the bears for years, so use caution with your food.

At Vidette Meadow the Rae Lakes Route leaves the JMT/PCT and heads west (right) down the spectacular Bubbs Creek Valley. After a 3-mile descent, the trail levels off in Junction Meadow (8,100 feet). The most popular campsites are located beyond the stock gate at the lower end of the meadow. The next camp is located 2.3 miles down the valley at the Charlotte Creek crossing and the last camp on the loop (or the first camp on the counterclockwise loop) lies at Sphinx Creek Trail junction, at the 42-mile point of the loop. The trail then descends out of the Bubbs Creek valley to complete the 46-mile loop at Roads End.

# 62  WOOD CHUCK LAKE

**Round trip: 18 miles**
**Hiking time: 2–3 days**
**High point: 9,812 feet**
**Elevation gain: 3,380 feet**

**Hikable: mid-July through**
**September**
**Backpack**

**Maps: USFS John Muir Wilderness (Central Section); USGS Rough**
**Spur and Courtright Reservoir**

Reservations and Information: Prather Ranger Station and Dinkey
Creek Ranger Station (Case 8)

Located in the midst of rolling ridges, small meadows, and shady
forest, Wood Chuck Lake is the largest of the picturesque lakes in scenic Woodchuck Basin. Although lacking in broad vistas or moonlike
landscapes of the High Sierra, the lake and basin area is ideal for hikers throughout the entire summer.

**Access.** Drive Highway 168 northeast from Fresno to the center of
Shaver Lake, then go right on Dinkey Creek Road and head east. After
12.1 miles turn right on the McKinley Grove Road, following the signs
to Wishon Reservoir for the next 18 miles. At the reservoir, drive
across the spillway then continue on 0.2 mile to the Woodchuck
Trailhead (6,660 feet).

The hike begins with a quick ascent up the rocky hillside. At 0.5
mile the trail intersects a dirt road. Cross the road and rejoin the trail
a few feet to the right, then head north in a long, rolling traverse above
the reservoir. At 2.5 miles the trail turns east, enters the wilderness,
then descends for 0.5 mile to Woodchuck Creek (7,300 feet) and a
couple of campsites. The trail crosses the creek, then follows it up the
forested hillside to Woodchuck Basin, passing several campsites.

At 6.5 miles the trail divides. The right fork follows Woodchuck
Creek to Chuck Pass creating all sorts of loop possibilities. However,
for now, go left on the Crown Pass Trail. The climb is steady and the
forest broken by rocky ribs and grassy meadows. At 7.2 miles (8,840

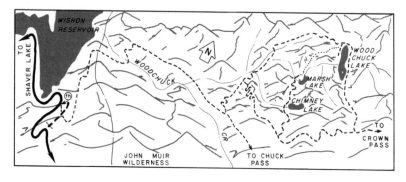

feet) leave the Crown Pass Trail and go left toward Wood Chuck Lake. The trail descends to cross a creek and passes several small campsites before it begins a steady climb through thinning forest to reach Wood Chuck Lake (9,812 feet) at 9 miles. The lake is pleasantly nestled among granite boulders and rolling granite domes with just enough trees to provide shade on a hot day. Campsites are located on the west shore.

For your return trip you have three routes to choose from. You may return the way you came; you may continue around the east shore of Wood Chuck Lake and follow the trail until it rejoins the Crown Pass Trail 3 miles above the point where you originally left it; or you may try a cross-country route.

The cross-country route begins from the camp area at the northwest end of Wood Chuck Lake. Look down through the trees and spot a large meadow with two small ponds to the southwest. Descend to the meadow, then follow the outlet stream from the ponds down to Marsh Lake (9,330 feet). Walk to the west side of Marsh Lake to find a well-used trail and follow it over a small rise to Chimney Lake. Continue on this trail until you intersect the Crown Pass Trail, 2 miles below Wood Chuck Lake. Go right and descend 1.5 miles to close the loop at the Wood Chuck Lake intersection.

*Wood Chuck Lake*

*Campsite at Disappointment Lake*

# 63 DISAPPOINTMENT LAKE

**Round trip: 27 miles**
**Hiking time: 3–4 days**
**High point: 10,420 feet**
**Elevation gain: 3,020 feet**

**Hikable: mid-July through**
**September**
**Rackpack**

**Maps: USFS John Muir Wilderness (Central Section); USGS Courtright Reserv., Ward Mtn., and Mt. Henry**

Reservations and Information: Prather Ranger Station and Dinkey Creek Ranger Station (Case 8)

From its beginning among the granite domes of the exotic Courtright Reservoir to its objective, Disappointment Lake, set in the green meadows at the edge of the rocky world of the High Sierra, this is a remarkable hike.

**Access.** From Fresno, drive northeast on Highway 168 to the town of Shaver Lake. At the center of town, go right on Dinkey Creek Road for 12.1 miles. At Dinkey Creek the road divides. Go right on McKinley Grove Road for 14.2 miles, then turn left following the signs to Courtright Reservoir for another 7.7 miles. At the reservoir go right and cross the dam to reach the road's end at the Maxson-Dusy Trailhead in 1.3 miles (35.3 miles from Shaver Lake). The trailhead has rest rooms but no running water (8,150 feet).

The jeep road, hikers trail, and horse trail start from three different locations around the parking area and come together at the base of the first hill. Follow the jeep road up the nearly level valley for 1 mile. At Maxson Meadow, the road and trail part company at an intersection marked with a small sign reading "Trail."

Head to your right, crossing Maxson Meadow then climbing the forested hillside to the crest of an 8,900-foot ridge and an intersection with the Hobler Lake Trail at 3.7 miles. Stay right and descend to Long Meadow and the first campsites with water on this hike.

At the lower end of Long Meadow, cross a creek (expect damp feet), then continue down-valley on a horse-churned trail. At 7 miles, ford Post Corral Creek to find campsites, mosquitos, and an intersection at the edge of Post Corral Meadow (8,220 feet). Go left on a trail signed to Red Mountain Basin and begin your climb to the High Sierra on a dusty horse trail.

At 9 miles, cross a granite ridge, then follow a narrow, forested bench into the Fleming Creek drainage. The climb resumes again near the 10-mile mark. At 11.3 miles the trail passes subalpine Fleming Lake (9,724 feet) and several enticing campsites.

Cross the Fleming Lake outlet and head through meadows for 0.2 mile to the Rae Lakes intersection. To the left are sheltered base camps for extended stays in this area. From the Rae Lakes intersection go right and cross Fleming Creek. The trail then heads steeply uphill, passing a spur trail to Dale Lake. Shortly after cross a 10,240-foot saddle, then enter Red Meadows Basin.

Follow the trail across a granite-dotted meadow fringed by the barren summits of the Le Conte Divide to the east and an unnamed line of summits stemming from 11,998-foot Mt. Hutton to the south. At 13 miles, the trail crosses a small creek and arrives at an intersection. Stay left toward Hell For Sure Pass and follow the faint trail over granite slabs for 0.5 mile to a sandy, unmarked intersection on the bench above. Go right to Disappointment Lake, which has excellent campsites (10,360 feet).

Check your map for other lakes to explore in the basin and do not miss the view from Hell For Sure Pass. On your return trip, consider doing a loop by heading to Devils Punchbowl Lake then descending 5 miles to the North Fork Kings River. Head north for 4 miles to close the loop at Post Corral Meadows.

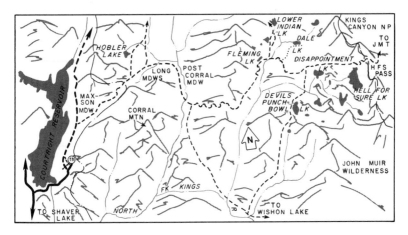

# 64  DINKEY LAKES

**Loop hike to Island Lake: 9 miles**
**Hiking time: 5 hours**
**High point: 9,810 feet**
**Elevation gain: 1,250 feet**

**Hikable: July through**
**mid-October**
**Day hike or backpack**

**Maps: USFS Dinkey Lakes Wilderness; USGS Dogtooth Peak**

Permits and Information: Prather Ranger Station (Case 8)

In comparison with the hundreds of other lakes in the Sierra, the Dinkey Lakes are nothing out of the ordinary. The lakes are subalpine with trees and spectacular walls of granite along one or more shores. The meadows around the lakes are grassy, festooned with Labrador tea and a profusion of flowers such as colorful paintbrush, monkey flower, primrose, pentstemon, and shooting star blooming in mid-July.

What makes this area so unusual is the short and easy access to the lakes and views. It is a great area for a day hike, an ideal place to take beginners backpacking, and a wonderful trail for families.

**Access.** From Fresno drive Highway 168 northeast through Clovis to the town of Shaver Lake. Continue to the center of town, where you will take a right on Dinkey Creek Road. After 9.1 miles turn left on rough, semi-paved Rock Creek Road for 6 miles. At a signed T intersection, go right for an even rougher 4.7 miles to the crest of a wooded ridge. Turn right again on an extremely rough, steep, and narrow spur road for 2 miles. When the road divides, stay left for a final rocky descent to a surprisingly busy parking area (8,560 feet).

The trail begins with a short, steep drop to Dinkey Creek. Cross the creek then follow it up-valley in the cool shade of the forest. At 0.5 mile you will recross the creek and enter the wilderness. The climb remains gradual but steady to the first of many intersections at 1.3 miles and the beginning of the loop portion of this hike.

For now stay left on the well-graded trail to First Dinkey Lake. At 2.9 miles pass a marshy lake and shortly after you will arrive at a junction. Stay right and walk along the shore of First Dinkey Lake, passing several signed and unsigned junctions on your way to Second Dinkey Lake.

Second Dinkey Lake and the Island Lake intersection are reached at 3.1 miles. Go right along the shore of Second Dinkey then head steeply up over a band of rocks. Once on top of the rocks the ascent is gradual for the remainder of the way to Island Lake (9,810 feet), reached at 3.6 miles. Tucked into the base of the Three Sisters, Island Lake is the rockiest and wildest lake in the wilderness. Camping is excellent.

On your return, descend from Second Dinkey Lake to find an intersection (unsigned at the time of this writing) at 9,325 feet, just before the trail enters the meadows that surround the First Dinkey Lake. Go left on a well-trampled path through the forest for 0.5 mile to South

*Island Lake*

Lake. After enjoying the serenity of this area, head west across the outlet creek then over a forest ridge. The trail then descends steeply to Swede Lake, another place to linger, although the fishing is reported to be bad.

From Swede Lake the trail drops over the hill to reach Mystery Lake 1.2 miles from South Lake. Walk along the northeast side of the lake to its outlet, then descend again to close the loop at the Dinkey Lake Trail, 1.9 miles from South Lake. Go left and head back to find the trailhead.

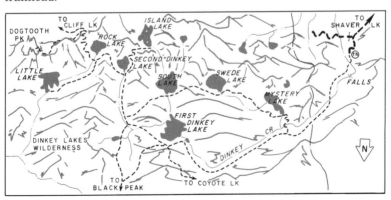

# 65 KAISER LOOP TRAIL

**Loop hike: 15 miles**
**Hiking time: 9 hours**
**High point: 10,310 feet**
**Elevation gain: 3,110 feet**

**Hikable: late June through**
  **mid-October**
**Day hike or backpack**

**Maps: USFS Kaiser Wilderness; USGS Kaiser Peak and Huntington Lake**

Reservations and Information: Prather Ranger Station (Case 8)

The Kaiser Loop is a strenuous trail that combines a climb to an outstanding panoramic view of the High Sierra from the summit, Kaiser Peak, with a tour through the forest and meadows of the lower portions of the Kaiser Wilderness.

Backpackers may find it difficult to obtain permits as the Deer Creek Trailhead (where the loop begins) has a daily quota of six people. However, Billy Creek is a good second choice and adds only 1.8 miles to the total loop.

**Access.** From Fresno drive northeast on Highway 168 for 71 miles to its end at Huntington Lake. Go left on Huntington Lake Road for 1 mile to Kinnikinnick Campground, then turn right on Upper Deer Creek Road, following the signs to the stables for 0.6 mile. Just before you reach the pack station, find the hikers' parking on the left (7,200 feet).

From the parking area walk up the road to the trailhead at the upper end of the pack station. Head uphill 100 yards to intersect the Kaiser Loop Trail. You will return to this point by the trail to your left. For now go straight.

Near the 0.6-mile point, pass an unmarked intersection with the Potter Pass Trail. Continue straight and shortly afterward the steep climb will give way to well-graded switchbacks. At 1.9 miles a rocky

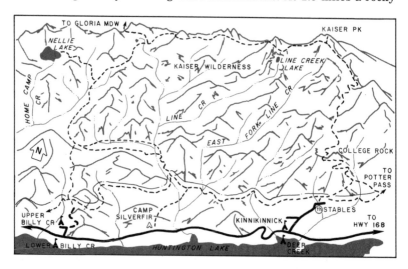

outcropping offers your first view of Huntington Lake. The trail levels off in a small basin at 3.5 miles, but soon resumes climbing with a final steep push to the open crest of the ridge. Walk past a carpet of miniature alpine flowers to a saddle overlooking George Lake, then follow the ridge to an intersection at 5.3 miles, just a few feet below the summit of 10,310-foot Kaiser Peak. Go left to the high point for a view of the High Sierra and the great reservoirs: Shaver, Huntington, Mammoth Pool, and Thomas A. Edison.

From Kaiser Peak the loop trail heads west, descending for 0.5 mile to Line Creek Lake. When the weather is good, this is a great campsite. Continue west along the ridge then switchback down to a small meadow, where you will find an unsigned intersection. Stay left, and continue your descent to a small creek and signed junction with the Gloria Meadow/Hidden Lake Trail at 8.8 miles (8,800 feet). Go straight and cross the creek then head down the forested valley, passing the Nellie Lake intersection at 9.6 miles.

At 11.3 miles (8,140 feet), leave the Kaiser Loop Trail temporarily and go left on Marys Meadow Trail. Descend the forested hillside for 0.3 mile to Marys Meadow, where the trail disappears. Walk around the left side of the meadow, crossing first a marshy creek then a seasonal creek, to the northeast end where you will find a trail on the left that heads into the forest and divides. Take the right fork and continue down-valley, paralleling a small creek.

At 12.2 miles (7,850 feet) the trail crosses Line Creek, then descends, often steeply, for 0.7 mile until it intersects the Kaiser Loop at 12.9 miles (7,540 feet). Go left for a final 2.1 miles of forest walking. Several signed and unsigned spur trails branch off to the right; ignore them. At Bear Creek the trail intersects an old road. Go right 10 feet then left back onto the trail. The loop ends at 15 miles.

*View from summit of Kaiser Peak*

# 66 GEORGE LAKE

**Round trip: 9.6 miles**
**Hiking time: 5 hours**
**High point: 9,100 feet**
**Elevation gain: 1,460 feet in;**
    **480 feet out**

**Hikable: mid-June through**
    **October**
**Day hike or backpack**

**Maps: USFS Kaiser Wilderness; USGS Kaiser Peak and Mt. Givens**

Reservations and Information: Prather Ranger Station (Case 8)

Granite-speckled lakes and a grand vista make this low-mileage trek a great day hike or an easy backpack, perfect for families and beginners. Of course this ideal hiking area is very busy on weekends, so backpackers should reserve their permits as early as possible.

**Access.** From Fresno drive northeast on Highway 168, passing through Clovis, Prather (where backcountry permits are picked up),

*Granite boulders near Upper Twin Lake*

then Shaver Lake before reaching Huntington Lake at 71 miles. When Highway 168 ends, go right and head up Kaiser Pass Road 4.8 miles. The trailhead is a large dirt turnout on the right (south) side of the road marked by a sign that reads "Riding and Hiking Trail 24E03." A small pit toilet is the only facility (8,120 feet).

Cross Kaiser Pass Road to find the trail on the north side and begin your hike with a climb through mixed coniferous forest. Around 1 mile you will cross a creek and walk past the first of many meadows. Wildflowers attempt to grow here in early summer; later the cows trim the meadows to a uniform size and color.

The trail crosses a saddle where a couple of old roads and some large stumps indicate logging activity in the not-too-distant past. Continue on with a nearly level traverse into the Potter Creek drainage. Watch for views to the west, which extend all the way to the San Joaquin Mountains.

The ascent resumes and at 2 miles you will arrive at 8,990-foot Potter Pass. Walk by the signed intersection with the Potter Creek Trail then enter the Kaiser Wilderness. An unsigned trail to Idaho Lake branches off to the right near the wilderness sign. To the northeast, 13,157-foot Mt. Ritter and the Minarets stand proud on the horizon.

From the pass, the trail heads steeply down a dusty hillside. Descend 480 feet through forest and meadows in the next 0.7 mile to an intersection. Go left here, heading to Twin Lakes.

The shallow Lower Twin Lake with its headwall of tumbled granite is reached at 3.3 miles. Continue on another 0.3 mile to Upper Twin Lake (8,601 feet). Campsites are numerous and excellent on the rocky shelves above the upper lake, larger than those found ahead at George Lake.

The George Lake Trail follows the east shore of Upper Twin Lake to an unmarked intersection at the upper end. Go left and climb steeply to a flower-covered ridge crest, where you will pass an unmarked trail to Walking Lake. Continue straight to reach the shores of George Lake (9,100 feet) at 4.8 miles. Pick a glacier-polished granite slab for a picnic lunch or search around the rocky shores for one of the two good campsites.

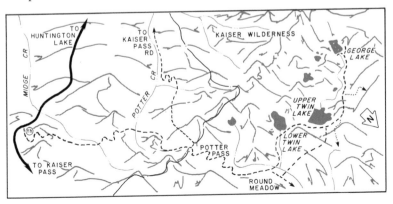

# 67 BLAYNEY MEADOWS HOT SPRINGS

Round trip: 18 miles
Hiking time: 2–3 days
High point: 7,790 feet
Elevation gain: 780 feet

Hikable: mid-August through
  mid-October
Backpack

Maps: USFS-John Muir Wilderness (North Section); USGS Florence
  Lake and Ward Mountain

Reservations and Information: Prather Ranger Station and High Sierra Station (Case 8)

Because of a dangerous ford of the South Fork San Joaquin River, the extremely popular Blayney Meadows Hot Springs is a late summer destination. However, if you skip the hot springs and simply enjoy a hike in the scenic South Fork River valley to excellent fishing, wide meadows, and shady riverside campsites, then this trail is ideal from the time the snow melts in June until it falls again in October.

The hot-springs hike is long but not strenuous. In midsummer this 18-mile trip can be shortened to 8 miles by taking advantage of the hikers' ferry up Florence Lake.

**Access.** From Fresno, drive northeast on Highway 168 for 71 miles to Huntington Lake Reservoir. When the highway ends, go right on Kaiser Pass Road. At 16.2 miles from Huntington Lake, pass the High Sierra Ranger Station and at 17.2 miles the road divides. Stay right and head to Florence Lake for another 6.1 miles to the hikers' parking area (7,360 feet).

Hikers making use of the ferry service should take the road at the lower left side of the parking area. If hiking the entire distance, go right and descend through the picnic area, then walk the paved road past a gate and Crater Lake Trail to reach the Florence Lake Trail at 0.2 mile. Go right and climb to a bench where the trail traverses

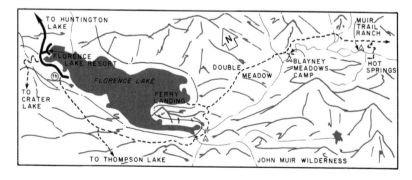

the west side of the lake with views of the dam, Ward Mountain, Mt. Shinn, Mt. Darwin, and Mt. Mendel.

Climb a granite ridge where an unmarked trail branches right to Thompson Lake and Hot Springs Pass, then descend to the upper end of the lake, where the trail divides. Stay left for a bridged crossing of Boulder Creek, which is followed by a bridged crossing of the South Fork of the San Joaquin River. Pleasant campsites are located on either side of the river.

Once across the river, climb a sparsely forested hillside to intersect the trail from the ferry at 5.5 miles. Shortly beyond you will cross a 4x4 road (one of those strange wilderness anomalies). The trail and 4x4 road are intertwined for the remainder of the hike. The climb ends at 7,790 feet and the trail levels off, passes Double Meadow, then descends.

At 7.6 miles pass a signed trail on the right to Blayney Meadows camp area, a delightful site along the edge of the river. Continuing up the nearly level valley pass Lower Blayney Meadow then enter the private land holding of the Muir Trail Ranch (the Double D). Once through the stock gate, hikers are requested to stay on the trail and hike without stopping, picnicking, camping, or otherwise lingering for the next 1.2 miles.

*Blayney Meadows Hot Springs*

At 8.3 miles the trail divides. Go left and in a few feet exit the private land by a second gate. Just 150 feet beyond is an intersection. Go right for 10 feet, then left and descend to the campsites along the river.

Cautiously ford the river, walking with a stick for balance and shoes for traction on some of the most slippery and rounded boulders found anywhere. Once across, head through a couple of campsites then to the right on a boot path. Following the fence line across a damp meadow, you will pass two small pools before reaching the deep hot springs pool. The path continues another 100 feet to end at a small, clear lake at the base of Ward Mountain.

# 68 DEVILS BATHTUB

**Round trip: 10 miles**
**Hiking time: 6 hours**
**High point: 9,167 feet**
**Elevation gain: 1,327 feet**

**Hikable: July through**
  **mid-October**
**Day hike or backpack**

**Maps: USFS-John Muir Wilderness (North Section); USGS Sharktooth Peak and Graveyard Peak**

Reservations and Information: Prather Ranger Station and High Sierra Station (Case 8)

If the devil really did pick this lake for a bathtub, he obviously prefers scenery to such amenities as hot water and smooth porcelain. The bathtub picked out by the devil has a necklace of granite boulders along a narrow band of trees, with the imposing wall of the Silver Divide and Graveyard Peak dominating the horizon.

**Access.** Drive Highway 168 northeast from Fresno for 71 miles to Huntington Lake. When the road ends at a T intersection, go right on the Kaiser Pass Road. The first 5.9 miles are easy driving, then the road narrows to a paved single lane that twists and winds over Kaiser Pass and passes the High Sierra Station (where backpackers can pick up their wilderness permits) to reach an intersection at 17.2 miles from Huntington Lake. Go left toward Lake Thomas A. Edison. At 6 miles the road divides at the base of the dam. Go left and after 0.5 mile go left again, following signs to the High Sierra Pack Station. Pass the Vermilion Valley Resort to reach the campground entrance in 1.8 miles. Go left again then stay right at all the remaining intersections for the final 0.3 mile to the large trailhead. Pit toilets, picnic tables, and fire pits are available (7,840 feet).

With two trails beginning from the same trailhead there can be a bit of confusion. The Devils Bathtub Trail begins from the upper, left-hand side of the sign and follows the route of an old road. After a nearly level

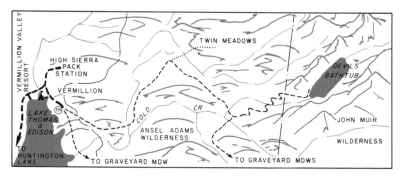

*Graveyard Peak overlooks Devils Bathtub*

0.3 mile, the trail crosses an unmarked horse packers' trail. Go right for 20 feet then go left back on the trail.

Due to heavy use by feet, horses, and cattle, the trail bed has been beaten to a fine powder. Battle your way through the dust, climbing gradually up the forested hillside. At 1.1 miles the trail levels off on a broad bench then fords Cold Creek (7,980 feet). Find a convenient log to cross the creek, then follow the trail as it wanders through the forest before passing the lower end of a large meadow. Stock herders have built a small dam here, providing a constant flow of water.

Climb to a platform where you leave the old road for good at 2 miles. Shortly after, the trail levels off on a bench covered with lodgepole pines. At 3.2 miles (8,340 feet) reach an intersection with a trail to Graveyard Meadows. Go left and continue across the forested bench.

At 4 miles the trail begins to climb again. The soft soil makes this last mile slow going as you head steeply up. At 4.8 miles begin paralleling the Devils Bathtub outlet creek. Campsites are located here and around the lakeshore, which is reached at 5 miles (9,167 feet).

# 69 SILVER DIVIDE LOOP

Loop hike: 27.2 miles
Hiking time: 4–5 days
High point: 10,970 feet
Elevation gain: 4,527 feet

Hikable: August through
  September
Backpack

Maps: USFS-John Muir Wilderness (North Section); USGS Sharktooth
  Peak and Graveyard Peak

Reservations and Information: Prather Ranger Station and High Sierra Station (Case 8)

Six beautiful lakes, two passes (both near 11,000 feet in elevation), and flower-covered meadows make this loop one of the best hikes in the area. Part of this loop follows the route of the combined John Muir Trail/Pacific Crest Trail (JMT/PCT), which is well maintained and easy to follow even in early season. However, the Goodale Pass Trail, the return leg of the loop, is designed for stock rather than human use and has several difficult fords of Cold Creek, making late season the best time for the complete loop.

**Access.** Follow the driving instructions given in Hike 68.

This hike description assumes you are planning to walk the entire loop. However, if you choose to ride the hikers' ferry from Vermilion Valley Resort to the upper end of Lake Thomas A. Edison, you can cut 5 miles off your trip total. The ferry departs daily at 9:00 A.M. and 4:00 P.M. from July 1 to the middle of September.

*Campsite near Silver Pass Lake*

The official start of the loop is from the upper end of the parking lot (7,840 feet). Take the lower of the two trails that start here, signed to Graveyard Lakes and Quail Meadows. This dusty trail descends gradually along the north shore of the Lake Thomas A. Edison. At 0.3 mile an unsigned trail from the pack station joins in from the left and shortly after, the trail divides. Stay left and cross Cold Creek on a horse bridge. The intersection at 0.8 mile marks the start of the loop. Stay right; you will return to this point by the trail on the left.

Before long the trail leaves the dense lodgepole forest and begins a roller-coaster traverse of the granite slabs that comprise the shore of Lake Thomas A. Edison. Views from the slabs are a delightful reward for hiking instead of taking the boat. Pass several tempting campsites overlooking the lake before you reach the upper end and the trail from the ferry landing at 5 miles.

The trail crosses a seasonal creek (a difficult ford during early summer runoff), then climbs steadily for the next mile along boisterous Mono Creek to Quail Meadows (7,820 feet). The meadows are mostly forested and campsites are numerous though uninspiring. At the upper end of the meadows the Lake Edison Trail meets the JMT/PCT and ends. Continue straight ahead on the JMT/PCT, following signs to Silver Pass. The trail climbs steadily up the rapidly narrowing valley to reach the Mono Creek Trail intersection at 7.5 miles (8,380 feet). Continue straight on the JMT/PCT.

The climb steepens as the trail switchbacks up a granite headwall then levels out to traverse Pocket Meadow, passing several inviting campsites and thousands of mosquitos along the way. At 9 miles reach the upper end of the meadows, where the 1.8-mile spur trail to Mott Lake branches right.

The loop route continues straight, crossing North Fork Creek then climbing the steep cliff on the west side of the valley. At 9,530 feet you will arrive at the top of the cliffs and pass the first of several meadows along Silver Creek. The climb remains steady as you go up this beautiful valley, gradually leaving the forest and heading into the open

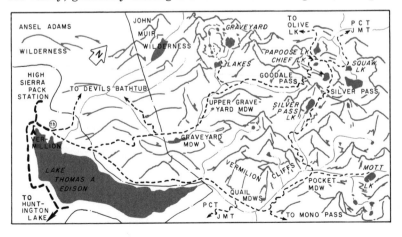

*Upper Graveyard Lakes Basin*

wonderland that is the High Sierra. Silver Pass Lake (10,380 feet), lying to the left of the trail in the shadow of the jagged crest of the Silver Divide, is passed at 12 miles. Several excellent campsites are located here.

From Silver Pass Lake the trail crosses open meadows then climbs to a false pass. Go right and continue up to the real 10,880-foot Silver Pass and view of Mt. Ritter and the Minarets to the north.

From the pass the trail descends over an almost permanent patch of snow, then passes rocky Warrior and Chief Lakes to reach an intersection at 14 miles (10,475 feet). At this point the loop route leaves the JMT/PCT and goes left, descending 0.3 mile to Papoose Lake. Small, rocky, and very scenic campsites may be found around all these lakes.

At Papoose Lake the trail crosses the outlet then climbs to an intersection. The loop route goes straight, heading steeply up to Goodale Pass. After climbing the first pitch the trail levels in an open gully. An unsigned spur trail branches right here, descending to Lake of the Lone Indian. Ahead on an open bench is a false summit where the trail bends left then splinters as stock and hikers take different routes around lingering snowfields.

Crest the 10,970-foot summit of Goodale Pass at 15.8 miles. At this point the trail crosses back to the south side of Silver Divide and begins a rocky, switchbacking descent into the Cold Creek Valley. The trail stairsteps past several small meadows, crossing a couple of streams to reach Upper Graveyard Meadow and the Graveyard Lakes Trail intersection at 18.7 miles (9,355 feet).

Although off the main loop, Graveyard Lakes are an essential part of this trip. So go right for 1 mile and trudge up the rough trail to lower Graveyard Lake (9,900 feet). Campsites are numerous around the shore of this large subalpine lake. Anglers and view seekers will want to follow the trail on for another 0.3 mile to its end in the basin above, where two smaller lakes are located. Cross-country hikers can continue on climbing northeast to a larger lake with an incredible view of the peaks of the Mono Divide to the southeast.

The loop route returns to the Goodale Pass Trail at 20.7 miles then continues down the valley, descending gradually to Graveyard Meadows. Due to overuse, the trail does not enter the meadows; that privilege is left for the cows. Instead, the trail makes two difficult fords of Cold Creek. Numerous forested campsites may be found in this section.

At 23.5 miles, just before the second Cold Creek ford, an unsigned but well-defined trail branches off to the right to join the Devils Bathtub Trail. Stay left and follow the trail down through a couple pocket-sized meadows to reach the Lake Edison Trail at 26.5 miles. Go right for the final 0.8-mile, slightly uphill trudge back to the parking lot to complete your hike at 27.2 miles.

*Alpine columbine*

# 70 POST PEAK LOOP

**Semi-loop: 25.1 miles**
**Hiking time: 3–4 days**
**High point: 10,800 feet**
**Elevation gain: 4,040 feet**

**Hikable: mid-July through**
   **September**
**Backpack**

**Maps: USFS Ansel Adams Wilderness; USGS Timber Knob and Mt. Lyell**

Reservations and Information: North Fork Ranger Station or Oakhurst Ranger Station (Case 8)

From the soft green forest to the rugged High Sierra, this loop has something for every hiker. Although the recommended hike is a semi-loop, a complete loop around Post Peak is possible. The full loop is 31.2 miles long and involves several miles of walking on forest roads. Most hikers prefer to do a car shuttle between trailheads and spend their extra time exploring the high country.

**Access.** From the town of North Fork, drive north on Minarets Highway for 54 miles following signs to Mammoth Pool and Clover Meadow. When the pavement ends, go right on Forest Road 5S30 for 1.8 miles to the Clover Meadow Station (7,001 feet). Continue on Forest Road 5S20 for 0.5 mile then go left for 2.4 miles following signs to Isberg Trailhead (7,040 feet). If hiking the full loop, park at Clover Meadow Station and walk the road to the trailhead. Car shuttlers should park their second vehicle at Fernandez Trailhead.

The trail begins with a 1.5-mile climb to the Ansel Adams Wilderness boundary at The Niche (8,000 feet). Soon after entering the wilderness you will pass two junctions. Stay left at the first and right at the second following the Cora Lakes signs.

At 3.2 miles the trail skirts forested Cora Lake (8,400 feet). (Camping is allowed on the west shore only.) At 3.7 miles pass a trail to Chetwood Cabin on the right and 100 feet beyond pass a second, unmarked trail, also on the right.

Following signs to Sadler Lake, continue the generally gradual ascent. Campsites are nonexistent along the seasonal creeks. At 6.2 miles, a 1-mile side trail takes off left to pretty Joe Crane Lake. At 7.8 miles reach the turnoff to Sadler and McClure Lakes. The very popular Sadler Lake (9,345 feet) is located 100 feet west of the junction. Camping is prohibited on the north and east sides of the lake. Dazzling McClure Lake is located 0.7 mile beyond Sadler Lake.

Continuing on, reach the high alpine country around Lower Isberg Lake (9,920 foot) and campsites at 9 miles. From Isberg Lakes, the trail climbs 2.4 miles to the crest of 10,560-foot Isberg Pass and outstanding views. From the pass you must descend to the Post Peak Pass Trail, then climb back up to reach 10,800-foot Post Creek Pass at 13.2 miles. (If the trail is blocked by snow, stay right and ascend the rocky hillside to the ridge crest above the pass.)

From the pass, descend to Porphyry Lake, which has only limited

*Rocks near Porphyry Lake*

camping among the fascinating boulders. Good campsites can be found 2 miles below at the Post Creek crossing. If the creek is dry, you must continue on another mile to two small tarns. Water and campsites can be found at Fernandez Creek (8,640 feet) at 18.5 miles. Continuing down, pass junctions to Fernandez Pass, Rainbow Lake, then Lillian Lake. At the Lillian Lake junction you can choose between two routes. If time allows, go right to Lillian, Stanford, Chittenden, Lady, and Vandeburg Lakes. If you are in a hurry, take the left fork and continue your forested descent. At the Walton Trail junction go left and, after 0.3 mile, ford Fernandez Creek. The trail traverses the forested hillside to the Fernandez Trailhead. If hiking the full loop, follow the horse trail through the forest to Clover Meadow Campground.

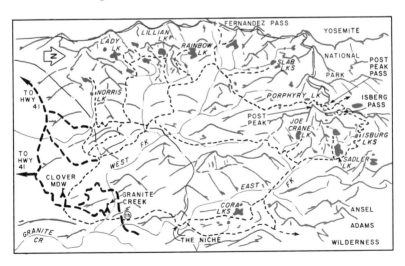

# 71 CHAIN LAKES

**Round trip: 13.8 miles**
**Hiking time: 2 days**
**High point: 9,050 feet**
**Elevation gain: 1,850 feet**
**Hikable: July through**
  **mid-October**
**Backpack**

**Maps: USFS Ansel Adams**
  **Wilderness; USGS Sing Peak**

**Loop hike: 17.4 miles**
**Hiking time: 2–3 days**
**High point: 9,050 feet**
**Elevation gain: 2,450 feet**
**Hikable: August through**
  **mid-October**
**Backpack**

**Maps: USFS Ansel Adams**
  **Wilderness; USGS Sing Peak**

Reservations and Information: Oakhurst Ranger Station or North Fork Ranger Station (Case 8)

*Middle Chain Lake lies in a broad basin below Gale Peak.*

The remote southwest corner of Yosemite National Park is the location of the three superb subalpine lakes that compose the Chain Lakes group. Although quite isolated, these lakes are not the place to look for solitude; they are much too pretty. The basic trip is a very agreeable weekend outing; however, if you want to add an extra zing to your hike, consider the longer loop, which offers a few more miles of granite-plated landscape, an extra view or two, and a side trip to a small soda spring.

**Access.** Drive Highway 41 north from Fresno or south from Yosemite to the northeast side of Oakhurst. Turn east on Bass Lake Road No. 222 and follow it for 6 miles, then go left on Beasure Road No. 7. Stay on this road for the next 20.7 miles, following signs to Beasure Meadows and then to Clover Meadow and Granite Creek. The pavement ends at mile 20.3; continue on for another 0.4 mile to the Globe Rock and take a left turn on Road 5S04. At 2.4 miles you will reach the Chiquito Lake Trailhead (7,200 feet).

The trail is located across from the parking area and the first 0.2 mile is on a 4x4 road. When the road ends the trail climbs steeply over a rocky outcropping, then levels off in a forested valley. At 2 miles you will arrive at the swampy shores of Chiquito Lake (7,960 feet). Campsites are located at the south end of the lake; mosquitos can be found anywhere.

Head around the west side of the lake, passing the first of several unsigned trails on the left to the Quartz Mountain Trailhead, then make a short climb to 8,039-foot Chiquito Pass at 2.5 miles. Ignoring the spur trails on the left, cross the pass and enter Yosemite National Park. Pass through an old cattle fence, then take an immediate right on the Chain Lakes Trail.

The trail remains nearly level as it passes through forest and small meadows. At 3 miles you will cross the outlet creek from Spotted Lake, then begin a gradual climb along an old moraine. The trail traverses a meadow at the top of the moraine (8,540 feet) then descends, gradually, to cross the Chain Lakes outlet creek at 6 miles (8,575 feet).

On the north side of the creek the trail divides. Go left and climb steadily for the next 0.5 mile to reach the lower Chain Lake (8,845 feet) at 6.5 miles. Located in a delightful granite saucer, this lake has several protected campsites. To reach the upper lakes, follow the trail along the north side of the lower lake, then climb the rocky hillside to the island-studded middle lake (9,050 feet). The trail continues, climbing past several marshy tarns and crossing the outlet creek before entering the granite bowl at the base of Gale Peak that holds the rugged upper lake (9,300 feet).

If you choose to return by the loop route, go right at the outlet creek intersection. At 2.7 miles pass the Soda Springs Trail. The springs are located 200 yards off the trail in a small meadow with several campsites.

The next intersection is reached at 5.8 miles (8,030 feet). Go left (southeast) over granite ridges covered by a thin veneer of soil and trees. Shortly after passing Swamp Lake at 7.6 miles the trail reaches Gravelly Ford, where you will get your feet wet crossing the South Fork Merced River. The trail then climbs 1.1 miles back to Chiquito Pass at 8.9 miles from the Chain Lakes intersection.

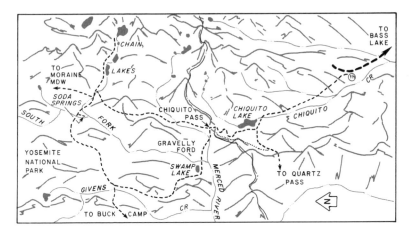

# 72 BUENA VISTA LAKES LOOP

**Loop hike: 28.1 miles**
**Hiking time: 4 days**
**High point: 9,315 feet**
**Elevation gain: 2,400 feet**

**Hikable: July through**
    **mid-October**
**Backpack**

**Maps: Wilderness Press Yosemite; USGS Half Dome and Mariposa**
    **Grove**

Reservations and Information: Wawona and Wilderness Office in
    Yosemite Valley (Case 9)

This rambling forest walk explores six of the lesser known lakes
along the southern border of Yosemite National Park. While there are
a few magnificent vistas and two of the lakes are certifiably subalpine
gems, it is the colorful flowers that cover the meadows and forest floor
that make this an outstanding hike.

Water is the chief problem on this loop. In early season the streams
flood and are miserable to ford. By mid-September these same creeks
dry up and the lakes are the only reliable sources of water.

**Access.** Drive Highway 41 north from Oakhurst 33 miles, then go
right on Glacier Point Road for 9.4 miles to the Ostrander Lake
Trailhead (7,000 feet).

Follow the nearly level Ostrander Lake Trail through fire-damaged
forest and meadows for 1.5 miles to an intersection. Go right, toward
Bridalveil Campground, for 0.2 mile. After fording Bridalveil Creek
(not difficult) reach a second intersection where you go left toward
Buck Camp and Wawona for the next 0.8 mile. After fording another
small creek at 2.5 miles, arrive at a third intersection. Stay right and
head through meadows of waist-high lupine, columbine, mountain
bluebells, sneezewort, and corn lilies (to name a few).

At 3.5 miles the trail fords (easily) two small creeks and passes a
small campsite. Soon after you will climb to the crest of a dry ridge

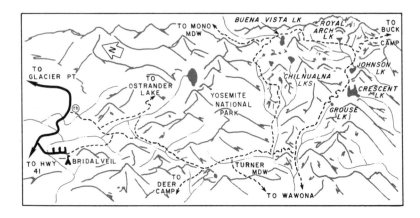

(7,640 feet), then descend back to verdant forest. The Deer Camp Trail branches off to the right at 4.9 miles. Continue straight, descending to good campsites at Turner Meadow (no water in late summer).

The descent eases at 6.2 miles after a lateral trail to Wawona is passed. At 7 miles you will reach the Chilnualna Lakes Trail intersection (7,300 feet), which is the start of the loop portion of this hike. Go straight and ford rocky Chilnualna Creek (a hazardous crossing in early season), then head up a forested ridge to a second Wawona junction at 7.7 miles (7,590 feet). Go left and climb through forest wildflower gardens. After 2 miles, pass little Grouse Lake and several campsites to the right. At 10.7 miles the trail passes another campsite at marshy Crescent Lake (8,380 feet).

Prepare to battle mosquitos as you walk the next mile to campsites at Johnson Lake. From there it is just 0.5 mile to the Buck Camp Trail intersection. Stay left for a 0.7-mile climb to Royal Arch Lake (8,700 feet) and more campsites. The name comes from the distinctive wall arch on the granite hillside above the lake.

From Royal Arch Lake, climb over granite slabs then through parklike forest to 9,315-foot Buena Vista crest. The trail then descends to scenic Buena Vista Lake (9,090 feet) at 15.5 miles. Campsites can be found along the north shore and on the granite shelves above the south side of the lake.

Beyond Buena Vista Lake, descend 0.5 mile to the Buena Vista Trail junction then go left down the Chilnualna Creek valley. The trail is steep and rocky as it descends past Upper Chilnualna Lake and several campsites at 16.7 miles. A mile beyond you will pass the shallow lower lake. From this point the descent is gradual through brightly colored meadows to reach the intersection with the Bridalveil Campground Trail, where the loop portion of the hike ends at 21.1 miles. Go right and retrace your steps for the final 7 miles back to the Ostrander Trailhead.

*Royal Arch Lake*

# 73 OSTRANDER AND HART LAKES

Ostrander Lake
Round trip: 12.4 miles
Hiking time: 7 hours
High point: 8,600 feet

Elevation gain: 1,560 feet
Hikable: mid-July through
    September
Day hike or backpack

Maps: Wilderness Press Yosemite; USGS Half Dome and Mariposa
    Grove

Hart Lake
Round trip: 15.4 miles
Hiking time: 2 days
High point: 9,040 feet

Elevation gain: 2,000 feet
Hikable: August through
    September
Backpack

Maps: Wilderness Press Yosemite; USGS Half Dome and Mariposa
    Grove

Reservations and Information: Wawona or the Wilderness Office in
    Yosemite Valley (Case 9)

The powerful beauty and peaceful setting attract year-round visitors
to Ostrander Lake. This granite-rimmed, tree-fringed lake is an ideal
weekend family outing or long day trip for the hardy hiker. However,
if you have some cross-country experience, you may escape the crowds
by heading through the forest to equally appealing, but little-known,
Hart Lake.

**Access.** Drive Highway 41 north from Oakhurst 33 miles, then turn
right on the Glacier Point Road for 9.4 miles. Park at the small, dirt-
surfaced Ostrander Lake Trailhead (7,040 feet).

The hike begins with a level stroll through fire-scarred forest and
grassy meadows. After 0.7 mile of easy going, the trail gradually begins to climb. At 1.5 miles the trail divides; stay left. You will come to a
second junction at 2.3 miles. Once again, stay to the left.

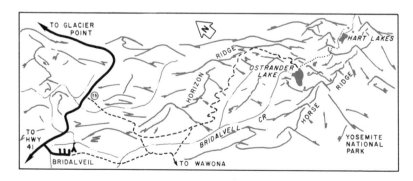

*Ostrander Lake*

Shortly after the second junction the trail begins ascending Horizon Ridge on an old road bed. Head southeast following the old road first through forest then up the dry, rocky ridge to an 8,641-foot high point with a stunning view of Half Dome, Liberty Cap, and Star King.

At 6.2 miles the trail reaches Ostrander Lake (8,580 feet). To the right is the large stone ski hut, which is usually locked during the summer. Campsites are located along the north, east, and west sides of the lake. If continuing to Hart Lake, head east from the ski hut along the north shore of Ostrander Lake, passing several forested campsites. When you have walked about halfway around the east shore, turn left (east) and head up through the forest. If you keep Horse Ridge in sight on the right, you will not get lost. Pass a small frog pond then a larger forested tarn at 0.5 mile. Climb to the top of a rocky ridge where you will get your first view of Hart Lake in the basin below, then pick your way down the rocky slope to the lakeshore and campsites (8,640 feet).

# 74     YOSEMITE POINT

**Round trip: 8.4 miles**
**Hiking time: 6 hours**
**High point: 6,935 feet**
**Elevation gain: 3,040 feet**

**Hikable: mid-June through**
   **October**
**Day hike or backpack**

**Maps: Wilderness Press Yosemite; USGS Half Dome and Yosemite Falls**

Reservations and Information: Yosemite Wilderness Office, Yosemite
   Valley (Case 9)

One of the most popular activities for visitors to Yosemite National
Park is to stand in the valley with necks arched back and look up at
the Lower Yosemite Falls. Bending their necks a little more they can
see Upper Yosemite Falls free-falling down massive granite walls in
delicate plumes. With a final stretch of the neck muscles they can see
all the way to the top of the falls, where the glowing granite meets the
blue sky.

The strenuous hike to Yosemite Point offers you a chance to reverse
this activity and look down from the top of the granite walls to the
green valley below. Start early in the day to avoid the heat, and carry
plenty of water.

**Access.** Parking is a problem in the valley. If you arrive early in the
day, drive to Yosemite Falls and park in the large lot. If you start later,
leave your car in any available parking area and ride the shuttle to the
falls (3,990 feet).

Begin your hike with a short side trip to the base of Yosemite Falls,
then walk back to the parking area and go west on a trail that parallels the highway for 0.3 mile to Sunnyside Walk-In Campground. Go
right and head up the first of hundreds of switchbacks. Much of the
trail is paved with slick stone cobbles which, in turn, are covered with
an even slicker dusting of sand. Watch your step.

Pass the first viewpoint, Columbia Rock (5,031 feet), at 1.2 miles.
Soon after, the trail levels then, appallingly, descends for 0.2 mile.

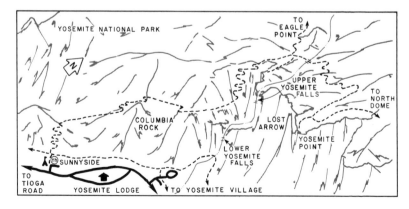

*Hiker high above Yosemite Valley*

Pass below a near-vertical cliff, then resume the climb at 1.7 miles near the base of Upper Yosemite Falls. In early season a cooling mist from the falls can blow across the trail as the water tumbles freely for 1,430 feet to crash on the rocks near your feet.

The climb continues and so do the switchbacks until you reach an intersection at 3.4 miles. Go right toward Yosemite Point. In 100 feet pass some excellent campsites to the left of the trail. Continue on another 150 feet to a second intersection. One hundred yards to the right is an unprotected viewpoint over the Upper Falls and the valley.

Continuing on, your trail heads east over a small rise then drops to cross Yosemite Creek. Ascend again to reach a junction with the North Dome Trail at 4.2 miles, then continue straight for a final 100 yards to Yosemite Point (6,936 feet). Walk to the railing and gasp at the view. Half Dome and North Dome dominate the eastern horizon. To the south are Glacier Point and Sentinel Rock. The top of Lost Arrow and the granite walls of the Three Brothers are visible to the west. For the ultimate thrill, look down and watch the cars and people scurrying around in the valley below your toes.

*Cable route to summit of Half Dome*

# 75     HALF DOME

**Round trip: 16.4 miles**
**Hiking time: 9 hours**
**High point: 8,842 feet**

**Elevation gain: 4,870 feet**
**Hikable: July through September**
**Day hike or backpack**

**Maps: Wilderness Press Yosemite; USGS Yosemite Falls and Half
    Dome**

Reservations and Information: Wilderness Permit Office in Yosemite
    Valley (Case 9)

Some people hike to the summit for the view. Others go to the top just
to say they did it. No matter what your reason, it is important to understand that the climb to the top is not for everyone. The final ascent of the
dome requires strong arms to pull yourself up a set of near-vertical
cables. The exposure is extreme. Being caught on the top in an electric
storm and having to descend wet rock holding onto slippery cables is
also a potential danger. If you are not comfortable with extreme exposure or cannot recognize an impending electric storm, do not go.

**Access.** Drive through Yosemite Valley and park at the large lot at
Curry Village. Wilderness permit holders can continue down the road
to the backpackers' lot (3,970 feet).

If you are getting an early start you must walk up-valley 0.8 mile to

Happy Isles. A shuttle bus is available later in the day. At Happy Isles head up-river to the concession stands, then go left. Cross the Merced River on a wide bridge, and head to the right climbing steeply on a paved trail. At 1 mile recross the Merced River just below Vernal Falls to reach an important junction on the opposite side. Both trails lead to the top of Nevada Falls. On the right, the John Muir Trail (JMT) climbs the steep hillside with well-graded switchbacks. To the left the Mist Trail climbs with incredible steepness, making giant steps up the rock. The Mist Trail is wonderfully scenic and a whole mile shorter, but it requires a great deal of concentration with each foot placement.

At 2.5 miles from Happy Isles the Mist Trail rejoins the JMT (6,000 feet). Go left and continue the climb on well-graded switchbacks to the entrance of Little Yosemite Valley, where the trails levels off and parallels the Merced River. At 4.4 miles the trail splits (6,285 feet). To the right in 0.3 mile is a large camp area. Half Dome is to the left. Both trails rejoin 10 feet north of the solar toilet.

At 6.2 miles (7,000 feet) the JMT and Half Dome Trails divide. Go left and continue the ascent for another 1.5 miles up the forested hillside. At 7.9 miles (7,860 feet) you leave the forest and begin the assault of Half Dome. The climb begins with a series of steep granite steps that lead to the top of a small granite dome at the eastern base of Half Dome. Cross the top of this dome, then descend to a saddle (8,400 feet) where you will find the cables that will guide you to the summit.

At the base of the cable is a pile of used work gloves. If you did not bring a pair of your own, grab a pair to spare your hands from cable burns, then grasp the cables and begin hauling yourself up the final 442 feet to the summit. Before you go too far, stop and ask yourself if you really want to go on, because this is the last convenient turn-around point.

Once on the broad 8,842-foot summit, make a full tour for the complete 360-degree view. Stay away from the edges; it is a long drop to the valley. No camping is allowed on the summit.

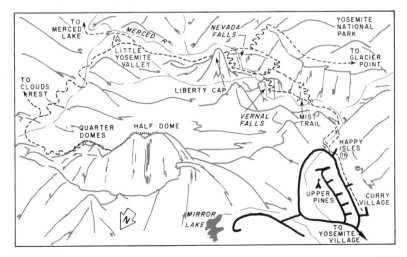

# 76 MERCED LAKE

**Round trip: 27.4 miles**
**Hiking time: 3–4 days**
**High point: 7,216 feet**
**Elevation gain: 3,181 feet**

**Hikable: mid-June through**
    **September**
**Backpack**

**Maps: Wilderness Press Yosemite and Merced Peak; USGS Half Dome, Merced Peak**

Reservations and Information: Wilderness Permit Office in Yosemite Valley (Case 9)

Granite surrounds you. You walk on granite and climb granite stairways. Huge walls of granite tower to lofty heights above you, the river below you cascades over a bed of granite, and everywhere you look there are slabs of granite, granite domes, and even massive blocks of granite.

The trail to Merced Lake is not an easy one, climbing steeply for extended periods, but you will be amply rewarded for your efforts by marvelous scenery. If possible, plan to do most of this hike either early in the morning or late in the afternoon to avoid the midday sun.

**Access.** Drive to Yosemite Valley and pick up your wilderness permit at the window on the left-hand side of the Visitor Center. Leave your vehicle at Curry Village or the backcountry hikers lot, then either walk or catch a shuttle bus for the 0.8 mile to Happy Isles (4,035 feet).

From the road, walk toward the Happy Isles Trail Center. Just before the turn-off to the Nature Center, go left. Cross the Merced River on a wide bridge, then go right on the John Muir Trail (JMT). The JMT is steep, wide, and partially paved. At 0.9 mile cross the Vernal Fall bridge to an intersection with the Mist Trail. Here you must choose between the steady grade of the JMT or the steep and often slippery ascent of the Mist Trail.

The two trails rejoin at the top of Nevada Fall (5,980 feet) at 3.5 miles by the JMT from Happy Isles. Continue on the JMT for 0.7 mile to an intersection at the entrance to Little Yosemite Valley. Stay right to reach the extremely popular Little Yosemite Campground at 4.7 miles (6,300 feet).

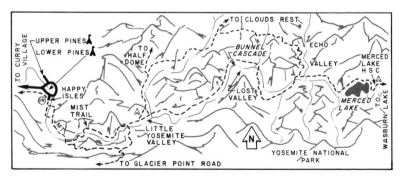

*Merced River valley from Bunnell Point*

At the campground the trail divides again; stay right. The next nearly level 2 miles is a no-camping zone. At 6.7 miles the valley narrows. The trail passes a forested camp area, then enters a zone of granite. Climb briefly to enter Lost Valley, another no-camping area, and walk for the next mile under a canopy of sugar pines, sequoias, lodgepole pines, and incense cedars.

At the upper end of Lost Valley, the trail passes a small camping area then heads steeply up a granite wall, climbing past Bunnel Cascade before leveling out again (6,500 feet). At 8.9 miles pass another camp area on the left, then cross to the south side of the valley. The next stage is a steep climb over the granite flank of Bunnell Point. At the crest, walk across sloping granite before descending to recross the river (7,000 feet).

The trail continues up the nearly level valley, passing several appealing campsites. At 10.8 miles, pass the trail to Sunrise High Sierra Camp and Sunrise Creek (an excellent alternate return route). Continue straight, crossing Echo Creek on three major bridges, then walk on up-valley for another mile before beginning your final climb at 11.9 miles.

The valley narrows and the walls tower above you on both sides. The trail reaches the west end of granite-bound Merced Lake at 12.8 miles. No camping is allowed along the lakeshore, so walk 0.3 mile to reach the official campsite at 13.1 miles, located next to the Merced Lake High Sierra Camp (7,216 feet). Food storage boxes, a pit toilet, and running water (when the camp is open) are provided.

# 77 GRAND CANYON OF THE TUOLUMNE

**Loop hike: 48.8 miles**
**Hiking time: 5–6 days**
**High point: 9,840 feet**
**Elevation gain: 6,935 feet**

**Hikable: July through
    mid-October**
**Backpack**

**Maps: Wilderness Press Tuolumne Meadows and Hetch Hetchy
    Reservoir; USGS Falls Ridge, Hetch Hetchy Reservoir, Tamarack
    Flat, Ten Lakes, Tenaya Lake, and Yosemite Falls**

Reservations and Information: Wilderness Permit Office, Yosemite
    Valley (Case 9)

Hikers who follow the Tuolumne River past foaming cascades, thundering waterfalls, and deep placid pools on its turbulent journey down the Grand Canyon must be prepared for the incessant roar of the river as the noise reverberates off magnificent walls of granite that rise a breathless 4,000 feet above the canyon floor. The most pleasing way to do this hike is as a loop that includes a trek to Ten Lakes. However, using the park's excellent transportation system (summer only) the Grand Canyon may also be hiked as a one-way trip from Tuolumne Meadows to White Wolf.

**Access.** From Yosemite Valley, drive east on Tioga Pass Road

*Upper Grand Canyon of the Tuolumne River near Glen Aulin*

(Highway 120) to the White Wolf Campground exit. Go left and descend 1.1 miles to the White Wolf Trailhead (7,840 feet).

Head east through forest, skirting the campground to reach an intersection at 0.4 mile, then go right toward Ten Lakes on a trail that climbs through alternating whispering pines and small meadows ablaze with wildflowers. At 5.5 miles your trail intersects the Ten Lakes Trail. Go left and ascend to the crest of a 9,690-foot ridge and magnificent views at 8.3 miles. The trail then descends 600 feet to Ten Lakes Basin, reached at 9.7 miles. From the basin the trail heads into the South Fork Cathedral Creek valley, then climbs around the southeast flanks of Tuolumne Peak to the hike's 9,840-foot high point on an open ridge. The trail then descends to the May Lake Trail junction and on to reach the Polly Dome Lakes/Tenaya Lake junction at 21 miles (8,700 feet). Good campsites may be found near Polly Dome Lakes.

Continue the gradual descent to reach McGee Lake at 24.1 miles and the very popular Glen Aulin at 25.3 miles (7,840 feet), where you will find a High Sierra Camp and a 30-site backpackers' camp with running water.

The loop route crosses the Tuolumne River on a bridge, then turns left and climbs a rocky rise to a view of the upper Grand Canyon. Descend into the canyon, passing California Falls and Le Conte Falls before reaching the famous Waterwheel Falls at 28.6 miles. Watch for rattlesnakes on or near the trail as you descend and check your campsite before setting your pack down.

At 39.4 miles the trail reaches Pate Valley, a junction, and a popular camp area (4,400 feet). Below Pate Valley the trail crosses the Tuolumne River on a footbridge, then continues down the nearly level canyon for another 1.3 miles before starting the long, steep grind out of the valley. There are two main camp areas on the way up; one at 5,690 feet and the second at 6,780 feet. At the 45.6-mile point the trail reaches a junction (6,970 feet). Go right for the final 3.2 miles on trail and dirt road, passing swampy Lukens Lake and the sewage treatment area to reach White Wolf at 48.8 miles.

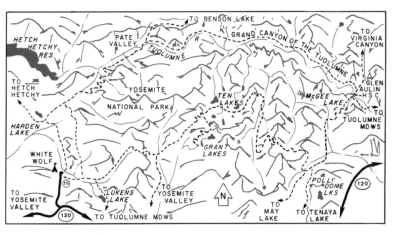

# 78     TEN LAKES

**Round trip: 12.6 miles**
**Hiking time: 7 hours**
**High point: 9,690 feet**
**Elevation gain: 2,190 feet in;**
   **750 feet out**

**Hikable: July through**
   **mid-October**
**Day hike backpack**

**Maps: Wilderness Press Tuolumne Meadows; USGS Yosemite Falls and Ten Lakes**

Reservations and Information: Wilderness Permit Office in Yosemite Valley (Case 9)

This is a hike to an isolated basin tucked precariously beneath towering granite walls and above precipitous granite cliffs that plunge 3,000 feet into the Grand Canyon of the Tuolumne River. The isolation and beauty of this lake-dotted basin attract large numbers of visitors, so plan to reserve your permit well ahead of time.

**Access.** Drive the Tioga Pass Road east 5.3 miles from the White Wolf Campground exit to Yosemite Creek/Ten Lakes Trailhead and park on the south side of the road. The trail begins on the north side of the road (7,520 feet).

The trail heads away from the road for 75 feet to reach its first

*Hikers at vista point above Grand Canyon of the Tuolumne River*

junction. To the left a trail descends 11.5 miles to Yosemite Valley. Go right, following the signs to Grant Lake and Ten Lakes, and begin a steady climb.

Before long the trail leaves the forest then continues its ascent on barren granite slabs. At 2 miles pass the trail from White Wolf Campground on the left and continue the climb. A brief descent at 4 miles leads to Half Moon Meadow, a lush green patch of earth that is an ideal resting spot (if the bugs do not run you out) before the final climb.

After skirting the meadow, the trail heads steeply up, using several switchbacks to complete the 700-foot grind. At 4.8 miles, just below the crest of the ridge, pass

*Leaves of corn lily*

the Grant Lakes Trail on the right. This 1-mile side trip is an ideal day hike from the lakes basin; it also is a good destination for hikers who prefer to avoid the crowds.

At 5 miles the Ten Lakes Trail reaches the crest of the ridge and 9,690-foot high point of this hike. Walk across the lupine-covered saddle to view a seemingly endless succession of ridges filling the northern horizon. Just as the trail begins its descent, a boot path branches off to the left leading to a rock outcropping with a breath-stopping view over Ten Lakes Basin and into the Grand Canyon of the Tuolumne.

The next mile is spent in a 750-foot descent to one of the largest of the Ten Lakes (8,940 feet). If you do not like the campsites at this first lake, move on and descend a terrace to the next lake. You have seven large lakes and several small ones to choose from.

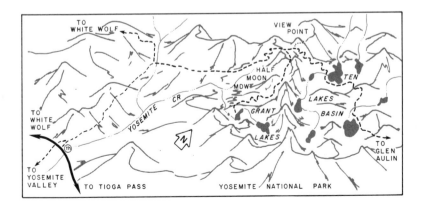

*View of Yosemite Valley from Clouds Rest*

# 79 CLOUDS REST

**Round trip: 14 miles**
**Hiking time: 8 hours**
**High point: 9,926 feet**

**Elevation gain: 2,300 feet**
**Hikable: July through September**
**Day hike or backpack**

**Maps: Wilderness Press Tuolumne Meadows; USGS Tenaya Lake**

Reservations and Information: Wilderness Permit Office in Yosemite Valley, (Case 9)

Most veteran Yosemite Park hikers consider the view from Clouds Rest to be the best in the park. What more needs to be said?

This is a long trip and many hikers prefer a backpack trip over a one-day marathon hike with a chance of thunderstorms rather than views at the end. No water is available on the dry summit ridge that leads to Clouds Rest. The closest water and comfortable campsites are located 3 miles below the summit along a tributary of Tenaya Creek.

**Access.** Drive Highway 120 (Tioga Pass Road) west for 8.9 miles from the Tuolumne Meadows Store or east 16.6 miles from the White Wolf exit to the Sunrise Trailhead at the west end of Tenaya Lake (8,150 feet).

From the parking area head east on a paved road for 200 feet, then go right on the trail signed to Sunrise High Sierra Camp (HSC). Follow this trail out into a meadow for 300 feet to a junction where you will then go left. After just 500 more feet the trail crosses Tenaya Creek then heads right to another intersection. Go straight, still following signs to Sunrise HSC.

The trail crosses a second stream then begins a rocky ascent of a forested hillside. After 1.5 miles the ascent becomes even more aggressive, and at 2.8 miles the trail attains the crest of a broad, sandy ridge where there is a junction (9,200 feet) at which the trail to the Sunrise HSC goes to the left. Continue straight and descend from the ridge, losing 280 feet of hard-earned elevation.

Once down, the trail heads northwest over a broad bench, winding in and out of forest interspersed with verdant meadows. Pass a small tarn at 4 miles and 0.5 mile beyond cross a small, unnamed tributary of Tenaya Creek. This is the last camp area with water before Clouds Rest. One site is located below the trail, and several sites may be found above.

At 5 miles the trail to Sunrise Creek heads off to the right (9,120 feet). Continue straight and begin a steady climb through thinning forest cover. Your goal, a bald, rocky ridge, can be seen to the west. At 6.7 miles the trail arrives at the crest of the ridge (9,766 feet). At the last large tree, the trail splits. Stock goes left while sure-footed hikers stay right, ascending slabs of granite that look like stacks of pancakes to reach the summit of Clouds Rest at 7 miles (9,926 feet).

To the north and east are Tenaya Lake, the Cathedral Range, and a sea of granite domes and jagged ridges. To the west lie Little Yosemite Valley and Merced Lake. However, the most impressive view is to the southwest over Half Dome to Yosemite Valley. Your eye can trace the path of the glaciers from Tuolumne Meadows to the valley. While absorbing the view, keep a weather eye open for thunderstorms, and leave as soon as you spot even a slightly suspicious cloud.

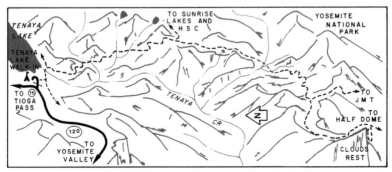

# 80 CATHEDRAL LAKES TRAIL

**Cathedral Lakes**
**Round trip: 7 miles**
**Hiking time: 4 hours**
**High point: 9,580 feet**

**Elevation gain: 1,010 feet**
**Hikable: July through September**
**Day hike or backpack**

**Maps: Wilderness Press Tuolumne Meadows; USGS Tenaya Lake**

**Sunrise High Sierra Camp**
**Semi-loop: 12.8 miles**
**Hiking time: 7 hours**
**High point: 9,850 feet**

**Elevation gain: 1,760 feet**
**Hikable: July through September**
**Backpacker**

**Maps: Wilderness Press Tuolumne Meadows; USGS Tenaya Lake**

Reservations and Information: Wilderness Permit Office in Yosemite
Valley (Case 9)

From the stately spires of Cathedral Peak rising from parklike
meadows to cleave the deep blue sky, to the serene lakes in broad granite saucers, the lavish scenery on the Cathedral Lakes Trail is guaran-
teed to please even the most jaded hiker.

The Cathedral Lakes Trail offers hikers a choice of scenic destinations. The Cathedral Lakes are an ideal destination for a day hike or a
low-mileage backpack. Hikers looking for a longer trip may continue
on to campsites at Sunrise High Sierra Camp, then complete their trip
by making a semi-loop to Tenaya Lake. The summer shuttle bus will
solve any transportation difficulties involved in starting and ending at
different trailheads.

**Access.** Drive Highway 120 (Tioga Pass Road) west 1.6 miles from
the Tuolumne Meadows Store or east from White Wolf for 23.9 miles.
Park at the small Cathedral Lakes Trailhead (8,570 feet). During the
summer months you may leave your car at the Wilderness Permit
Booth in Tuolumne Meadows and ride the free shuttle bus to the
trailhead.

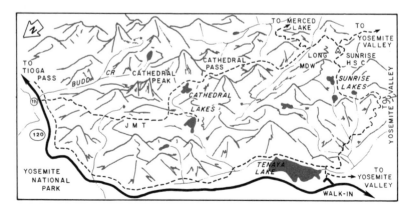

From the parking area, follow the trail into the forest for 500 feet to a four-way junction. Go straight on the John Muir Trail (JMT) and begin your climb toward Cathedral Lakes. The trail is steep and rough, ravaged by excess stock use. This first climb is short, and soon you are heading across the broad bench between Fairview Dome and Cathedral Peak. A second climb takes you to the forested crest of a 9,540-foot saddle.

From the saddle the trail descends gradually to an intersection at 3 miles. To the right, a 0.5-mile spur trail descends to lower Cathedral Lake (9,250 feet), where broad slabs of granite invite you to relax and contemplate the meadows and needlelike Cathedral Peak. Campsites are located in a grove of trees at the lake's northeast corner.

To reach the Sunrise High Sierra Camp, stay on the main trail, which climbs to upper Cathedral Lake and more campsites at 3.5 miles. A short climb above the lake leads to Cathedral Pass (9,700 feet). The trail continues its well-graded ascent above the pass, traversing the flanks of Tresidder Peak to a saddle on the

*View of Cathedral Peak from Cathedral Pass*

side of the Columbia Finger. The view is impressive; to the south and east, looking like waves on the ocean, are endless rows of granite ridges.

From the saddle, descend through coniferous forest to an intersection at the northern end of Long Meadow at 7.4 miles. Go straight for a final 0.4-mile stroll over the open meadow to Sunrise High Sierra Camp (9,300 feet). Several trails branch off to the right. The first is the horse access to the camp, the second is for hikers. Just beyond is a major intersection where you leave the JMT. Go right, uphill, for 100 feet then go right again to the backpacker camp, toilet, running water (midsummer only), and bear bar.

To complete the semi-loop, continue up the Clouds Rest/Tenaya Lakes Trail. Climb to a saddle, then descend past the three Sunrise Lakes to intersect the Clouds Rest Trail. Go right and descend to Tenaya Lake 5 miles from Sunrise High Sierra Camp.

# 81 NELSON LAKE

**Round trip: 12 miles**  **Hikable: July through September**
**Hiking time: 7 hours**  **Day hike or backpack**
**High point: 10,170 feet**
**Elevation gain: 1,720 feet in;**
  **750 feet out**

**Maps: Wilderness Press Tuolumne Meadows; USGS Vogelsang Peak
and Tenaya Lake**

Reservations and Information: Wilderness Permit Office in Yosemite
  Valley (Case 9)

In a park that is known for its beautifully constructed and well-signed trails, the hike to Nelson Lake is an anomaly. This trail is a boot-beaten route with no signs or markings. In fact the trail does not even appear on most maps. As a result, the hike to this spectacular lake has all the elements necessary for a true wilderness adventure.

**Access.** From the Tuolumne Meadows Store, drive east for 100 yards to Tuolumne Meadows Campground and go right. Pass the entrance booth and take the first right. At site B38 turn left. Park at the rest room across from site B49 (8,592 feet). (Note: Parking in the campground is for day hikers only. If planning to spend a night at the lake, you must park either at the base of Lembert Dome or near the Wilderness Permit Booth located 0.4 mile west and walk back to the trailhead.)

The trail begins on the left (uphill) side of site B49 and immediately begins a gradual climb of the forested hillside. At 0.1 mile, cross the valley trail and continue straight, following the signs to Elizabeth Lake. The next 1.4 miles are spent in an ascent through a forest of hemlocks and lodgepole pines.

At 1.5 miles the climb eases when the trail enters meadows where the views begin. As you near the northeast end of Elizabeth Lake (9,580 feet) at 2.3 miles, the granite massif of Unicorn Peak fills the

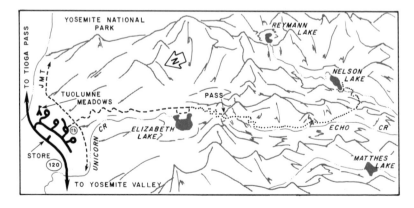

horizon to the right and the trail divides. Elizabeth Lake lies 100 yards to the right. Just 100 yards beyond, a second spur trail to the lake branches off to the right. Stay left and continue south along the edge of the meadow.

At 2.6 miles the trail reenters the trees and begins to climb steeply toward an unnamed pass in the Cathedral Range. Near the top, the trail splits and heads up several different gullies, avoiding snow patches that linger through July. The main trail stays to the left and climbs a wide, open gully. Just before you reach the top, veer right onto a sandy saddle then continue up to reach the unnamed 10,170-foot pass at 3.5 miles.

The trail descends into Echo Valley, staying to the right of Echo Creek. Pass vertical walls of granite, then head down through forest to the lupine-covered meadows below. At 5.4 miles, near the base of the second meadow, the trail leaves the valley floor and heads uphill to the east. After ascending partway up a ridge and gaining about 100 feet of elevation, the trail begins to contour to the south until it abruptly disappears at the edge of a large granite slab. Walk up the slab, angling to the left on a route that is marked by an occasional duck. Cross the top of the ridge and head east, descending gradually for 100 yards into a forested gully where the trail will reappear. Follow the trail up a final ridge to reach Nelson Lake (9,636 feet) 6 miles from the start.

Subalpine Nelson Lake is surrounded by meadow and dominated by towering walls of granite and has excellent camping at the south end.

*Echo Valley*

# 82 VOGELSANG LOOP

**Loop hike: 20.9 miles**
**Hiking time: 2–4 days**
**High point: 10,600 feet**
**Elevation gain: 2,300 feet**

**Hikable: July through**
 **mid-October**
**Backpack**

**Maps: Wilderness Press Tuolumne Meadows; USGS Tioga Pass and
 Vogelsang Peak**

Reservations and Information: Wilderness Permit Office in Yosemite
 Valley (Case 9)

Tucked away in a rocky basin at the foot of the Cathedral Range,
Vogelsang Lake is an ideal place to set up a base camp for several days
of exploring one of the most outstanding backcountry areas of
Yosemite National Park.

**Access.** From the Tuolumne Meadows Store, drive east on Highway
120. After 1.4 miles turn right and follow the signs to the Wilderness
Permit Booth. You may park next to the booth or continue on 0.4 mile
to a second parking area (8,640 feet).

From the second parking area, descend to the combined John Muir
Trail/Pacific Crest Trail (JMT/PCT) at the edge of Dana Fork Creek
and go left. At 0.2 mile cross the Dana Fork on a footbridge, then stay
right at the Gaylor Lakes Trail junction. Follow the JMT/PCT across
upper Tuolumne Meadows and cross the Lyell Fork of the Tuolumne
River on a second footbridge.

Shortly after crossing the Lyell Fork, a trail from Tuolumne Meadows Campground joins in from the right. Stay left following the JMT/
PCT for another 0.4 mile to the Rafferty Creek junction, where the loop
portion of this hike begins. Leave the JMT/PCT here and go right following the signs to Vogelsang High Sierra Camp. For the next couple
of miles the trail climbs steadily through the forest to reach the mead-

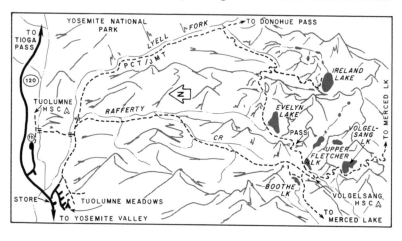

ows and dramatic views of Fletcher Peak at 4 miles. Rafferty Creek, which slices through the heart of the meadow, may run dry in late summer.

At 6.1 miles crest the 10,000-foot summit of Tuolumne Pass and arrive at an intersection. Go left and continue to climb for another 0.8 mile to Vogelsang High Sierra Camp (10,160 feet). Walk straight past the camp and continue 0.7 mile on the Vogelsang Pass Trail to wildly beautiful Vogelsang Lake (10,341 feet) and peaceful wilderness campsites.

To continue the loop, retrace your steps from Vogelsang Lake to the High Sierra Camp, then go right (northeast) to Upper Fletcher Lake and a very busy camp area. The trail ascends a low saddle, then drops down to reach Evelyn Lake at 9.8 miles. The lake, located on a barren plateau, is an excellent location for a camp.

Continuing on, the trail takes you over two more low ridges then begins the long descent into Lyell Canyon by zigzagging down granite ledges. At 11.8 miles you will pass the Ireland Lake Trail junction (10,420 feet). Ireland Lake, located 2.5 miles to the south, is an excellent side trip and delightful place to camp.

Below the junction the trail heads into forest, paralleling Ireland Creek into Lyell Canyon, where you will intersect the JMT/PCT at 15.7 miles. There is an excellent campsite at the intersection.

From the intersection, go left and follow the JMT/PCT down the canyon through beautiful meadows along the Lyell Fork. The loop portion of the hike ends after you cross Rafferty Creek on a wide bridge at 19.8 miles. Follow the JMT/PCT back to the parking area to end your hike at 20.9 miles.

*Vogelsang Lake*

*Lower Young Lake and Mount Conness*

# 83 YOUNG LAKES

**Loop hike: 12.9 miles**
**Hiking time: 7 hours**
**High point: 10,095 feet**
**Elevation gain: 1,485 feet**
**Hikable: mid-July through September**
**Day hike or backpack**

**Maps: Wilderness Press Tuolumne Meadows; USGS Tioga Pass and Falls Ridge**

Reservations and Information: Wilderness Permit Office in Yosemite Valley (Case 9)

Young Lakes lie in a broad basin surrounded by jagged ridges, shear cliffs, and towering mountains. From Tuolumne Meadows there are two trails to the lakes, creating a delightful loop. Adventurous route finders can have the added pleasure of a cross-country segment that climbs to a memorable view from a saddle on Ragged Ridge.

**Access.** Drive to the Dog Lake/ Lembert Dome Trailhead (8,610 feet) on the north side of Highway 120 (Tioga Pass Road) located 0.3 mile east of the Tuolumne Meadows Store or 0.4 mile west of the backcountry permit office.

Begin your loop with a walk north on the stables' access road. When the road divides at 0.3 mile, go straight past a gate, then head across Tuolumne Meadows following signs to Glen Aulin. At 0.6 mile pass the Soda Spring, then leave the road and head uphill on a wide trail. Walk over a low ridge, then descend to cross Delaney Creek (an easy boulder hop except in early season). At 1.7 miles the trail divides; go right toward Young Lakes.

The Young Lakes Trail climbs to the crest of a 9,700-foot ridge then levels off. After descending to cross a creek at 5 miles, the trail divides. Go left toward Young Lakes (the trail on the right is used when you loop back to the parking area). The final 1.5 miles to Lower Young Lake (9,850 feet) is an easy stroll around the base of Ragged Ridge. Campsites are located along the north shore of the lake.

To reach the upper two lakes, go around the north side of the lower lake and cross the outlet. When the trail divides, stay left for about 0.2 mile to a second junction where you will go right. From the middle lake, simply follow the creek up-slope to the upper lake (10,230 feet).

To complete the loop by trail, from Lower Young Lake descend 1.5 miles back to the intersection and go left. The trail climbs over a 10,095-foot ridge, then descends open hillsides. Cross Dingley Creek, then leave the meadows heading northwest through forest to a long meadow where the trail crosses Delaney Creek and arrives at an unmarked intersection. Stay left and continue descending to reach the Dog Lake intersection at the 11.4-mile point of the loop. Dog Lake (9,240 feet) is a pleasant 0.2-mile side trip.

A couple hundred feet below the Dog Lake Trail is an intersection with the Lembert Dome Trail. Stay right and descend steeply along the west side of the dome. Pass three more intersections and, following signs to the parking area, stay left at the first two intersections and right at the third.

The cross-country route begins from the southwest corner of Lower Young Lake. Your goal is the saddle on the ridge about 600 feet above. Find a path that heads steeply up through a fringe of trees, staying to the right side of the broad gully. Above the trees the path climbs through heather and boulders. It is steep. You will reach a bench about ⅔ of the way up; stay right and climb to the large cairn at the crest of the 10,540-foot saddle. To the east is an eye-catching view of the Young Lakes and Roosevelt Lake at the base of Mt. Conness. However, the most expansive panoramic views are at the west side of the broad saddle. From the viewpoint go left and descend a rocky hillside to a broad meadow. Continue down to the lower end of the meadow, where your cross-country route meets the trail and ends. Go left and follow the trail back to the parking lot.

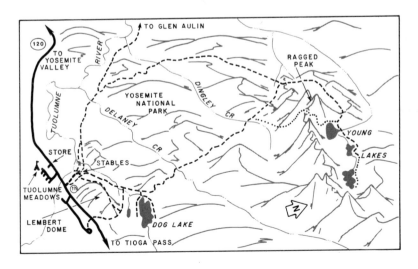

# 84 GLEN AULIN AND McCABE LAKES

**Glen Aulin**
**Round trip: 11 miles**
**Hiking time: 6 hours**
**High point: 8,610 feet**

**Elevation loss: 770 feet**
**Hikable: July through**
**mid-October**
**Day hikle or backpack**

**Maps: Wilderness Press Tuolumne Meadows; USGS Tioga Pass and Falls Ridge**

**McCabe Lakes**
**Round trip: 29 miles**
**Hiking time: 3–4 days**
**High point: 9,900 feet**

**Elevation gain: 2,060 feet**
**Hikable: mid-July through**
**mid-October**
**Backpack**

**Maps: Wilderness Press Tuolumne Meadows; USGS: Tioga Pass, Falls Ridge, and Dunderberg Peak**

Reservations and Information: Wilderness Permit Office in Yosemite Valley (Case 9)

The hike to Glen Aulin is a classic. Wide meadows, sweeping vistas of rounded granitic domes, and pulsating waterfalls on the Tuolumne River all combine to make this an exceptional hike.

Even if this trail were not so spectacular it would still be very popular. Glen Aulin lies on the Pacific Crest Trail (PCT) and the Tahoe–Yosemite Trail, and is also a pivotal point for many hikes on the east side of the park. Because of the popularity of this area, make your backpacking reservations early.

If you would like to see more of this beautiful area and less of your fellow visitors, continue on from Glen Aulin to the relative peace of the subalpine McCabe Lakes.

**Access.** Drive Highway 120 (Tioga Pass Road) to Tuolumne Meadows. At 0.3 mile east of the Tuolumne Meadows Store or 0.4 mile west of the Wilderness Permit Office, turn north on a small dirt road, signed to the stables. When the road makes a sharp turn to the right at 0.3 mile, find a parking place along the edge (8,610 feet).

*Chipmunk, always ready to steal crumbs or sneak into the food bag*

*Hiker in Tuolumne Meadows*

**Glen Aulin.** Following signs to Glen Aulin, walk around the gate and begin your hike on a road that heads across Tuolumne Meadows. This is a popular short-hike area and the meadows are laced with well-signed trails. At 0.3 mile pass the famous Soda Springs. Just ahead is Parsons Memorial Lodge. At this point, the Glen Aulin Trail leaves the road and climbs over a low hill where you will pass a spur trail to the stables. The trail fords a couple channels of Delaney Creek (easy crossings except during the early season snowmelt) and at 1.5 miles passes the trail to Young Lakes (Hike 83). Stay left and continue the nearly level trek along the edge of meadows.

The trail stays in the forest, skirting the meadows. Below you will see the Tuolumne River as it meanders over the level plain. Cross several slabs of granite where the trail disappears on the hard rock. In these areas you must follow a scattered line of boulders to find the trail in the soft soil beyond. Pay attention to the trail when you are crossing the sheets of sloping granite; it is easy to meander off the route while paying more attention to the scenery than to where you are going.

When the valley narrows, the hike gets exciting. The trail heads

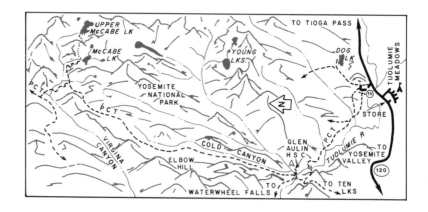

along a ledge of granite at the edge of the Tuolumne River. Steep and somewhat slippery ramps of cobblestones have been built to aid hikers and horses on and off the granite. As you walk, look west across the river for a view of the Little Devils Postpile, an anomalous wall of columnar basalt set in a granite landscape. At 3.8 miles cross the Tuolumne River on two bridges and begin the descent to Glen Aulin. Keep your eyes on your feet along this rough section of trail and not on the expanding view over the upper Grand Canyon of the Tuolumne River. Descend past Tuolumne Falls then by the frothy White Cascade

*Leopard lily*

to reach an intersection with the May Lake/Ten Lakes Trail at 5.3 miles. Go right and descend for the final 0.2 mile to the large pool and waterfall that keynote Glen Aulin.

Recross the Tuolumne River on a large bridge to reach a four-way intersection (7,840 feet). To the right is the Glen Aulin High Sierra Camp and a 30-site backcountry campsite with a solar toilet, running water, and a bear bar. To the left is the Tuolumne River Trail. The 3.3 miles down the Grand Canyon of the Tuolumne to Waterwheel Falls makes an excellent side trip from Glen Aulin. On the way the trail passes three waterfalls and several campsites before reaching its objective.

**McCabe Lakes.** From Glen Aulin go straight at the four-way junction, following the PCT north up Cold Canyon. The trail climbs

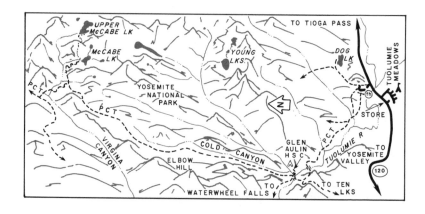

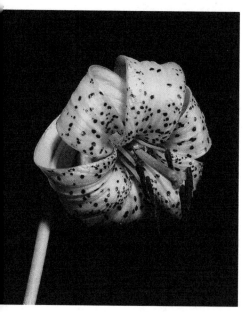

*Leopard lily*

*Beautiful meadow near Elbow Hill*

granite slabs to expanding views of Cathedral, Echo, Cockscomb, and Unicorn Peaks to the south. Ragged Peak, Mt. Conness, and Sheep Peak fill the northeastern skyline.

The trail passes a couple of damp meadows—mosquito havens and potential campsites in July—then ascends to an 8,800-foot defile between two granite domes at 3.3 miles from Glen Aulin. A short descent leads to a mile-long meadow, which ends opposite Elbow Hill. This meadow offers your best chance for water before the lakes.

The trail resumes its gradual climb as it heads back into the forest, and at 7 miles from Glen Aulin it arrives at the McCabe Lakes intersection (9,215 feet). Leave the PCT here and go right on a narrow trail that climbs gradually up the forested hillside. At 9 miles from Glen Aulin, the trail ends at lower McCabe Lake (9,900 feet). The lake is ringed by the granite slopes of Sheep Peak on two sides and by trees and boulders around the other two sides. Campsites are located on both sides of the outlet. No wood fires are allowed.

No maintained trail exists between the lower and upper McCabe Lakes; however, there is a well-traveled route that traverses along the north shore of lower McCabe Lake then ascends through the forest. Pass a couple of tarns, then continue up to the crest of a saddle marked by cairns. Head east from the saddle to the outlet of the upper McCabe Lake.

# 85     MONO PASS

**Round trip: 9 miles**
**Hiking time: 5 hours**
**High point: 10,599 feet**
**Elevation gain: 902 feet**

**Hikable: mid-July through**
    **September**
**Day hike or backpack**

**Maps: Wilderness Press Mono Craters; USGS Tioga Pass and Koip Peak**

Reservations and Information: Wilderness Permit Office in Yosemite Valley (Case 9)

The trail to Mono Pass offers a remarkably easy entry into the starkly beautiful world of the High Sierra. Meadows, lakes, long-abandoned miners' cabins, and views attract crowds of visitors. Hikers seeking solitude are advised to go elsewhere.

*Old Golden Crown Mine cabins at Mono Pass*

**Access.** Drive Highway 120 (Tioga Pass Road) west 1.4 miles from Tioga Pass summit or east 6 miles from Tuolumne Meadows Store to Mono Pass Trailhead located in the forest on the south side of the road (9,697 feet).

The trail begins by descending on an old road through Dana Meadows. Once in the meadows, the trail leaves the road and goes left to cross the Dana Fork of the Tuolumne River (usually a simple matter of hopping boulders). The trail crosses a couple of old moraines, then settles into the gradual but steady climb.

At 2 miles pass an old miners' cabin and 0.3 mile beyond reach your first intersection (10,060 feet) with the Spillway Lake Trail. Stay left and continue up through the forest. Walk by the ruins of a second cabin shortly before the trail reaches the Parker Pass intersection at 3.7 miles (10,540 feet). In 1993, this intersection had neither a sign nor a visible trail. However, by looking across the meadow you can spot the Parker Pass Trail on the far hillside.

To reach Mono Pass, stay left and continue climbing for another 0.3 mile. The trail divides again, a few feet below the crest of the pass. The right fork leads across the meadow to an old miners' encampment. The trail on the left continues up to 10,599-foot Mono Pass. For the best views continue beyond the pass for another level 0.5 mile to glacier-polished rocks overlooking Upper Sardine Lake, Bloody Canyon, Mono Lake, and the Great Basin. No camping is allowed in the pass area; however, there are excellent campsites at Upper Sardine Lake.

If you have extra time, walk over to the miners' cabins. Silver was discovered in the Mono Pass area in 1879 and the cabins were part of the Golden Crown Mine. Long winters made mining difficult and eventually the project was abandoned.

To escape the crowds, head over to 11,100-foot Parker Pass. The pass is just 2 miles from Mono Pass and is very different in appearance. Parker Pass is dry and open with unobstructed views. No camping is allowed at the pass; however, you can descend south 0.2 mile into the Ansel Adams Wilderness and find poor campsites near several of the small tarns.

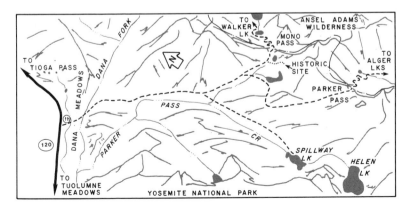

# 86 BUTANO RIDGE LOOP

**Loop trip: 14.3 miles**
**Hiking time: 8 hours**
**High point: 1,920 feet**

**Elevation gain: 1,960 feet**
**Hikable: All year**
**One day or backpack**

**Maps: Portola and Pescadero Park maps; USGS: Mindego Hill, Big Basin, and La Honda**

Reservations and information: San Mateo County Government Center (Case 10)

The Butano Ridge Loop begins in the cool shade of the redwoods, then passes through several forest life zones to reach the summit of Butano Ridge. Along the way, the trail wanders along bubbling creeks and through flower-covered grasslands.

The trails that make up this loop are well graded and the entire hike can be completed in a single day. Or with a base camp at Tarwater or Shaw Flat Trail Camps, this loop can be turned into an enjoyable weekend outing. The trail camps do not supply drinking water. Water is seasonally available from nearby creeks. Campfires are not allowed and all cooking must be done on a camp stove.

**Access.** Drive Highway 35 (Skyline Boulevard) 7.1 miles south of Highway 84 or 6.2 miles north from Highway 9. Turn west on Alpine Road and descend 3.1 miles to Portola State Park Road. Continue down for another 3.5 miles to the Visitor Center. Pay your fee then park where directed (400 feet).

The loop begins just above the Visitor Center, on the west side of the road. Start out by following the Iverson Trail for 0.2 mile then go straight on the Pomponio Trail, passing Tarwater Trail Camp at 1.2 miles to reach Shaw Flat Trail Camp at 2.6 miles. The route is mostly

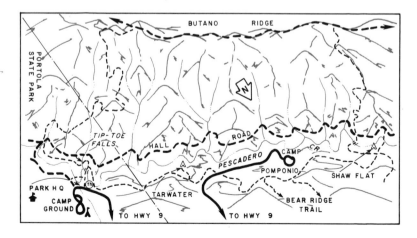

on trail, occasionally wandering onto or crossing old logging roads. Check the giant old tree stumps for springboard notches, a sign of days gone by.

From Shaw Flat Trail Camp, walk down to Pescadero Creek on the Shaw Flat Trail. (The bridge is removed in the winter, but the ford is easy except after a rainstorm.) Once across the creek, follow the trail up to the old Haul Road Trail. Cross the road then head up the Butano Ridge Loop Trail on the opposite side.

The 2.5-mile climb to the top of Butano Ridge is well graded, perfect for early season training. Once up, head left on the old ridge-crest logging road, which behaves like a roller coaster. Views along the ridge top are of the peekaboo variety, to be searched out between the trees.

After 2 miles on the ridge crest, the route leaves the road and heads back down with a series of well-graded switchbacks. If you carried all your overnight gear to the top of the ridge, follow the Basin Trail down to the Old Haul Road, then continue straight ahead to find the Iverson Trail on your left. Return to the Visitor Center via delicate Tip-Toe Falls. If you did not carry your gear around the loop, stay on the Butano Ridge Loop Trail to its end then follow the Old Haul Road back to your camp.

*Tip-Toe Falls*

# 87 PETERS CREEK GROVE

**Round trip: 12 miles**
**Hiking time: 7 hours**
**High point: 1,440 feet**

**Elevation gain: 1,040 feet in;**
**760 feet out**
**Hikable: All year**
**Day hike or backpack**

**Maps: Portola State Park map; USGS: Mindego Hill (trail not shown)**

Reservations and Information: Portola State Park (Case 11)

Like all of the old and magnificent trees, the tall trees of Peters Creek show signs of the fires and floods they have survived. However, the most amazing story of survival is their miraculous escape from the axes that leveled most of the forests in this area before the turn of the century.

The entire hike may be done in one day, or it may be spread out over two days with an overnight stop at Slate Creek Trail Camp. No drinking water is available at the trail camp. All water must be packed in or taken from less-than-pristine Slate Creek, a 0.4-mile walk from the campsite.

**Access.** Drive Highway 35 (Skyline Boulevard) south 7.1 miles from Highway 84 or 6.2 miles north from Highway 9. Follow Alpine Road for 3.1 miles then take a left on Portola State Park Road and descend, steeply, for 3.5 miles to the Visitor Center. Day hikers park in the picnic area; backpackers park behind the Visitor Center (400 feet).

Walk the main road downhill from the Visitor Center. Cross Peters Creek and head up to an intersection. Follow the road to the right for 300 feet, then go left and head uphill on the Slate Creek/Old Tree Trail.

After an initial 0.1-mile climb, reach an intersection. Go left on the Slate Creek Trail and contour north for 0.2 mile to a second intersection. Take the right fork and begin a slow, steady climb through mixed

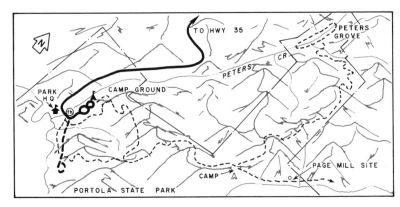

*Hillside of redwood sorrel in Peters Creek Grove*

forest of redwood, Douglas fir, oak, and madrone trees. At 1.5 miles the trail reaches a narrow saddle (920 feet) and a third intersection. To the right, the Summit Trail offers an alternate descent route. For now, continue on the Slate Creek Trail for another 1.5 miles to the trail camp and intersection (1,020 feet).

From the trail camp, go left and follow the Bear Creek Trail along an old road grade. At 4 miles from the Visitor Center, the road disappears and a narrow trail continues on through open shrub land where you must watch for poison oak and ticks. After 0.5 mile the trail reaches a 1,440-foot high point, then begins a very steep descent to the redwood grove. The state park owns a very narrow strip of land here and the trail builders were forced to forgo switchbacks.

The grove is reached at 5.2 miles (800 feet). Walk the 0.5-mile loop trail around the grove or just sit by the creek and enjoy the peacefulness of the area. At the base of the these hardy trees is a verdant carpet of ferns, redwood sorrel, miners lettuce, and, in early spring, trilliums.

# 88 SKYLINE TO THE SEA TRAIL

**One-way hike: 32.5 miles**  
**Hiking time: 3–4 days**  
**High point: 3,214 feet**

**Elevation gain: 673 feet;**  
  **loss: 3,887 feet**  
**Hikable: All year**  
**Backpack**

**Maps: Skyline to the Sea Trail Maps 1 and 2; USGS Castle Rock Ridge, Big Basin, Franklin Point, Ano Nuevo**

Reservations and Information: Big Basin State Park (Case 12)

From the crest of the Santa Cruz Range to the shores of the Pacific Ocean, the Skyline to the Sea Trail is the crowning achievement of the elaborate Santa Cruz Mountains trail system. The first segment of this trail, from Saratoga Gap to Big Basin Redwoods State Park, was constructed in 1969 by 2,500 enthusiastic volunteers in a single weekend. Since that time the idea has grown and the trail has been extended to the ocean.

When started at Castle Rock, the trail is 32.5 miles long and has six trail camps located at uneven intervals along the route. Two other trail camps, Sunset and Lane, are located on scenic variants off the main route. All camps require advance reservations except Castle Rock Trail Camp, which is on a first-come basis. Fees are charged at all the camps. Drinking water is currently available at the first three camps (Castle Rock, Waterman Gap, and Jay Camp). At the other camps, water must be carried in. No campfires are allowed, so carry a backpacking stove for cooking.

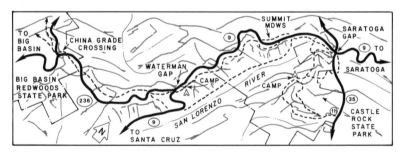

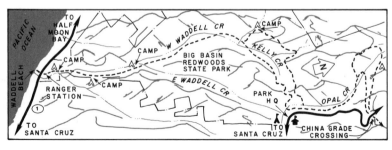

As this is a one-way hike, transportation must be arranged ahead of time. No overnight parking is allowed at Saratoga Gap, so cars are left at Castle Rock State Park. If you have trail camp reservations, a second car may be left at Rancho del Oso Ranger Station, located 0.2 mile east of Highway 1. If you are to be met at the end of the hike, you must walk out to Highway 1 and find your ride at Waddell Beach. Bus Service is available from Waddell Beach to Santa Cruz. For information call Santa Cruz Metropolitan Transit District at (408) 425-8600.

**Access.** Drive to Saratoga Gap at the intersection of Highway 9 and Skyline Drive (Highway 35). Head south on Skyline Drive for 2.6 miles, then turn left to the trailhead parking at Castle Rock State Park (3,060 feet).

The Skyline to the Sea Trail route begins by following the Saratoga Gap Trail past a waterfall then along the side of an open ridge with excellent views west over forested hills to the Pacific Ocean. At 2.8 miles reach Castle Rock Camp. From the camp follow the Loghry Woods and Skyline Trails along the ridge crest for 3.4 miles to Saratoga Gap.

At Saratoga Gap, pick up the official Skyline to the Sea Trail for the 6.3 mile descent to Waterman Gap. Unfortunately, the public right-of-way is

very limited in this area and the trail closely parallels Highway 9, crossing it several times. If you prefer a more wilderness feel to your walk, follow the Saratoga Toll Road stock trail for at least part of your descent.

From Waterman Gap the trail wanders through dense forest while paralleling Highway 236 for the next 4.5 miles to China Grade (a road crossing). You then descend through Big Basin Redwoods State Park past the headquarters to reach Jay Camp at 22 miles.

From Jay Camp to the ocean, hikers must choose between three scenic routes: 1) the Howard King Trail, which has outstanding views; 2) the Sunset and Berry Creek Falls Trails, which pass three unique and beautiful waterfalls; and 3) the Skyline to the Sea Trail, which winds through majestic redwood groves. The three routes rejoin for the final 6-mile descent along Waddell Creek to the ocean.

*Trail's end at Waddell Beach*

# 89 BERRY CREEK FALLS LOOP

| | |
|---|---|
| **Loop trip: 11 miles** | **Elevation gain: 1,300 feet** |
| **Hiking time: 6 hours** | **Hikable: All year** |
| **High point: 1,340 feet** | **One day or backpack** |

**Maps: Big Basin Redwoods State Park; USGS Big Basin**

Reservations and Information: Park Headquarters, Big Basin Redwoods State Park (Case 12)

The highlights of this very popular hike through the redwoods are three waterfalls. Berry Creek Falls appears as a lace curtain in a fern- and moss-covered grotto, beautiful Silver Falls plunges down a sheer cliff, and Golden Falls Cascade is exotic and extremely colorful.

The entire loop can be hiked in one day or divided into two leisurely days with an overnight stop at Sunset Trail Camp. Backpackers must carry their own stove (no open fires are permitted) and either carry their own water or be ready to boil, filter, and then purify the water from nearby Berry Creek.

**Access.** From Saratoga Gap, at the intersection of Highway 35 (Skyline Boulevard) and Highway 9, drive west on Highway 9. After descending 5.8 miles, reach Waterman Gap and turn right on Highway 236, and follow it to Big Basin Redwoods State Park Headquarters (1,001 feet).

The hike begins opposite the Visitor Center, next to the amphitheater. The trail starts off by cutting its way between two impressive redwood groves. Several trails branch off to the right and left, heading into the groves; however, for the loop you need to go straight and cross the Opal Creek bridge then go left on the Skyline to the Sea Trail.

For the next 3.7 miles, stay on the Skyline to the Sea Trail as it climbs over a ridge then descends through redwood groves first along Kelly Creek then along Waddell Creek. At one point the trail divides and the right fork crosses the creek to wander through another grove of redwoods before rejoining the main trail in 0.3 mile.

At the Berry Creek Trail junction (360 feet), go right and begin the

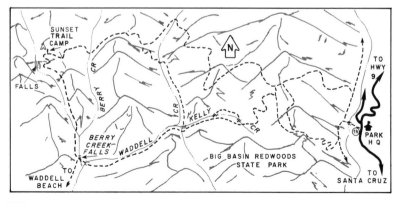

*Berry Creek Falls*

climb past Berry Creek Falls, Silver Falls, and Golden Falls Cascades. The final ascent is in a narrow valley where you climb steps cut into the sandstone at the edge of Berry Creek.

At 5.5 miles (800 feet) a trail branches left to Sunset Camp. Unless you are overnighting, continue straight ahead on Sunset Trail, which climbs then descends several times before reaching the trip's 1,340-foot high point on Middle Ridge. Walk across an old fire road, then descend to the Skyline to the Sea Trail at 10.7 miles. Go right and walk along Opal Creek for the final 0.2 mile to the bridge and the Visitor Center.

*Opal Creek*

# 90   NORTH RIM TRAIL

**Loop trip: 13.5 miles**
**Hiking time: 7 hours**
**High point: 2,282 feet**

**Elevation gain: 1,282 feet**
**Hikable: All year**
**Day hike or backpack**

**Maps: Big Basin Redwoods State Park; USGS Big Basin**

Reservations and Information: Park Headquarters, Big Basin Redwoods State Park (Case 12)

From redwood groves to grand vistas, this semi-loop along the north rim of Big Basin Redwoods State Park offers excellent scenery and delightful walking. Between the redwood groves and the vistas, the hike passes oddly weathered sandstone formations and an old mill site, and rambles through a wide variety of ecosystems. In late winter and early spring, add bubbling creeks and a scattering of wildflowers to the list.

The North Rim Trail may be hiked in one day or spread out over a two-day weekend with an overnight stop at Lane Trail Camp. Backpackers must carry a camp stove (no wood fires are allowed) as well as all water needed for the night.

**Access.** Drive to Big Basin Redwoods State Park (see Hike 88) and park near the Visitor Center (1,001 feet).

The hike begins opposite the amphitheater. Follow the trail across the Opal Creek bridge, then go right on the Skyline to the Sea Trail. The route parallels Opal Creek and North Escape Road, which is gated beyond the picnic area. Head through redwood groves and past the sight of the Maddock's Cabin, where the Maddock family built a home from a single giant redwood tree.

The trail brushes along the edge of North Escape Road at several points then shares a bridge over Rogers Creek. At 2.2 miles pass a fancy information board and picnic table, then use the road a second time to cross Opal Creek. Once over the bridge, go left and follow the trail into a redwood grove.

At 2.7 miles (1,320 feet) the trail divides. Leave the Skyline to the Sea Trail and go left on Hollow Tree Trail. After climbing toward the ridge tops for 1.4 miles, the trail divides again at 1,830 feet. Stay on the Hollow Tree Trail and begin a traverse along the northern boundary of the park. Much of this trail parallels China Grade Road, a rarely used access into the backcountry of the Santa Cruz Mountains.

The trail traverses oak- and madrone-covered hillsides, passing a lumber mill site with plenty of old relics to gawk at. Reach the 2,282-foot Lane Trail Camp at the 6-mile mark. The camp is located on the crest of the ridge, ideally placed to take advantage of the afternoon breezes.

From the camp, follow the Basin Trail past several Pacific Ocean vistas and across a couple of weathered sandstone formations. One of these sandstone areas is so steep that steps had to be cut into the rock. The Basin Trail ends at 9.2 miles (1,920 feet). Go right on the Skyline to the Sea Trail for the final 4.3 miles back to the Visitor Center.

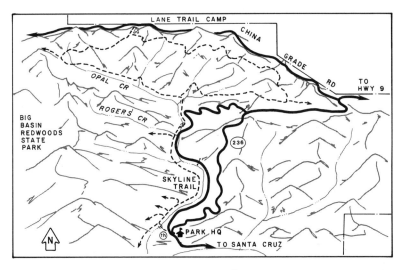

*Indian grinding hole where, in the past, native women ground acorns into flour*

# 91 MOUNT CARMEL

**Round trip: 9 miles**
**Hiking time: 5 hours**
**High point: 4,430 feet**
**Elevation gain: 2,580 feet**
**Hikable: March through October**
**Day hike or backpack**

**Maps: USFS Ventana Wilderness;**
**USGS: Big Sur and Mt. Carmel**

Information: Monterey Ranger District (Case 13)

Views, views, views, and more views. There is a 360-degree panorama of views from the summit of Mt. Carmel, but you had better hurry. Since the fire lookout burned down in the 1950s, the brush has slowly been reclaiming the best viewpoint in the northern Los Padres National Forest. Nowadays, in order to gaze north over the Monterey Peninsula, east across the Carmel Valley to the Sierra de Salinas Range, south over the Santa Lucia Range, or west across the seemingly endless expanse of the Pacific Ocean, you must scramble up a boulder pile or scale a rickety old telephone pole. In another ten years this outstanding view may be gone.

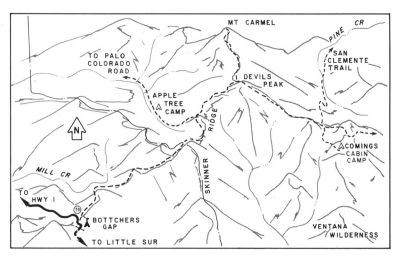

**Access.** Drive south from Monterey on Highway 1. Check your odometer as you pass the Highway 68 West exit, then continue down the coast for 14 miles. Turn left on Palo Colorado Road for 7.8 miles to its end at Bottchers Gap. Park at the small walk-in campground (2,050 feet).

The trail begins at the upper left-hand corner of the parking lot and climbs above the walk-in campsites. The grade varies from moderate on the chaparral-covered hillside to steep in the oak- and madrone-filled Mill Creek Valley. There are two creek crossings before the trail reaches the 3,450-foot crest of Skinner Ridge at 2.5 miles.

On the ridge crest, swing north, entering the Ventana Wilderness, then wander through an arcade of giant oak and madrone trees. After 0.2 mile, leave the ridge and descend to the Turner Creek Junction (3,200 feet) at 3 miles. To the left a trail descends 300 feet in 0.3 mile to forested Apple Tree Camp.

Continue straight ahead and switchback up the steep hillside. At the top of the first knoll is an intersection. The right fork follows the fire break straight up to the top of the ridge. The official

*Seeking an unobstructed view from summit of Mount Carmel*

trail stays to the left, making the same climb with the aid and comfort of switchbacks and shade.

At 4 miles cross the 4,158-foot summit of Devils Peak. Views are only moderate here, so continue on. When the trail traverses around the second summit of Devils Peak, go left on a well-worn path heading up the meadow-covered hill. Follow this path for 30 feet, then go left on a faint path covered with California blue oak leaves. After a few feet the trail improves. Descend to a small saddle, then head up through manzanita for 0.5 mile to the 4,430-foot lookout site on the summit of Mt. Carmel. The final portion of the trail is often very brushy, so have your long pants handy.

Backpackers should return to Devils Peak and continue on for another 1.2 miles to scenic Comings Cabin Camp. Water is usually available at the camp for the entire summer.

# 92    MANUEL PEAK

**Round trip: 9 miles**
**Hiking time: 5 hours**
**High point: 3,379 feet**

**Elevation gain: 3,039 feet**
**Hikable: All year**
**Day hike**

**Maps: USFS Ventana Wilderness; USGS Pfeiffer Point and Big Sur**

Information: Monterey Ranger District (Case 13)

Outstanding views keynote this hike, which begins in the redwood groves of Pfeiffer Big Sur State Park and ends overlooking the endless expanse of the Pacific Ocean.

Much of this hike is spent on the open and dry expanses of the chaparral-covered hillsides, so during the warm summer months plan to start your hike early and be sure to carry plenty of water.

**Access.** Drive Highway 1 south from Carmel 25 miles to Pfeiffer Big Sur State Park. At this point you have three options. You may pay the day-use fee and drive into the park to Picnic Area 3, where the trail begins (340 feet). Or you may find a parking place in one of the turnouts just outside the park and walk in for free. The third option is to park 0.5 mile south of the state park at the Big Sur Ranger Station, pay a $2.00 a day parking fee, then walk through forest and the campground to reach the trailhead at the picnic area.

From Picnic Area 3, the hike begins by rounding a gate and heading up a paved road through an oak grove. After 500 feet go left on a wide trail, passing a pioneer cabin then climbing through a beautiful oak arbor. At 0.5 mile from the picnic area is the intersection with the trail from Pfeiffer Falls. Go straight ahead on a wide, well-graded trail, leaving the state park and entering the Los Padres National Forest.

The views begin immediately as the trail switchbacks up the hillside. At first you are overlooking only the park. Soon the steep-walled canyon of the Big Sur River becomes visible and views expand over Island Mountain deep into the Santa Lucia Range. Not long after, the Pacific Ocean comes into view.

At 2.4 miles the trail rounds a rocky rib, then heads into a deep cut in the hillside. At the shadiest point is a redwood grove and a small, unreliable spring. When you reach the summit ridge at 3 miles, the Mt. Manuel Trail turns north for the final push to the crest of Manuel Peak.

Manuel Peak has many summits. The trail passes to the west of the first summit, descends, then climbs to a forested saddle. Go left on a narrow trail, passing a military-looking apparatus to the open and rocky crest of the 3,379-foot second summit. This is a great place to eat lunch and enjoy the view.

The trail continues on. In the next mile, it crosses over two more major summits and one lesser summit before dropping down to the Little Big Sur River. However, there is no substantial improvement in the view beyond the second summit.

*Unobstructed view of Pacific Ocean from Manuel Peak trail*

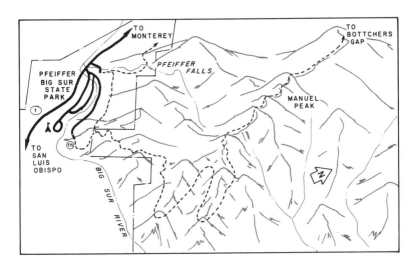

# $\underline{93}$     SYKES CAMP—THE HOTSPRINGS HIKE

**Round trip: 19.5 miles**
**Hiking time: 3–4 days**
**High point: 1,640 feet**

**Elevation gain: 2,100 feet**
**Hikable: April through October**
**Backpack**

**Maps: USFS Ventana Wilderness; USGS Pfeiffer Point, Partington Ridge, and Ventana Cones**

Information: Monterey Ranger District (Case 13)

The Pine Ridge Trail from Big Sur to Sykes Camp is the most popular hike in the Ventana Wilderness. Its popularity has nothing to do with the excellent trail, views of the forest and ocean, the Big Sur River with its deep pools of clear water, or the towering groves of redwoods,

*Big Sur River*

although these things help. The reason so many people make the long trek to Sykes Camp is the famous natural hot springs.

With endless streams of people trekking in to soak in the pools, this is not the place to go if you are looking for solitude. However, if you are looking for a good introduction to the spectacular variety of flora and fauna of the Ventana Wilderness, this place is hard to beat. (Note: Although the Pine Ridge Trail is hikable year-round, crossing the Big Sur River may be a problem after any rainstorm. If planning a winter hike, contact the Forest Service for up-to-date conditions before starting.)

**Access.** Drive Highway 1 south 25.5 miles from Carmel. At 0.5 mile south of the entrance to Pfeiffer Big Sur State Park, turn left to the Big Sur Forest Service Station. Follow signs to the trailhead and overnight parking area (320 feet). A fee is charged for parking.

From the ranger station, follow the Pine Ridge Trail through the redwood forest around the edge of the state park campground. The trail descends, crosses Post Creek, then heads steeply up through the chaparral. At the end of the first mile you will enter the Big Sur River Valley. A rock outcropping (880 feet) provides an open vantage point to Island Mountain and the Santa Lucia Range.

The trail contours the hillside, winding in and out of small redwood groves and entering the Ventana Wilderness at 2.5 miles. The next point of interest is an unmarked intersection at 4.2 miles. To the left a spur trail drops 700 feet in 1 mile to Ventana Camp, a scenic backcountry camping area on the edge of the Big Sur River.

The Pine Ridge Trail continues up-valley and at 5.4 miles passes Terrace Creek Camp in a redwood grove. A trail branches off on the right here, ascending to the Coast Ridge Trail.

From Terrace Creek Camp, the Pine Ridge Trail climbs a bit then descends to 900 feet and crosses Logwood Creek. At 7 miles you will arrive at Barlow Flat, where the trail brushes the shores of the Big Sur River for the first time. A camp area is located across the river. The trail climbs back to 1,400 feet to cross a rocky rib, then descends to ford the Big Sur River at 9.7 miles. Sykes Camp (1,100 feet) and the hot springs can be reached only by crossing the river. Once camp is set up, follow the footpath down-river for 600 feet to the hot spring pools for a long soak in the 100-degree water.

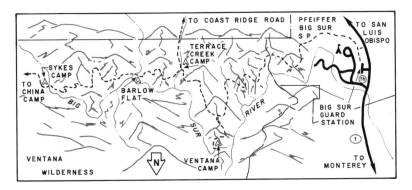

# 94 VICENTE FLAT

**Round trip from Kirk Creek:** **Elevation gain: 2,070 feet**
  **10 miles** **Hikable: March through November**
**Hiking time: 6 hours** **Day hike or backpack**
**High point: 2,200 feet**

**Maps: USFS Ventana Wilderness; USGS Cone Peak and Lopez Point**

Information: Big Sur Ranger Station or King City Ranger Station
(Case 13)

Meadows, open ridges, secluded redwood groves, and panoramic
views over the rugged Monterey coast combine to make the hike from
Kirk Creek to Vicente Flat one of the most scenic hikes in the Ventana
Wilderness. (Note: This area is known for ticks, especially in the
spring. Take all the usual precautions.)

**Access.** Drive Highway 1 south from Carmel 53 miles to Kirk Creek
Campground. The trailhead parking area is a moderate-sized turnout
on the east side of the highway, opposite the campground entrance
(130 feet).

The trail climbs the steep hillside above the highway through a band
of low scrub brush (replete with poison oak) into open meadows. Views
begin almost immediately. After the first 0.5 mile, the trail heads
north, following the undulations of the steep hillside and passing
through small groves of redwoods in the deepest folds before swinging
out into open meadows.

By 3 miles the trail has gained nearly all of its elevation. It then
swings northeast, contouring high above Hare Canyon for 1.5 miles. In

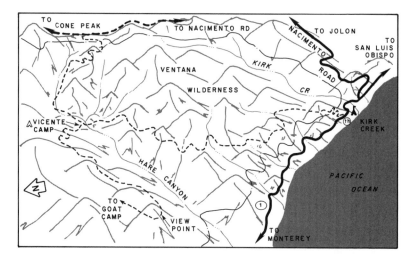

*View south along coast from open hillside above Kirk Creek*

this section you will reach the trip's 2,200-foot high point, then at 4.5 miles begin a steady descent that ends on the valley floor at the lower end of a large redwood grove. Walk up through the grove to an intersection. Keep left for 200 feet to reach the central portion of the sprawling Vicente Camp at 5 miles (1,570 feet).

If overnighting at Vicente Camp, plan to spend a couple of hours exploring. The cool, shady redwood grove above the camp area is an excellent place to wander on warm days. For views, head back to the intersection below the camp area and follow the Stone Ridge Trail for 1.5 miles north to an outstanding viewpoint on the open ridge crest.

A popular alternative to the round-trip hike from Kirk Creek is a one-way hike descending from Cone Peak Road (also called Coastal Ridge Road No. 20505) to Highway 1. This is a 7-mile hike that can be done easily in a day, providing a car shuttle can be arranged.

*Giant foothill pine* (pinus sabiana) *cone*

# 95　ARROYO SECO

| | |
|---|---|
| **Round trip to ridge: 10 miles** | **Hikable: mid-March through** |
| **Hiking time: 5 hours** | **October** |
| **High point: 4,420 feet** | **Day hike** |
| **Elevation gain: 2,320 feet** | |

**Maps: USFS Ventana Wilderness; USGS Cone Peak and Lopez Point**

| | |
|---|---|
| **Round trip to Cook Camp:** | **Elevation gain: 2,600 feet** |
| **12 miles** | **Hikable: mid-March through June** |
| **Hiking time: 6 hours** | **Backpack** |
| **High point: 4,700** | |

**Maps: USFS Ventana Wilderness; USGS Cone Peak and Lopez Point**

Information: Monterey Ranger District (Case 13)

It is the view from the crest of the Santa Lucia Range that inspires hikers to make the long climb from the valley floor to the top of the ridge. Although you cannot see all the way to China, on a clear day you can see freighters heading in that direction.

The Arroyo Seco Trail climbs along the Arroyo Seco River to the crest of the range, where it meets the North Coast Ridge Trail. Except for an absence of bridges, this is an excellent trail. However, since this area was swept by fire in 1985, storms bring down a new batch of dead and dying trees every winter. Brush grows rapidly in the burned area, particularly the chemise, manzanita, and the prickly leaved ceanothus. The Forest Service clears out the trail as often as possible, but expect some rough going in the spring.

**Access**. Drive to the end of the paved road at Santa Lucia Memorial Park (see Hike 96 for details). Go past the campground. When the road divides, find a place to park that will not block other traffic (1,980 feet).

The hike begins by following the gated road on the left. Walk around the gate, then head up-valley a short distance to a group of cabins. The official trailhead is located opposite the second building.

Watch out for poison oak as you walk along the shaded valley floor to reach the first unbridged crossing of Arroyo Seco River at 0.2 mile. The ford is deep and the water fast, so look for logs to help with the crossing. At 1.8 miles the trail arrives at Forks Campsite, an open area along the river with a year-round water supply and fire ring. Just 500 feet beyond the camp, the trail divides. To the right, Rodeo Flat Trail follows an old fire break steeply uphill to meet the North Coast Ridge Trail. Your trail heads left and recrosses the Arroyo Seco River (2,580 feet). Once across, head uphill and soon cross the Arroyo Seco River for the third and last time.

At 3 miles, pass Madrone Camp, which has a year-round water source and a fire box. At this point the trail begins to climb through the old burn, leaving the river and poison oak and entering an area of dense scrub brush. Views begin here and extend across the valley to Junipero Serra Peak, the highest summit in the wilderness.

Following a line of burned telephone poles, the trail reaches the 4,420-foot ridge crest at 5 miles. Go left on the North Coast Ridge Trail for 100 feet for the first views west over the ocean and a great picnic site. Backpackers should continue west along the ridge for another mile to the Cook Springs intersection (4,700 feet). Go left here and descend to the camp. Water supply at Cook Springs is not reliable after midsummer.

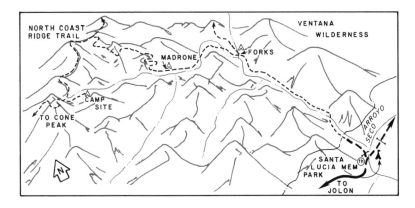

# 96  LOST VALLEY

**Round trip: 11 miles**
**Hiking time: 6 hours**
**High point: 2,852 feet**

**Elevation gain: 1,372 feet in;**
**760 feet out**
**Hikable: April through October**
**Day hike or backpack**

**Maps: USFS Ventana Wilderness; USGS Junipero Serra Peak and Tassajara Hot Springs**

Information: Monterey Ranger District (Case 13)

Extensive meadows and a reliable water source make Lost Valley a popular destination for day hikers and backpackers throughout the hiking

*Field of shooting stars along Lost Valley trail*

season. However, regular visitors all agree that springtime is the best, when wildflowers carpet the valley and hillsides, turning the meadows into a brilliant afghan of yellows, blues, and reds. If you wish to time your visit to enjoy the wildflowers, check ahead with the ranger office.

Once the rains begin in the fall (usually in October or November), the last 3 miles of road to the trailhead are gated and must be walked. The road is usually reopened by the first of May. However, peak wildflower season varies from mid-March to early May and when the flowers bloom early, the rivers along the trail still may be swollen from the winter rains and hard to cross.

**Access.** Drive Highway 101 to King City and take the Jolon exit, located 0.7 miles north of the Broadway exit, then head west on County Road G14 for 18.2 miles to Jolon. At the Jolon General Store, turn right on Mission Road. You must stop and check in at the Hunter-Leggett Military Reservation, then continue straight for 5 miles before turning left on Del Ventura Road, just opposite the mission. After another 17.7 miles reach the pavement's end at Santa Lucia Memorial Park Campground. During the rainy season, the hike begins here. When the road is open, continue up-valley another 3 miles to Escondido Campground. The trailhead is located at the far end of the campground access road (2,175 feet). (Note: The road through Hunter-Leggett has no bridges and is flooded after major rainstorms.)

Find the sign that says "Trail" and begin a one-mile descent to the Arroyo Seco River (1,680 feet). Once across the ford, spend the next 1.5 miles climbing. Watch for poison oak along the creek and for ticks on the dry hillside above. At 2,852 feet, the trail crosses an open divide with excellent views, then descends toward Lost Valley Creek. Just before the final descent to the valley floor, pass a waterfall with a deep bathing pool tantalizingly close to the trail. At 4 miles, cross a small creek to reach Fish Camp (2,030 feet).

The trail climbs again for 0.7 mile to an intersection on a dry divide with the Lost Valley Connector, a steep fire trail. The final leg of the hike is an easy descent to Lost Valley.

The upper Lost Valley Camp is located 0.5 mile below the divide, across a small creek from the trail. The main camp is located 0.2 mile further down. From your base camp, a day can be spent exploring the meadows and hiking to Higgins Camp and Indian Valley.

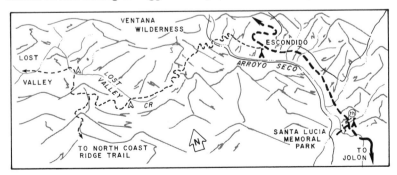

# 97 NORTH CHALONE PEAK

| | |
|---|---|
| **Round trip: 8 miles** | **Elevation gain: 2,004 feet** |
| **Hiking time: 4 hours** | **Hikable: November through May** |
| **High point: 3,304 feet** | **Day hike** |

**Maps: USGS Pinnacles National Monument or USGS North Chalone Peak**

Information: Pinnacles National Monument (Case 15)

On a normal day at North Chalone Peak lookout, there is a panoramic view of Pinnacles National Monument to the north, the Diablo Range to the east, and west over the Salinas Valley to the Santa Lucia Range. If the day is exceptionally clear, it is possible to see all the way to the Pacific Ocean. (Note: Although this trail is open for hiking the entire year, temperatures soar to uncomfortable levels in the summer. If hiking during the warmer months, plan to begin your hike at daybreak and carry a minimum of two quarts of water per person.)

**Access.** Drive Highway 101 for 2 miles south of Gilroy and take the Highway 25 exit. Head south through Hollister on Highway 25 for 42.6 miles. Turn right at the Highway 146 intersection for 5.2 miles to the Pinnacles National Monument Visitor Center. Park here or continue on another 0.3 mile to the end of the road (1,260 feet). If spending the weekend during the busy spring season, it is best to stop at the private campground just outside the monument, reserve a site, then take the shuttle bus to the trailhead. (From the south, drive Highway 101 to King City then go east on Highway 613 to Highway 25. Head north to the Highway 146 intersection.)

The trail begins near the entrance to the upper parking lot. Head up the valley, following signs to Bear Gulch Reservoir. After 0.2 mile the

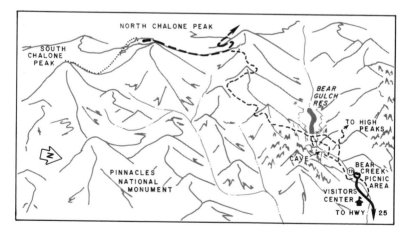

trail divides, offering you three different routes to the reservoir. To the left the Bear Gulch Caves Trail follows the creek up through deep caves. This trail requires much stooping, crawling, and walking in water, as well as a flashlight. Also to the left is the Moses Spring Trail, which is very scenic, with several overlooks of Bear Gulch. This trail has only one short section where body and pack must be wriggled through a narrow crevice. Finally, if neither of these two trails are to your taste, stay right at the intersection and follow the High Peaks Trail up for another 0.3 mile, then take the Rim Trail to Bear Gulch Reservoir.

From the reservoir a broad, well-graded trail climbs the chamise- and buckbrush-covered hillside to ever-expanding views of the monument. At 3.5 miles the trail passes through a gate and heads left up a fire road. After 200 feet the fire road joins the lookout road (gated at the bottom and open to lookout vehicles only). The lookout is now straight ahead and is reached after another 0.5 mile of following the road along the scenic ridge crest.

The 3,304-foot summit of North Chalone Peak provides a great place to relax and eat lunch. Rest rooms are located just below the summit on the south side. To the south, South Chalone Peak dominates the skyline. The peak can be reached by an easy-to-follow, unmaintained, 1.6-mile trail. To reach the trail, head back down the road past the switchback to

*Hiker on trail through Bear Gulch Caves*

find the unmarked trail on the left. The trail descends along the fence line to a 2,620-foot saddle, then climbs back to the 3,269-foot summit of South Chalone Peak. The view from the south summit is not much better than from the north peak; it simply offers a lot more solitude.

# 98    HIGH PEAKS LOOP

**Loop trip: 6.7 miles**
**Hiking time: 4 hours**
**High point: 2,580 feet**

**Elevation gain: 1,580 feet**
**Hikable: All year**
**Day hike**

**Maps: USGS Pinnacles National Monument or USGS North Chalone Peak**

Information: Pinnacles National Monument (Case 15)

From shaded creeks and narrow canyons to cliffs, crags, spires, and panoramic views, this loop across the crest of Pinnacles National Monument offers endless variety. Spring is one of the best times to hike here as temperatures are cool, flowers are blooming, and birds are everywhere: nesting on cliffs, in the trees, and on the chaparral-covered hillsides. Climbers also take advantage of the season and hikers are likely to see incredible feats of strength and flexibility on the sheer rock walls and pinnacles. If you hike here during the summer, start early to avoid the heat of the day and carry a minimum of two quarts of water per person.

**Access.** From Highway 101 follow Highway 25 to the Highway 146 intersection. Head west 4 miles into the east side of Pinnacles National Monument. When the road divides, go right 0.3 mile and park at the Chalone Creek Picnic Area (1,030 feet).

From the picnic area entrance head west, crossing Chalone Creek on a pair of bridges, to find an intersection and the start of the loop on the west side of the creek. Go left on Bear Gulch Trail, which heads down-valley through heavy vegetation. Watch for poison oak and rattlesnakes. At 0.6 mile, shortly after crossing the park road, the trail divides. Go right and head up Bear Gulch past pools, waterfalls (in the spring), and several impressive sycamore trees.

At 1.2 miles, walk by the Visitor Center, then cross the road and

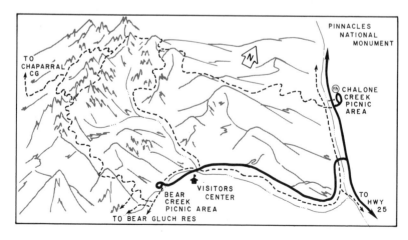

*Hiking through pinnacles on High Peaks Trail*

continue straight, paralleling the road. Follow the trail through the picnic area to reach the end of the road where the fun begins.

Cross the road for the last time and head up, following signs for the High Peaks Trail. The climb is steady as the trail heads to the ridge crest and the pinnacles. Reach a 2,100-foot saddle at 3.4 miles from Chalone Creek Picnic Area. Take a break on a handy bench and enjoy the view west to the Salines Valley and the Santa Lucia Range.

At the crest of the saddle the trail divides, giving you two choices. The right-hand fork is the High Peaks Trail, the shorter, easier, and more scenic of the two trails. This is the best choice if, and only if, you have a good head for heights. The trail has several narrow and extremely exposed sections where you must climb over the rocks with man-made hand- and toeholds. The alternative is to descend 600 feet in 0.6 mile, then climb back up on the Tunnel Trail.

At 4.2 miles the Tunnel Trail joins the High Peaks Trail. Continue on the High Peaks Trail, which begins a steady descent along the ridge crest, winding around the pinnacles to open meadows (covered with shooting stars in the spring) then down to chaparral-covered hillsides, passing an intersection with the Condor Gulch Trail. At 6.7 miles, the loop ends at Chalone Creek. Go left, cross the bridges, and return to your car.

# *99* NORTH WILDERNESS LOOP

**Loop trip: 9.9 miles**      **Elevation gain: 983 feet**
**Hiking time: 7 hours**      **Hikable: All year**
**High point: 2,083 feet**    **Day hike**

**Maps: USGS Pinnacles National Monument or USGS North Chalone
Peak and Bickmore Canyon**

Information: Pinnacles National Monument (Case 15)

The trail along the north boundary of Pinnacles National Monument
offers a chance to get away from the crowds and explore the chaparral
ecosystem. This is a wilderness trek that wanders along creek bottoms
richly covered with grasses, gray foothill pines, junipers, and oaks,
then climbs to an impenetrable mixture of chamise, buckbrush, and an
occasional manzanita on the ridge crest. In the early spring, wildflowers cover the valley floor and ridges with colorful carpets of yellow,
white, and blue.

The North Wilderness Trail has been designated as "unmaintained,"
which means trailheads are not signed, sections of the trail are steep,
and maintenance is limited. Hikers must be prepared to crawl over
fallen trees and wade shallow creeks. However, when equipped with
a map, compass, plenty of water, and a flashlight for the caves, you
can hike this trail with little difficulty. (Note: In the summer, carry a
minimum of two quarts of water per person and start early to avoid
the heat.)

**Access.** Drive Highway 101 to Soledad, then head east on Highway
146 for 12 miles to the road's end at Chaparral Campground (1,407
feet). (The campground is closed Friday through Sunday from Presi-
dents Day weekend through Memorial Day weekend.) From the east

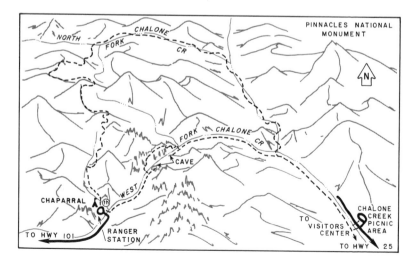

side of the monument you may start the loop from Chalone Creek Picnic Area, adding 2 miles to the total.

From the end of the Chaparral parking area, walk by the rest room, then follow the wide trail to the northwest corner of the walk-in campground where an opening in the fence marks the start of the trail. Head up-valley on a faint but discernible path through the deep grass. Points of confusion are marked with white-topped metal fence posts.

After the first mile, the trail heads to the ridge tops and views of the entire park. Once up, the trail traverses the ridge crest to a 2,083-foot high point. Watch for diggings made by wild pigs in this area. The park is working to fence these nonnative animals out, but it is a big job.

From the high point, descend steeply to North Fork Chalone Creek. The trail then heads down-valley, an easy walk except for the fifteen creek crossings. Watch for poison oak.

At 7.6 miles the trail crosses the West Fork Chalone Creek for the last time, then intersects the Old Pinnacles Trail (1,100 feet). Go right, and head up-valley on a broad, well-used path for 1.3 miles, crossing several more creeks. At 8.9 miles the trail divides. The Balconies Caves Trail goes straight, remaining in the cool shade of the valley floor. A flashlight is required to help you negotiate your way around and under the giant boulders that created the caves. The Balconies Cliffs Trail goes right, making a longer but much easier traverse across the dry slopes above the valley. Once the two trails rejoin, it is a quick 0.6 mile to the end of the loop at the Chaparral parking area.

*Shooting stars cover hillsides and forest floors in spring*

# ︲︱○○ POVERTY FLAT LOOP

**Loop trip: 10 miles**       **Elevation gain: 2,300 feet**
**Hiking time: 6 hours**       **Hikable: October through June**
**High point: 3,040 feet**       **Day hike or backpack**

**Maps: USGS Mt. Sizer and Mississippi Creek**

Reservations and Information: Henry W. Coe State Park Headquarters
    (Case 14)

    Between the coastal range and the Central Valley lies a group of rolling mountains known as the Diablo Range. This is a beautiful area with steep-sided hills and narrow valleys covered with Pacific madrones, feathery foothill pines, and majestic oaks. Springtime has the added enchantment of green hillsides spotted with colorful flowers.

*Hiker on Middle Ridge Trail*

While most of the Diablo Range is pastureland and the hillsides are cut by roads, a section has been preserved in Henry W. Coe State Park, which includes the 23,000-acre Orestima Wilderness. The park offers trails and roads for the non-motorized uses of hiking, mountain biking, and horseback riding. The trails are often steep and narrow. The roads (occasionally used by authorized motor vehicles) are narrow and frequently steeper than the trails.

The Poverty Flat Loop is just an introduction to this large park. Longer hikes of a week or more are easy to plan. Although trails are open year-round, hiking is best in the cooler months. creeks and some springs dry up in the late spring and summer, making backpacking difficult.

**Access.** Drive Highway 101 to Morgan Hill. Take the East Dunne Avenue exit and go east through a residential area then up a steep hill. At the top, the road divides. Stay right on Dunne Way, a narrow winding road that ends 12.5 miles from the freeway at the Visitor Center and campground (2,640 feet).

Begin the loop by walking back up the road for 200 feet from the Visitor Center. Go right and skirt around a gate, then head up the Pacheco Route, a jeep road, for 400 feet to the Monument Trail. Go left. At 0.6 mile from the parking lot, the trail divides. Go right for a visit to the Henry W. Coe Monument and viewpoint, then follow the road over the crest of the hill (3,040 feet). Descend, then climb to reach Frog Lake (2,440 feet) and two backcountry campsites at 1.6 miles. Here you may choose between a steep trail or the road for the climb to 2,899-foot Middle Ridge.

At the summit of Middle Ridge turn right on the Middle Ridge Trail and follow it southeast along the ridge crest then down to the Little Coyote Creek canyon (1,200 feet). Ford the creek at its confluence with Little Fork, then continue down the canyon 0.2 mile and ford the creek again. Watch for poison oak when looking for a dry place to cross.

At 5.5 miles from the Visitor Center, the Middle Ridge Trail ends. If spending the night on the trail, go left, crossing the creek one more time, to reach grassy meadows and five campsites at Poverty Flat. The

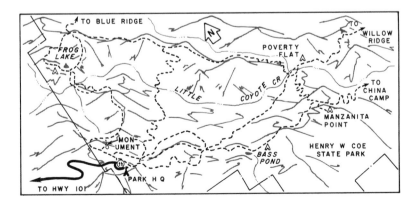

*Madrone and oak trees grow side by side*

loop route goes straight on the Cougar Trail. Before long, the trail divides. Stay right for a steep 0.9-mile climb to the crest of a manzanita- and madrone-covered ridge and an intersection with the China Hole Trail (1,840 feet). Go right and keep climbing to reach a road and the Manzanita Point group camps. Hike the road along the ridge crest for a mile, then go left on Springs Trail, which contours pleasantly along the hillside. At 9.4 miles, Springs Trail becomes Corral Trail and climbs a forested gorge to end the 10-mile loop at the Visitor Center.

# APPENDIX

## Wilderness Permits

In the overused areas of the national parks and the national forest wilderness areas, quotas have been set on the number of backpackers that can start their hike from a given trailhead on a given day. Once you have your permit, you are free to hike as long and as far as you wish during the time you specify. Your next trip requires a new permit. If your hike passes through more than one forest or through a forest and a national park you need only obtain one permit, issued from the forest or park where your trip begins.

In some high-use areas, such as Paradise Valley in Kings Canyon National Park and Glen Aulin in Yosemite National Park, backcountry camping is limited to numbered sites. When these sites are full, you are required to move on to find a legal and vacant site somewhere else. On busy weekends, searching for an open campsite may require a lot of extra miles or cross-country travel.

Except for hikes in the Toiyabe National Forest and Ventana Wilderness, advance reservation for permits for the National Forest wilderness trails begins March 1 and ends May 31. Permit requests received before or after these dates will be returned. It is a good idea to write for the regulations and the proper form no later than January. A fee of $3.00 per person is charged for each permit issued in advance.

 Backpackers with reservations may pick up their permits 24 hours before their trip (exceptions are noted below) and must pick up permits by 8:00 A.M. on the day of their hike. Backpackers without reservations may obtain a day-of-hike permit, issued only on the day that the trip begins. These permits are available at the district ranger offices as well as the seasonal ranger offices and at some information centers; see listings below for the individual hikes. (Note: The Inyo National Forest and Sequoia and Kings Canyon National Parks are experimenting with a new day-of-hike permit policy and in some areas will be issuing these permits up to 24 hours in advance. Call ahead to check on current policy.)

**Case 1:** Mokelumne, Carson-Iceberg, and Emigrant Wilderness permits are required between April 1 and November 1. As of 1994 no quota system had been established, so you may count on picking up your permit on the day of your hike from the nearest or most convenient ranger station along your route to the trailhead. If you prefer, you may write ahead and have your permit issued by mail for no fee. (Call ahead; this system may see some changes in the next few years.)

**Hikes 1–3 and 5**: Send permit requests to the Amador District Ranger Station, 26820 Silver Drive, Pioneer, CA 95666; phone (209) 295-4251.

**Hikes 6 and 7:** Permits are issued from the Calaveras Ranger Station, Highway 4, P.O. Box 500, Hathaway Pines, CA 95223; phone (209) 795-1381.

APPENDIX

**Hikes 11-15**: Permits are obtained from the Summit Ranger District, 1 Pinecrest Lake Road, Pinecrest, CA 95364; phone (209) 965-3434.

**Case 2**: The only permit required for an overnight hike is a fire permit, which may be picked up at any Forest Service office or in July and August at the Information Center at the crest of Carson Pass between the hours of 8:00 A.M. and 4:00 P.M. For more information contact the USDA Forest Service, Lake Tahoe Basin Management Unit, 870 Emerald Bay Road, Suite 1, South Lake Tahoe, CA 96150; phone (916) 573-2600.

**Case 3**: In 1994, wilderness permits were obtained at the trailhead from a self-registration box.

**Case 4**: Although the Walker River Basin is not yet officially part of the Hoover Wilderness, wilderness rules apply. The trail quotas at this time are very generous and day-of-hike permits are usually not a problem except on holiday weekends. Day-of-hike permits are issued by the camp hosts at Leavitt Meadow Campground between 8:00 A.M. and 5:00 P.M. To arrange for a reserved permit write Bridgeport Ranger District, P.O. Box 595, Bridgeport, CA 93517; phone (619) 932-7070. Reserved permits may be picked up at the ranger station or at the campground.

**Case 5**: All reserved and day-of-hike permits are issued from the ranger station at Bridgeport. Make advance reservations with the Bridgeport Ranger Station, P.O. Box 595, Bridgeport, CA 93517. For questions call (619) 932-7070. Day-of-hike permits are issued from 6:30 A.M. to 4:30 P.M.

**Case 6**: Much of the area administered by the Inyo National Forest is extremely popular with hikers and stock users and quotas are in effect from the last Friday in June until September 15. To ensure that you will get the hike of your choice, reserve your wilderness permit ahead of time. One-half the daily quota of spaces are available by advance reservation, except on the Mt. Whitney Trail where all spaces are filled by advance reservation. The second half of the quota spaces are given out on a first-come, first-served basis the day of the hike at locations listed below. Popular hikes often have a line of people waiting all night for a permit. Send your reservations for **Hikes 20 and 21** to Mono Lake Ranger Station, Box 10, Lee Vining, CA 94541, phone (619) 647-6527; for **Hikes 22-25** to Mammoth Ranger Station, Box 148, Mammoth Lakes, CA 93465, phone (619) 934-2505; for **Hikes 23-41** to White Mountain Ranger Station, 798 North Main Street, Bishop, CA 93545, phone (619) 873-2500; and for **Hikes 42-47** to Mt. Whitney Ranger District, P.O. Box 8, Lone Pine, CA 93545.

**Hikes 20 and 21**: Reserved and day-of-hike permits are issued at the Rush Creek Trailhead from 6:30 A.M. to 3:30 P.M. Thursday through Monday. On Tuesdays and Wednesdays permits are issued from the ranger station in Lee Vining. (Check with the ranger station in Lee Vining to verify these hours and days, which may change from year to year.)

244

**Hikes 22-25**: Reserved and day-of-hike wilderness permits for the Mammoth Lakes area (that includes hikes in the John Muir and Ansel Adams Wilderness) are issued from the Mammoth Ranger Station Visitor Center. For hikes beginning from the Devils Postpile area **(Hikes 22, 23, and 24)**, there is a mandatory shuttle bus, fee charged, from the Mammoth Mountain Ski Area. The bus runs from 7:30 A.M. to 5:30 P.M. If you wish to drive to the trailhead you must either arrive before or after these hours or secure a site in one of the very busy valley campgrounds. During the summer, the Mammoth Ranger Station Visitor Center opens at 6:00 A.M. to allow wilderness users time to pick up permits and drive to the trailhead before the shuttle bus begins operation in the morning.

**Hikes 26-29**: Reserved and day-of-hike permits for hikes in the McGee Creek and Rock Creek drainages may be picked up at the Rock Creek Entrance Station near Tom's Place from the last Friday in June to September 15.

**Hikes 30-32**: Reserved and day-of-hike wilderness permits for the Pine Creek drainage are issued at the White Mountain Ranger Station in Bishop. However, if you are coming from the north you may arrange to pick up your reserved permit at the Rock Creek Entrance Station at Tom's Place.

**Hikes 33-38:** Bishop Creek is an extremely popular area; plan ahead and apply for your wilderness permit in March. From the last Friday in June through September 15, reserved and day-of-hike permits are issued from the Bishop Creek Entrance Station located 10.1 miles west of Bishop on Highway 168.

**Hike 39**: This trail does not enter the wilderness until it crosses the divide. If you camp at Green Lake you are in the forest and need only a fire permit, which may be obtained at the White Mountain Ranger Station in Bishop or Bishop Creek Entrance Station. If you go over the pass and camp in the Baker Creek drainage, you will need a wilderness permit. As this is a non-quota trail, you may pick up a permit on the day of your hike.

**Hikes 40 and 41**: Reserved and day-of-hike permits are issued by the camp host at the Sage Flat Campground from the last Friday in June to the middle of September. Call the White Mountain Ranger District in Bishop at (619) 873-2500 for current information on specific times for issuance of day-of-hike permits.

**Hike 42**: All permits for the Sawmill Pass Trail must be obtained from the Mt. Whitney Ranger Station in Lone Pine.

**Hikes 43 and 44**: Reserved and day-of-hike permits are issued from Mt. Whitney Ranger Station in Lone Pine between 7:00 A.M. and 3:30 P.M. Day-of-hike permits as well as reserved permits may be picked up 24 hours ahead of time.

**Hike 45**: Due to the popularity and the fragile nature of the area, the Mt. Whitney Trail is governed by an especially strict set of rules.

All wilderness permits are issued in advance. There is a 50-person daily quota on the trail and generally there are so many applications per day that your chances for a permit are only slightly better than the possibility of winning the lottery. Permits that remain unclaimed by 8:00 A.M. on the day of the hike are given out on a first-come basis at the Mt. Whitney Ranger Station in Lone Pine. Because these permits are in great demand, hikers sleep on the front porch of the ranger station to save a place in line. *Don't join their ranks.* It is much better to ensure the success of your hike by acclimating overnight at the trailhead. Trail quota limits apply from the last Friday in June through mid-October.

**Hikes 46 and 47**: Reserved and day-of-hike permits are available up to 24 hours in advance from the Mt. Whitney Ranger Station in Lone Pine between 7:00 A.M. and 3:30 P.M. Hikers hoping for a day-of-hike permit frequently sleep on the porch of the ranger station to ensure their place in line. When making advance reservations for Hike 46, request the Cottonwood Lakes Basin Trail on your reservation request form. For Hike 47 you must request the Cottonwood Pass Trail on the advance reservation request form.

**Case 7**: In Sequoia and Kings Canyon National Parks, reservations are accepted from March 1 through the end of August. You may make a reservation up to two weeks before the start of your hike by writing: Wilderness Permit Reservations, Sequoia and Kings Canyon National Parks, Three Rivers, CA 93271. Reserved permits are picked up at the closest ranger station to the start of your hike, up to 24 hours in advance. Reserved reservations must be picked up no later than 10:00 A.M. the day of your hike. Day-of-hike permits are issued 24 hours in advance.

**Hikes 48-51**: The Mineral King Ranger Station issues reserved and day-of-hike permits between 7:00 A.M. and 5:00 P.M.

**Hikes 52-55**: Day-of-hike and pre-reserved permits may be picked up at the Reservations Office at the Lodgepole Visitor Center from early June to the end of September. Office hours are 7:00 A.M. to 6:00 P.M. Off-season permits are issued from the Visitor Center.

**Hike 56**: No permits are required for backpacking in the Jennie Lakes Wilderness. However, if you are planning to pass through the wilderness and spend a night in Sequoia National Park, as is the case in Hike 56, you may either pre-reserve your permit through the park's reservation system or pick up a day-of-hike permit from either the Lodgepole Visitor Center in Sequoia National Park or Grants Forest Visitor Center in Kings Canyon National Park.

**Hike 57**: Pick up day-of-hike permits up to 24 hours in advance of your hike at the Grants Forest Visitor Center.

**Hikes 58-61**: In the Cedar Grove area most of the spaces on the popular trails, such as Woods Creek and Bubbs Creek (Hike 61), are given out by advance reservation. The few remaining spaces are doled out up to 24 hours in advance of your hike.

**Case 8**: In the Sierra National Forest, trailhead quotas for the John Muir, Ansel Adams, and Kaiser Wildernesses are in effect from the last Friday in June until mid-September. Reservations may be made by mail up to three weeks in advance of your trip date, from March 1 to August 15, at a cost of $3.00 per person. Advance reservations are available for ⅔ of the daily trail quota. Reserved permits may be picked up as much as 48 hours before the departure day and must be picked up by noon on the day of the hike. Day-of-hike permits are issued on a first-come basis for that day only.

**Hikes 62 and 63**: Make advance reservations by writing the Dinkey Information Station, 53800 Dinkey Creek Road, Dinkey Creek, CA 93664. Reserved and day-of-hike permits should be picked up at the Dinkey Creek Information Station.

**Hike 64**: At the time of this writing, no quota system was in effect for the Dinkey Lakes Wilderness. Each backpacking group must have a wilderness permit, which is issued at the Pineridge Ranger Station at Prather. This is a popular area and a quota system may be initiated in the near future, so you may want to call ahead to (209) 855-5355.

**Hikes 65-69**: Reservations for wilderness permits are made through the Pineridge Ranger District Office at Prather. Address your permit requests to Pineridge Ranger District, P.O. Box 559, Prather, CA 93651. Permits for Hikes 65 and 66 should be picked up at the ranger station in Prather. For Hikes 67, 68, and 69, pick up reserved and day-of-hike permits at the High Sierra Station on Kaiser Pass Road below Lake Thomas Edison and Florence Lake.

**Hikes 70 and 71**: Advance reservations are made through the Minarets District Office, North Fork, CA 93643. You can arrange to pick up your reserved permit in North Fork at the Minarets Ranger Station or at the Clover Meadow Information Station. From the last Friday in June to late-September, day-of-hike permits are issued at Clover Meadow from 8:00 A.M. to 12:00 P.M., and 1:00 P.M. to 5:00 P.M. Permits for Hike 71 may also be picked up at the Oakhurst Ranger Station located on Highway 41 just north of Oakhurst.

**Case 9**: In Yosemite National Park up to 50 percent of the daily trail quotas may be reserved in advance. Mail reservation requests between March 1 and May 31 to the Wilderness Office, P.O. Box 577, Yosemite, CA 95389. A fee (call for amount) will be charged for advance reservations. The remaining spaces are released on a first-come basis up to 24 hours before the start of the hike. It is best to be in line before the office opens the day before your hike to ensure you will get a permit. Call (209) 372-0310 for the most up-to-date information. Reserved and day-of-hike permits are issued in Tuolumne Meadows from a small booth in a parking area on the Tuolumne Lodge Road, in Yosemite Valley from the backcountry office at the Visitor Center, from the Ranger Station at Wawona, and from the Big Oak Flat entrance station on Highway 120. (Note: A party size limit of eight has been established for the Nelson Lake Trail, Hike 81.)

**Case 10**: A permit is required and a fee charged for all overnight stays at the trail camps. Reservations are made through the San Mateo Government Center, 590 Hamilton Street, Redwood City, CA 94063; phone (415) 363-4021.

**Case 11**: A permit is required and a fee charged for all overnight stays at Slate Creek Trail Camp. For reservations write or call Portola State Park, Box F, Route 2, La Honda, CA 94020-9717, phone (415) 948-9098.

**Case 12**: A permit is required and fee charged for use of all campsites in Big Basin Redwoods State Park and for all trail camps on the Skyline to the Sea Trail except in Castle Rock Trail Camp, which is on a first-come, first-served system. For reservations call Big Basin Redwoods State Park at (408) 338-6132.

**Case 13**: At the time of this writing, wilderness permits were not required for overnight hikes in the Ventana Wilderness. Fires are allowed only in designated trail camps. If camping at a nondesignated camp, you must use a camp stove. For more information contact the Monterey Ranger District Office, 406 Mildred Street, King City, CA 93930; phone (408) 385-5434. For **Hikes 91-94** the most current trail information can be obtained at the Big Sur Guard Station; phone (408) 667-5726.

**Case 14**: A permit is required and a fee charged for all overnight stays in the backcountry of Henry W. Coe State Park. The permits are issued on a first-come, first-served basis at the state park headquarters. On spring weekends it is best to arrive early to ensure you will get the permit you want. Reservations are required if you have more than ten people in your group. For information write Henry W. Coe State Park, P.O. Box 846, Morgan Hill, CA 95038 or call (408) 779-2728.

**Case 15**: No camping is allowed in the backcountry of Pinnacles National Monument. For further information write: Superintendent, Pinnacles National Monument, Paicines, CA 95043.

# Maps

Forest and Wilderness maps are available for a fee from the District Forest Offices or from the regional Forest Service office. Calling ahead for prices may help speed up the process.

USDA Forest Service
Pacific Southwest Region
Office of Information
630 Sansome Street
San Francisco, CA 94111
Phone: (415) 705-2879

Topographical maps, as well as Forest and Wilderness maps, may be purchased at many outdoor recreational supply stores. If you have plenty of patience, topographical maps also may be ordered directly from the U.S. Geological Survey.

Earth Science Information Center, U.S. Geological Survey
Customs House
555 Battery Street
San Francisco, CA 94111

Wilderness Press in Berkeley has a series of up-to-date 15-minute quadrangles which use USGS base maps. Write or call for these maps and a catalog of current publications.

Wilderness Press
2440 Bancroft Way
Berkeley, CA 94704
Phone: (800) 443-7227

For the Skyline to the Sea Trail and Big Basin Redwoods State Park, the Santa Cruz Mountains Natural History Association has produced two very informative maps. These maps may be purchased at the park or directly from the Natural History Association:

101 No. Big Trees Road
Felton, CA 95018

For Sequoia and Kings Canyon National Parks the Sequoia Natural History Association has produced a very helpful series of maps, which may be purchased at any of the visitor centers in the parks.

Sequoia Natural History Association, Inc.
Ash Mountain, Box 10
Three Rivers, CA 93271

## Addresses

Alpine Ranger Station (1 mile above Bear Valley on Highway 4) open June 1 through October 1; 8:00 A.M. to 5:00 P.M. daily
(209) 753-2811

Amador Ranger District
26820 Silver Drive
Pioneer, CA 95666
(209) 295-4251

Big Sur Guard Station
Highway 1
Big Sur, CA
(408) 667-2423

Calaveras Ranger District
Highway 4
P.O. Box 500
Hathaway Pines, CA 95232
(209) 795-1381

Big Basin Redwoods State Park
21600 Big Basin Way
Boulder Creek, CA 95006
(408) 338-6132

Bridgeport Ranger District
P.O. Box 595
Bridgeport, CA 93517
(619) 932-7070

Carson Ranger District
1536 South Carson Street
Carson City, NV 89701
(702) 882-2766
(702) 882-9211 (recorded message)

Castle Rock State Park
15000 Skyline Boulevard
Los Gatos, CA 95030-9404
(408) 867-2952

Henry W. Coe State Park
P.O. Box 846
Morgan Hill, CA 95038
(408) 779-2728

Lake Tahoe Basin Management
    Unit
870 Emerald Bay Road, Suite 1
South Lake Tahoe, CA 96150
(916) 573-2600

Markleeville Guard Station
Markleeville, CA 96120
(916) 694-2911

Mammoth Ranger District
Highway 203 - P.O. Box 148
Mammoth Lakes, CA 93546
(619) 924-5500

Minarets Ranger District
North Fork, CA 93643
(209) 877-2218

Mono Lake Ranger District
P.O. Box 10
Lee Vining, CA 93541
(619) 647-3000 or (619) 647-3001

Monterey Ranger District
406 South Mildred
King City, CA 93930
(408) 385-5434

Mt. Whitney Ranger District
P.O. Box 8
640 South Main Street
Lone Pine, CA 93545
(619) 876-6200

Pineridge Ranger District
P.O. Box 300
Shaver Lake, CA 93664
(209) 841-3311

Pinnacles National Monument
Superintendent
Pinnacles National Monument
Paicines, CA 95043

Portola State Park
Box F, Route 2
La Honda, CA 94020-9717
(415) 948-9098

San Mateo County Government
    Center
590 Hamilton Street
Redwood City, CA 94063
(415) 363-4021

Summit Ranger District
1 Pinecrest Lake Road
Pinecrest, CA 95364
(209) 965-3434

U.S. Forest Service
Pacific Southwest Region
Office of Information
630 Sansome Street
San Francisco, CA 94111
(415) 705-2874

White Mountain Ranger District
798 North Main Street
Bishop, CA 93514
(619) 873-4207

Yosemite National Park
Wilderness Permits
P.O. Box 577
Yosemite National Park, CA 95389
(209) 372-0310

# INDEX

*Vicky Spring, Tom Kirkendall, and the chief editor (son Logan)*

## About the Authors

Vicky Spring and Tom Kirkendall are both experienced outdoor people. The couple travel the hills in summer as hikers, backpackers, and cyclists on mountain bikes; when the snow falls, they pin on cross-country skis and keep on exploring. Both Tom and Vicky studied at the Brooks Institute of Photography in Santa Barbara, California, and are now building their careers together as outdoor photographers and guidebook authors.

Vicky is the author of *Bicycling the Pacific Coast* and *Cross-Country Ski Tours of Washington's North Cascades* and *Washington's South Cascades and Olympics.* Tom is author/photographer of *Mountain Bike Adventures in Washington's North Cascades and Olympics* and *Washington's South Cascades and Puget Sound,* all published by The Mountaineers.

THE MOUNTAINEERS, founded in 1906, is a nonprofit outdoor activity and conservation club, whose mission is "to explore, study, preserve, and enjoy the natural beauty of the outdoors. . . ." Based in Seattle, Washington, the club is now the third-largest such organization in the United States, with 15,000 members and five branches throughout Washington State.

The Mountaineers sponsors both classes and year-round outdoor activities in the Pacific Northwest, which include hiking, mountain climbing, ski-touring, snowshoeing, bicycling, camping, kayaking and canoeing, nature study, sailing, and adventure travel. The club's conservation division supports environmental causes through educational activities, sponsoring legislation, and presenting informational programs. All club activities are led by skilled, experienced volunteers, who are dedicated to promoting safe and responsible enjoyment and preservation of the outdoors.

If you would like to participate in these organized outdoor activities or the club's programs, consider a membership in The Mountaineers. For information and an application, write or call The Mountaineers, Club Headquarters, 300 Third Avenue West, Seattle, Washington 98119; (206) 284-6310; e-mail: clubmail@mountaineers.org.

The Mountaineers Books, an active, nonprofit publishing program of the club, produces guidebooks, instructional texts, historical works, natural history guides, and works on environmental conservation. All books produced by The Mountaineers are aimed at fulfilling the club's mission.

*Send or call for our catalog of more than 300 outdoor titles:*

The Mountaineers Books
1001 SW Klickitat Way, Suite 201
Seattle, WA 98134
1-800-553-4453 / e-mail: mbooks@mountaineers.org